PRAISE FOR
PASSIONATE TEACHING IN TROUBLED TIMES

"When books are pulled from shelves, when teachers are told what they cannot say, and when public education itself is under siege, Robert Fried offers an eloquent lifeline. Drawing on thirty years of classroom wisdom and the voices of today's most inspiring teachers, he makes a quietly radical argument: A teacher's passion for students and honest inquiry is not just good pedagogy. It is an act of resistance. A must-read for anyone who cares about education."

—TONY WAGNER, best-selling author
and senior research fellow,
Learning Policy Institute

"I've loved *The Passionate Teacher* and have recommended it for years. This new edition greatly enhances the book for today's educators, laypeople, and students because it underscores a simple truth about learning: Learn what you love and you will learn to love learning. The genius of the teachers and students highlighted in *Passionate Teaching in Troubled Times* is their ability to make the connections that ignite that passion. Most of all, this book should be required reading for all educators at every level and for those considering joining the profession."

—GREGORY PRINCE, president emeritus
of Hampshire College

"This new edition of Rob Fried's indispensable book—which has been a central feature of our new-teacher reading list for many years—addresses vital issues facing educators, recognizing the mounting complexities that teachers face while retaining the inspiring vision of teaching that made the original so powerful."

—PAGE TOMPKINS, president of the
Upper Valley Educators Institute

PRAISE FOR *THE PASSIONATE TEACHER*

"At a time when teachers find student thinking and analysis skills at an all-time low, Robert L. Fried's *The Passionate Teacher: A Practical Guide* is the pathway to student engagement. When I applied his ideas to my teaching, my discipline improved dramatically. Bringing Fried's techniques of passionate teaching into your classroom will give you control of your content and enhance your motivation. All students will be empowered as learners and thinkers to try things that seem difficult."

—LISA BROSE,
retired elementary teacher, Colorado

"Fried's *The Passionate Teacher* ingrained in me that teachers may often unwittingly remove the joy of their subject from their students by doing the hard work for them. It led me to understand that my job was to guide them as they did the work of the reader and the writer themselves, and not to spoil the fun by lecturing the answers. My students and I are all much more engaged when I allow them the time and space to be messy and develop their skills rather than to rush through material to 'cover' it. This book's teaching philosophy has definitely impacted my practice and therefore my students. It's hard to fathom the reach of its influence."

—KAREN BELL,
high school teacher, Indiana

PASSIONATE TEACHING *in* TROUBLED TIMES

ROBERT L. FRIED

BEACON PRESS, BOSTON

ALSO BY ROBERT L. FRIED

The Passionate Learner: How Teachers and Parents Can Help Children Reclaim the Joy of Discovery

The Game of School: Why We All Play It, How It Hurts Kids, and What It Will Take to Change It

The Skeptical Visionary: A Seymour Sarason Educational Reader

PASSIONATE TEACHING *in* TROUBLED TIMES

COMPELLING LESSONS FOR TODAY'S CLASSROOM

ROBERT L. FRIED

BEACON PRESS, BOSTON

BEACON PRESS
24 Farnsworth Street
Boston, Massachusetts
www.beacon.org

Beacon Press books
are published under the auspices of
the Unitarian Universalist Association of Congregations.

An earlier version of this book was previously published
under the title *The Passionate Teacher*.

Printed in the United States of America

29 28 27 26 8 7 6 5 4 3 2 1

This book is printed on acid-free paper that meets the uncoated paper
ANSI/NISO specifications for permanence as revised in 1992.

Text design and composition by Kim Arney

Library of Congress Cataloging-in-Publication
Data is available for this title.
ISBN: 978-0-8070-2533-8; e-book: 978-0-8070-2534-5;
audiobook: 978-0-8070-2541-3

The authorized representative in the EU for product safety and
compliance is Easy Access System Europe 16879218, Mustamäe tee 50,
10621 Tallinn, Estonia: https://beacon.org/eu-contact.

To my wife, Pat,
with enduring love

CONTENTS

PREFACE TO THE 2026 EDITION

"I Touch the Future"

"I touch the future; I teach!" With these words, teacher-astronaut Christa McAuliffe set forth on her fateful quest to be the first teacher in space. My son was in her son's third-grade class, and I had arranged with other kids' parents to have the whole class travel to Florida to watch the launch. We arrived in a spirit of adventure, excitement, and eagerness to be witnesses to history. We were given a special tour of the Kennedy Space Center and lectured to by NASA experts, all of whom exuded pride and confidence. After the explosion, we returned to Concord, New Hampshire, in a hail of press publicity. None of us has ever forgotten this moment when, to our children's unbelieving eyes, it seemed the best minds in America had gotten things so tragically wrong.

It may seem that way today, when our nation and our world are swept up in turmoil, antagonism, division, and what appears to be a rebellion by vast swaths of the population against science, against knowledge, against reason, against truth itself—all of which can manifest as being *against education*. There are demands by politically motivated citizen groups and reactionary politicians to divert funds from public schools to support private and parochial education, to pull books off library shelves, to purge historical truths, to deny opportunity to children who don't conform to traditional gender identities, to round up and deport immigrant children and their families, to rewrite curricula and make lesson plans "teacher-proof," and generally to restrict any teaching that might expose children to a less-than-heroic view of America.

But, despite all the hostility and divisiveness surrounding them in our society, *our teachers continue to touch the future: They teach.* They come to class ready to engage young minds, to shoulder the increasing burdens of being teacher, coach, counselor, remediator, advocate, and monitor of social media. They adjust their lessons to cope with students' often-diminished attention spans and the residue of COVID-era disruptions. They surround the children they teach with curiosity, inspiration, love and respect and, in so doing, they model those values for children who may be beset with over-stressed home environments, bullying in or out of school, and/or who have become victims of addictive social media algorithms that leave them alienated and depressed. These teachers do not give in or give up.

As Zachary Arenz, New York State 2024 Teacher of the Year, emailed me this summer:

> I've come to realize that my enthusiasm for teaching is rooted in being passionate about the work that I *get* to do every day. My passion isn't always loud or showy—it doesn't show up in the form of boundless energy, textbook-perfect lessons, or a picture-perfect classroom. It shows up in the form of consistency: the daily choice to show up and believe that what I do matters.
>
> What sustains my passion is connection. I get to teach something I love, music, and through that art form, I get to build relationships with my students. I see them light up when they realize they belong, when they create something beautiful, and when they feel seen and valued. Those moments are the heartbeat of my teaching.
>
> I have also learned that teaching is a long game. We keep our focus set on the belief that the seeds we sow today will bloom later on. Those seeds germinate in the form of students who are happy, proud, and successful.[1]

How beautifully said! Thirty years ago, Beacon Press published *The Passionate Teacher*, which introduced or highlighted concepts such as *Passion* as the heart of a teacher's approach to students, the *Game of School* as a subtle but devastating obstacle to learning, and the *Stance* as a physical, philosophical, and pedagogical positioning of a teacher within a classroom. These ideas and the stories of the inspiring teachers who embodied them are as vivid and pertinent today as they were in 1995, and the book has been used continuously as a foundational text in teacher education.

But so much has changed. New technologies both amplify and constrain the teaching/learning process. The emergence of LGBTQ awareness provides children and youth a new freedom to acknowledge their gender identities even as it has spurred a virulent backlash by conservative and fundamentalist forces. The COVID pandemic closed schools and forced students to try to learn from home. Many still haven't returned to classrooms, and those who have are often behind in reading and math. According to US Census estimates, public school enrollment declined by 1.2 million students (2.5 percent) in the years after the pandemic, while enrollment in private schools rose. Homeschooling has increased to more than 5 percent, up from 3.4 percent before the pandemic, particularly among families who resist the secular nature of public education and those who find traditional school confining or alienating for their children. Some charter schools have forged exciting new pedagogies, while others seem merely to siphon funds from already underfunded public schools. And social media has had a dramatic and often highly detrimental impact on the emotional well-being of our youth.

It is these occurrences that have led to a request for an updated and amplified new edition of *The Passionate Teacher*, despite the proliferation of important books that individually address many of these phenomena. As in the previous edition, I rely largely on conversations with today's educators—classroom teachers from at least a dozen states—who are working to maintain their idealism and enthusiasm despite the proliferation of challenges. I have also called on colleagues of many years, principally Deborah Meier and Tony Wagner, to lend their perspectives from many decades of reform work. I then worked to integrate the thoughts and experiences of all these folks within the core concepts of the original book, to revisit Passion, Game, and Stance through the eyes of today's inspired teachers who face obstacles, both new and persisting, as they work to create environments for learning that serve children and youth in our troubled nation and world.

I cannot, of course, address all the challenges and obstacles mentioned above, and it would be foolhardy to try. So, in this new edition,

I will focus on amplifying the original text by attending to issues that might be especially informed by Passion, Game, and Stance. Here are some of the issues I have chosen *not* to deal with:

- the consequences of artificial intelligence (AI) on learning from pre-K through graduate school
- the educational implications of the political fight against diversity, equity, and inclusion
- the impact of rising rates of students on the autism spectrum
- the ramifications of the emphasis on STEM education on the teaching of the classics and of the humanities
- the diminution of financial support for public schools and colleges
- the worsening impacts of underfunded schools and underpaid teachers
- the continuing constraints and debilitating effects of standardized testing (although I will address this later when discussing mastery and motivation)

To be sure, each is an important issue, and there are useful books that address them. This new edition *will*, however, offer useful suggestions on:

- determining what is essential to teach amid conflicting priorities, agendas, and curricular mandates
- helping students take ownership of their learning and assessing their learning in ways that promote such ownership
- working with students to create and maintain a learning environment of mutual respect and caring in the face of bullying and meanness
- nurturing in students a respect for truth and the ability to recognize and resist falsehoods
- teaching history and social studies in an intellectually honest way without getting fired.

I give the final words of this preface to two of the 2024 Teachers of the Year: Joshua Chard from Maine and De'Shawn Washington from Massachusetts:

> Teachers often describe themselves as "just a teacher," but the truth is that what we do every day—meeting basic needs, designing creative lessons, supporting every learner—is actually extraordinary. The impact of educators is found in the quiet, consistent ways we show up for our students, knowing their stories, challenging their thinking, and helping them see themselves as capable and valued. What may feel routine to us is, in reality, transformative for the children and families we serve—and this is, in fact, extraordinary.[2]

> Teachers, you are awesome—and you are the Changemakers. You are the Empowerers, the Inspirers, the ones who plant the seeds of truth, justice, and brilliance in every child you teach, coach, mentor, and connect with. The work you do each day is vital to the health, hope, and future of our children and this nation.[3]

As in the original edition, I rely on the wisdom of teachers like Joshua and De'Shawn who daily employ their skills, knowledge, experience, and, above all, their devotion to all the students whose future they strive to touch. For you, the teacher, administrator, parent, or student, I hope this book inspires you to strive for the essence of learning, which is to open your hearts and minds to the task of living meaningfully in a troubled world.

—ROB FRIED

FOREWORD TO THE FIRST EDITION, 1995

I remember the first draft of this book I received in the mail. I dutifully began a quick read because I knew and respected its author and figured it would be of interest—although I was longing instead to get into the garden. I had a hard time stopping. I rushed to the telephone to tell Rob he had to hurry up and get it published because I wanted every teacher I worked with to have it in their hands—on Monday morning past.

I still feel the same way. I know it is customary these days to tell teachers (and parents and administrators and district staff) to go away for a day and get themselves a "vision" or a "mission," no less. We're living in an age of inflated rhetoric, as though missions and visions were the result of deliberative processes, consensus arrangements, and a good agenda. Rob Fried makes it clear that such principles develop out of our lives; they take time to articulate and shape, but the wellspring can't be managed or mandated.

Passionate teaching of the kind described in this book is the work of learned craftsmanship. And it's made up of details. Having a wonderful idea is only the start. Good teaching emerges when passion is translated into a craft. This is an account of why it makes such a difference and how such craftsmanship gets shaped over time. It's a book filled with details—real stories, the tradeoffs and compromises that educators encounter daily, and the breakthroughs with students that can make teaching so rewarding. It's my ideal of a how-to book.

The only kind of school reform that can make a lasting difference is reform that helps create genuine learning communities—where adults are able to practice in real life what it is that we want children to care about: reasoned argument, independent investigation, initiative, experimentation, getting to the heart of things, acting on ideas. Until children are surrounded by an adult community that presents an attractive model of what all this "intellectual" stuff is about, we are wasting our time. That model of intellectual engagement is what passionate teaching is all about.

Passionate teaching is not a luxury, a frill we can do without. We can't afford to keep sending kids to schools that disrespect the qualities of heart and mind we claim to be promoting. It's like trying to teach kids to be musicians without letting them hear any music or see an expert musician at work. That's what we've done to our children. We've cut them off from the "real stuff" for twelve long years, then bemoaned their lack of enthusiasm and proposed substituting increasingly direr penalties for failure in lieu of offering reasons to aspire to excellence.

Passionate teaching is doable. It doesn't require exceptional teachers, although it will remain scarce until we change schools so that adults and children recapture their nascent passions. We've all got them. They've just gotten buried. Until we treat these passions not as embarrassments but as assets in the job of rearing the next generation, the kinds of stories and successes you will read about in this book will remain exceptions. Admired but not widely practiced. That's the challenge before us.

—DEBORAH MEIER

PART ONE

THE PASSION

1

TEACHING WITH PASSION IN TROUBLED TIMES

So, you still love teaching, but you feel increasingly caught in a bind. The walls around the profession you've devoted your life to seem to be closing in: books removed from the library, topics banned from the curriculum, undocumented students under threat of deportation, the US Department of Education itself being dismantled, America and the world in chaos.

Your students still astonish you: They bring into your classroom a freshness, an intriguing vulnerability and unpolished vividness (along with the traumas of growing up in a world they don't much understand, manipulated by social media algorithms that distort their reality).

The subjects you teach still enthrall you, continuing to remind you of how much you still seek to know; your discipline remains a gourmet meal that has delightful courses yet to be served if you're willing to work for your supper.

The world of nature and our fellow humans still astounds you: a walk in a nearby park, a hike in the mountains, a visit to a city environ rich with culture, a trip to the ocean, or tulips emerging in your garden from a winter's slumber offer a delight to your senses that, for a time at least, transcends the mess that we humans are making of our planet.

And you feel alive (if sometimes disheartened) in the knowledge that it is still in your wheelhouse to make a difference.

You are a passionate teacher who is justly concerned that the values that brought you into this profession—values that sustain you—are under siege. Lots of people out there seem eager to distrust education, repudiate science, and deny truth. Some in your immediate community—decent people who would gladly lend you a hand if they found you in trouble—have been taken captive by radical idealogues who seek to undermine public education. They are removing their own children from public schools not only to homeschool them or send them to private and religious institutions but also to limit their access to what they view as unpalatable truths about our history and to encounters with children from lower social classes and religious minorities. This is depriving a growing group of America's youth of the freedom to choose their identity, of the right to read books that offer diverse perspectives, of the celebration of our cherished democracy, to preserve our planet, and to enjoy the essence of our motto, E Pluribus Unum. These people, for the moment at least, appear to hold sway in our nation, in some neighborhoods, and on some of our school boards. They bring to mind an image of ignorance on the rampage. They make us afraid. And we should be afraid.

The threats to public education, while politically driven, go beyond politics. As I write this, a podcast called *The Daily* in today's digital edition of the *New York Times* (August 20, 2025) is titled "Why So Many Parents Are Opting Out of Public Schools," and it begins with this chilling note: "Across the country, public schools are facing massive declines in enrollment, while the movement to use public funds for private education grows." Let me first say that this book is for *all* educators, including parents of all political persuasions and teachers in public, private, and religious-based schools. True, my message in these pages comports closely with the Progressive Education movement spawned by Horace Mann and later by John Dewey in the mid-nineteenth and early twentieth centuries. But good education is good education, whether offered by the Jesuits, liberal-minded adults, or conscientious parents teaching their children at home. Still, the consequences of declining support for public schools are dire.

Ted Sizer, founder of the Essential Schools movement, with whom I worked on education reform in the 1990s, used to say, "When I was growing up, there were three places where people of all backgrounds would commingle and relate on a daily basis—except, of course, in communities where Jim Crow racism prevented this. The first was in small towns, the second was in the army, the third was in the public schools. These days, our small communities are being depleted as people migrate to the cities. Our armed forces are now solely voluntary, with the end of the draft. That leaves only our public schools to allow Americans from different social, economic, and cultural backgrounds to get to know one another." But now, it seems, we must contemplate the erosion of this last piece of common ground.

Not so long ago, "diversity" meant the opportunity to explore differing perspectives, cultures, and philosophies so we and our ethnically diverse neighbors might help one another enrich our understanding of the world. "Equity" meant being fair to all and acknowledging our duty to correct past and current wrongs done to our fellow citizens. And "inclusion" described both the goal of parents seeking fuller lives for their children with disabilities and the fervent hope of every child entering a new neighborhood or school to feel welcomed. Now these words feel like ashes in our mouths, relics of a bygone civilization, tenets of a faith that has been overwhelmed by alien orthodoxies.

HOPE IN TROUBLED TIMES

Yet, despite all, there is hope. And beyond hope, there are paths to sustaining oneself as a passionate teacher. It's not a certainty, not foolproof, not a guarantee of your freedom to be the teacher you have always striven to be. It's not without risk, and it may require a sober reassessment of the parameters and constraints on your liberty to teach to your passions. But it will allow you to remain as good a teacher as you can be, for as long as you remain in the classroom. Your passion will help you become better at your craft and enjoy your students more. It can help you to weather the current maelstrom of popular distrust and political oppression while you continue to offer to your students a light unto their future.

And the secret to this hope, this pathway, can be summarized in a few phrases that are easy to pronounce but hard to maintain as daily practice:

- showing your students that you respect them
- helping them learn to respect each other despite their differences

- letting them know that you are fascinated by how they think—even, or especially, when they do or say things that seem improbable
- posing questions that they know you cannot answer but that deserve being answered
- impressing upon them that you see amazing potential in them, even when they may not yet see it themselves
- telling that you are ready to work with them to help make their learning an adventure that brings them power, agency, confidence, hope, and even joy

In brief, you can remain a passionate teacher in these times if you can form a bond with your students that makes them (and their parents) feel proud of who they are and eager to gain the skills and knowledge to become more fully who they wish to be.

As one who, over eight decades of life, has faced countless obstacles, frustrations, and setbacks, and who, years after retiring, still has dreams in which I am in a classroom or a meeting unable to make myself understood, I continue to believe in the power of ideas and the vibrancy of the human spirit, and I invite you to a reprise of this thirty-year-old book in hopes that it may lend strength to the passionate teacher within you during troubling times.

What you will find in this new edition are the reflections of teachers who have entered the profession in the years since the book was first published in 1995, teachers who face challenges both *legendary* (student resistance to instruction, their fear of taking risks, inappropriate imposed curricula, standardized testing, underfunded schools, sorting and labeling of students, which stigmatizes even as it segregates, and your own isolation within the classroom); and *contemporary* (social media distractions, the vestiges of COVID shutdowns, online pedagogy, and the ascendency of a demagogic attack on liberal education).

I hope in these pages to identify practical ways for teachers in all fields and all kinds of schools to renew a passion for teaching that attracts young minds to a world of ideas and helps them put their new knowledge and skills into action, despite the social problems that surround them and the numbing distractions of popular culture. The book is divided into five parts—"The Passion," "The Game," "The Stance," "The Student," and "The Course"—that deal, in turn, with the passions we embody and the games we are forced to play, the stance we take regarding young people, and the growth we want them to acquire from the ideas and habits with which we inspire them—and, importantly, with the structures that make this growth happen. Each of these five parts has been augmented with a new chapter that brings these ideas and issues to the tasks that face us a quarter century into the new millennium.

"The Passion" analyzes what might seem to be a mysterious and indefinable trait. It argues that a teacher's love of subject matter and ability to take charge of the syllabus powerfully influences how students acquire the content and skills we think are most important for them to learn. The section ends with a detailed outline for turning any unit of instruction into one that translates our passions into student engagement.

"The Game" exposes a pernicious obstacle to students and teachers engaging in serious work together and offers strategies for getting out of that "game" and into something better.

"The Stance" looks at what it means to prepare ourselves intellectually and emotionally to face the students who wander into class each day, and it looks at student discipline with a view to helping teachers and students develop a higher level of mutual respect (and have more fun in the bargain).

"The Student" discusses what we might expect our young people to actually know and do in our classes and how teachers and parents can inspire students to do their best work.

"The Course" tries to nail down the practical steps to setting higher standards, organizing an entire course around its essential elements, and developing a grading system that puts teachers and students on the same side in the pursuit of high-quality work. A final chapter is dedicated to those entering the teaching profession, and the wisdom of those once-new teachers now in their prime should be an inspiration to veterans as well.

I anticipate that the ideas, practical applications, and inspiration of the many teachers who have been so generous in lending their experiences and their vision to these pages will coalesce around several key obstacles to passionate teaching today. We will try our best to offer techniques and strategies to surmount those obstacles. In this edition, some of the best minds of our times have contributed their perceptions of that struggle. But the basic task will remain: for each of us to summon the courage and confidence to win to the ranks of passionate learning the young people whom we must count on to lead us through troubled times.

2

THE ART OF ENGAGING YOUNG MINDS

We can all think back to a teacher who either, for better or worse, said something or made us feel some type of way that either fueled our desire to be a better person or squelched our enthusiasm for learning. I for one feel this pressure every day to be the person that fuels a fire of elevating humanity.

—TAYLOR BUSSINGER,
Kansas 2024 Teacher of the Year

To be a passionate teacher is to be someone in love with a field of knowledge, deeply stirred by issues and ideas that challenge our world, drawn to the dilemmas and potentials of the young people who come into class each day—or captivated by all of these. A passionate teacher is a teacher who breaks out of the isolation of a classroom, who refuses to submit to apathy or cynicism. I argue in these pages that only when teachers bring their passions about learning and life into their daily work can they dispel the fog of passive compliance or active disinterest that surrounds so many students. I believe that we all have it within ourselves to be passionate teachers, and that nothing else will quite do the trick.

As adults working with young people, our passions are key to their engagement. For almost thirty years, working in primary, secondary, undergraduate, and graduate schools, I have been polishing John Dewey's argument that nothing much of lasting value happens in a classroom unless students' minds are engaged in ways that connect with their experience. But I have learned that just talking to people about engagement doesn't work: one has to *engage* people first.

This book is the product of my struggle to do just that, to move from being a purveyor of good advice about teaching and learning to becoming an advocate for my own and other people's passionate approach to our work with students. It is much easier to give sermons on what ought to be than to put these notions into practice. So I rely, in these pages, on the stories and insights of a number of teachers who have inspired me. After many years of working with teachers and staff in their school settings, I became a full-time teacher and teacher educator at the university level and in a stand-alone training center for teacher and principal certification, where I worked hard to put this philosophy to work.

FOURTH GRADERS LOBBYING THE STATE FOR A SEATBELT BILL

For students, to *engage* is not what is usually called "time on task": responding to worksheets, recalling facts or dates, or reading chapters of a text and answering questions at the end. I want students to engage the way the clutch on a car gets engaged: an engine can be running, making appropriate noises, burning fuel, and creating exhaust fumes, but unless the clutch is engaged, nothing moves. It's all sound and smoke, and nobody gets anywhere.

In too many classrooms we see the sound and smoke of note taking, answer giving, homework checking, test taking, and the forgetting that so quickly follows. In the end, there is creativity and excitement for the few, compliance and endurance for most, and rebellion and failure for some; but not very much work of high quality is being produced, and not much intense engagement of the mind and spirit takes place.

A number of years ago, Tim Sullivan, a fourth-grade teacher here in Concord, New Hampshire, asked his class how they felt about a proposed state bill that would raise the age requirement for mandatory seat-belt use from three years to twelve years old.

> We decided to adopt the bill as a class project. We debated it in class, coached by a high school student who was on the debating team. The kids also contacted a pro–seat belt group who sent someone to talk to them

and brought along a seat-belt car crash simulator, called "the Convincer." My students invited our mayor, city council, school board, and several legislators, who came to our class to listen to the kids and take a ride on the Convincer.

Every student then wrote to the state legislators and 85 percent of them wrote back with personalized notes. When it came time for legislative hearings, I asked my kids if they wanted to testify before subcommittees of the House and the Senate. I thought I'd have to lean on them to volunteer, but every hand went up. And the kids found that because they had done their homework, they were able to respond to the legislators' questions and win their respect.

The bill passed both houses, and when Governor Sununu [John] vetoed it, the kids lobbied hard for the over-ride motion, which made it through the House and would have succeeded in the Senate if the governor hadn't personally intervened. We lost in the Senate by one vote. The kids were disappointed, but we knew all along we might lose. The whole point was to understand the process. Those kids came away with a better sense of how a bill becomes law than any class I've ever taught.[1]

Tim Sullivan's story shows us what it means when students *willingly* engage. They have to want to see where their ideas and energies might take them, to follow their curiosity and intuition to useful places. They have to get un-shy about being smart—to stop using their smartness to put each other down or to get around doing the work we assign them. But to stay "smart" in the face of all the obstacles to engagement, in school and out, today's students need help from teachers who are more than well prepared or genial or fair. They need teachers with passion.

Joanne Dunlap, who taught chemistry at the public high school in my town, suggested I ask teachers, "Think of the times when you accidentally did something *right*, when an incident you hadn't planned got kids really excited about learning and allowed them to connect with an idea or a skill or a project they might not otherwise have embraced. What made each of these accidents succeed? How did an unusual occurrence break the routine? What do these incidents tell us about engagement?"

Joanne's suggestion points to the discovery that lurks in moments of spontaneity. Her years of experience as a science teacher have taught her the value of looking at data in new ways and accepting unforeseen experiences as essential to greater knowledge. Her approach makes for good science and good teaching. I see these fortuitous moments, along with those planned lessons that succeed beyond our expectations, as more than just good pedagogy: They are windows into our most creative selves. They tap the sources of our potential power to help young people grow in wonderful ways and accomplish splendid things.

Teachers often tell me that they need practical answers to the many vexing problems they face. While "passion" is not a word that seems to lend itself to practical application, passion can be put to practical use. The core of this book is that passion is not just a personality trait that some people have and others lack, but rather something discoverable, teachable, and reproducible, even when the regularities of school life gang up against it. Passion and practicality are not opposing notions; good planning and design are as important as caring and spontaneity in bringing out the best in students. To convey this duality, I borrow practical examples and techniques that I have learned from teachers and students over the years.

THE BRIDGE THAT CONNECTS US TO OUR STUDENTS

Of course passion itself is not the goal of education. It is a bridge that connects us to the intensity of young people's thoughts and life experiences—things that they too rarely see as part of school. Once that connection has been made, we can help transfer passions about ideas into habits of hard work, discipline, and practice that will remain with them even when the going gets rough, when peers cajole them to "take it easy." Although not the whole story, passion, uncomfortable as that word may sound, is at the heart of what teaching is or should be—especially if we want to be mentors for young people who sorely need (but rarely seek) heroes of the mind to counterbalance the heroes of brute strength or trendy fashion, which surround them in the media.

Some critical readers have asked just what kind of book I am writing and who my audience is. Is this a theoretical book aimed at teachers-in-training at the undergraduate or graduate level? A hands-on tool for experienced practitioners trying to make things work better in the classroom? A philosophical or moral treatise on the aesthetics of teaching? Am I seeking only those who have energy for new challenges and approaches?

Or am I just as devoted to those who have been "burned" before by promoters of sure-fire solutions to the real dilemmas that teachers face each day? And what about parents, board members, and other citizens who are part of the growing public concern about education in our society—is it for them too, or only for those working inside schools?

I want to write for all these audiences. This book is first and foremost for teachers, with many practical suggestions concerning techniques of putting their passions to work in the classroom. But it may serve parents in guiding their children toward those teachers whose passionate regard for learning shines forth in even the most drab of school settings. I write as one who has faced the everyday challenges of being a student, parent, teacher, principal, university professor, school board member, bureaucrat, consultant to teachers and to school systems, and taxpaying citizen. I think all these audiences need to be invited into the conversation if teaching and learning are to improve significantly.

During the months I have spent putting together this new edition, and despite the challenges of intervening years, my optimism about the teaching profession remains. In school after school, spurred on by good news and bad, I see teachers breaking out of the constraints that have confined their spirits, isolated them, and depressed their passions. After reading a draft of the first edition of this book, Yvonne Griffin threw out the text in a course on sexuality and human relationships at Hartford Public High School and invited her students to redesign the course with her, from scratch, based on what they most wanted to learn about. She told me she was both exhilarated and "scared stiff" by the adventure but was very pleased with the way her students have responded.

This book owes much to the clarity of teachers like Yvonne Griffin, Tim Sullivan, Susan Lukas, Christine Sullivan, David Ervin, Ed Clarke, Maria Ortiz, Alfredo Fuentes, and Dan Bisaccio as well as the more recent contributions of teachers like Andrea Levin, Joshua Chard, Taylor Bassinger, and others whose visions and practical insights enliven these pages. Amid plenty of evidence that our schools are in crisis, the courage of teachers who are taking risks on behalf of better results for students says a lot about the potential not only for survival but for the triumph of liberal education in difficult times.

With all that is being written and legislated about changing entire educational systems—much of which shunts teachers to a subsidiary role in the debate about national standards and performance outcomes—I want this book to reaffirm the central role that a teacher's relationship with students, subject, and self plays in the pursuit of true excellence in the classroom. At the heart of the struggle for intense and humane schools in these tumultuous times is the passion that comes of a teacher's lifelong commitment to learning.

3

PASSIONATE TEACHING REVEALED

> *I believe I make a difference not only by helping kids connect math and science to their lives, but also in understanding how to reach their goals in life—how to be somebody.*
>
> —MARIA ORTIZ, middle school science teacher

HOW MARIA ORTIZ BECAME A TEACHER

The destiny of Maria Ortiz, whom I encountered in her twenty-second year of teaching science at Lewis B. Fox Middle School in an inner-city neighborhood of Hartford, Connecticut, was probably decided on the very day she entered first grade, back in the village of Canóvanas, Puerto Rico, and encountered the woman she still refers to as "Mrs. Betancourt."

> She was not only a teacher, but a kind of mother to us—so loving to each kid that I can remember almost every single moment of first and second grade (I had her for two years) even though it was more than forty years ago. Every morning, she was waiting for us outside in the school yard. She hugged each kid like we were her long-lost children. Then she would gather us around her, like a mother hen with her chicks, and lead us inside.
>
> And waiting for us would be hot cocoa and soda crackers—she didn't believe we should have to wait for midmorning snack time; we got our snack first thing. Then she would get us singing, all of us. And her songs were full of tricks to make us learn things even while we were singing and

having fun: songs about the alphabet, about animals and numbers. We would get so involved in her projects—drawing, building things, making a doll out of an old sock with buttons for its eyes—that we didn't realize how much we were learning. We knew we had to do schoolwork, but because of her warmth it didn't seem like work, it seemed like fun.

You see, I never planned to be a teacher. Since I liked science and was good at it, my parents wanted me to be a doctor. Instead, I studied pharmacology for four years in college and then started an apprenticeship in a drugstore. But as soon as I started practicing, I knew it wasn't for me. I didn't want to spend my life putting labels on bottles and selling them to customers for high prices.

So I went back to my dean and told him I was in the wrong profession and was quitting. He asked why, and I said, "A highly regarded doctor sent in a prescription for a woman, and although it was only for aspirin, he gave it a scientific name, and the druggist told me to cover over the 'Bayer Aspirin' label and charge her twenty dollars. I told him I wouldn't do it. If that's the kind of business it is, pharmacy is not for me. I have to have an opportunity to live!"

Then I thought I would change my major and become a science researcher. But my sister-in-law said, "Why don't you become a teacher?" Immediately Mrs. Betancourt flashed into my mind. And I said to myself: "Maybe that's what I really want to be—I want to be like her!"

So I began teaching right away. There was such a shortage of math and science teachers that they were willing to hire me even though I had never taken an education course and didn't know any methodology. I had to create everything myself, without relying on theories.

I started teaching science to students in grades 7 and 9, in a middle school in Hato Rey, near San Juan. As the newest teacher, naturally they gave me what they thought were the worst classes. (They didn't tell me that nine other teachers had already quit because they could not handle the kids.) I can still remember one of the students, Ismari Rivera. Our class was held in the art room, and when I came in, he was sitting atop the pottery wheel, slowly spinning around before an admiring audience of classmates. He gave me a look that said: "I dare you to get me off, or make me stop."

I decided to ignore him and busied myself at my desk. After a while, Ismari looked up and said: "Are you the new teacher?" I said, "Yes." He paused, and then asked, "Are you going to leave us, too?" I said, no, I wasn't going to leave. And he continued to spin on the wheel and I continued to ignore him and began talking to the kids.

For the first week or two, I said nothing at all about science. I was operating totally on instinct, and my instinct told me that I needed first of all to get to know who these kids really were. The principal had said that they were "mentally retarded," but I soon found out that they were not that at all, just angry. We talked about the kind of sports and music they liked, and they told me all about who was in their families, and of course they asked about mine, and I told them.

At the end of the first week, I knew *so* much about their lives, and somehow, *that* changed their behavior. They probably saw me as the kind of older teenager that they might want to be, and they were grateful that I was so interested in them. They saw themselves as rebels in the school because there was so much anger around them, in their lives, in school, in their homes.

After a while, I could tell them that I was a science teacher and that my job was to teach the science curriculum. But I promised that we would take one day each week and pull our chairs into a circle and talk about whatever was on their minds. We set some rules: everybody had to promise to listen to each other and to take turns if they wanted to talk. When somebody mentioned a problem they were having, onc by one the other kids could give suggestions or make helpful comments.

Ismari didn't like this. He had gotten down from the pottery wheel when the other kids stopped paying attention to him. But now he just sat in the corner and sulked. And I still decided it was best to ignore him. So eventually, he moved closer and closer, until he was in the circle.

I remember one girl, named Waleska, who told us she hated her father because he had killed her little sister. She said that he had backed up his car and it had run over her sister. She couldn't understand how he could have done that. And so we talked about it, and we all decided that it had been an accident, and that her father didn't mean it. Slowly, with our help, Waleska was able to understand this too. The circle gave them a chance to let their emotions out and deal with them. There was some crying, at times, by all of us. But there was also a lot of laughter.

And so I became a teacher, just like that. After a few years, I was offered a chance to come to America and teach for a year. I came to this school, in Hartford, in 1972. And I'm still here. I believe I make a difference not only by helping kids connect math and science to their lives, but also in understanding how to reach their goals in life—how to be somebody. It's strange. In Puerto Rico the kids seem so proud of themselves. But when they come here, they suffer a great blow to their esteem. We have to work very hard to help them convince themselves that their goals still matter, that nothing is impossible, that they can do it, that to be bilingual is to have power.

I don't feel fifty years old. I can still think like a teenager. There are three teachers in Hartford schools who were my students, here at Fox Middle, and another who's at the university, studying to be a teacher. And we owe it all to Mrs. Betancourt.[1]

FROM GREAT STORIES TO A USEFUL PEDAGOGY

When I hear stories like this—and almost every school has its stories of inspired and devoted adults who reach out in ways that change people's lives—it occurs to me that we educators and social scientists have not yet found a way to capture what we hear and see. When we try to synthesize what has inspired us, to generalize from these individual stories and draw them into a theory or a technique, the images don't survive, like certain wildflowers that won't bloom if you try to transplant them.

We boil the stories down into their essences but their power slips away. We try to draw from them a methodology that seems so personal as to be nearly impossible to transmit to others, leaving us with fleeting impressions that can only be admired from a distance. We hear about the legendary Mrs. Betancourt in Puerto Rico, or about the work of Maria Ortiz amid the urban challenges of Hartford, and we somehow end up putting a frame around their unique gifts and placing it up on a shelf, so it won't get trampled when the next bunch of kids comes storming or slouching into the classroom.

Our inability to translate great stories into a useful pedagogy is due to our encountering something that people find hard to identify, talk about, or hold onto intellectually. I believe that what we are dealing with is *passion*. And it all feels too special, too intense, too outside the boundaries of normal teacher talk.

But I am convinced that passion—our own as well as other people's—can be analyzed and put to work. The examples, strategies, and techniques I describe in these pages are instances of passion in action, ways of transforming those images into use in our daily work with children and young adults. I hope to celebrate passionate teaching and make it accessible to us in whatever roles we are called upon to play. My challenge is to enable readers to translate potentially exciting ideas and models into their own practical idioms, so that these will survive the inevitable clash with our workaday constraints.

WHAT'S THE BIG DEAL ABOUT PASSION?

Why passion, when we have so many other ways of thinking about teaching and learning? Passion seems a rather odd way to characterize what teachers ought to bring to their work. Bumping into one another on a Monday morning, not many of us are likely to ask: "So, are you feeling passionate enough for your classes today?" Isn't there enough irrationality and fool-headedness in education and most everywhere else these days without adding passion to the soup?

Yet after years of looking into hundreds of classrooms and watching teachers with all kinds of students, I have come to see it is a teacher's passion that makes the greatest difference in the quality of learning. More than knowledge of subject matter. More than variety of teaching techniques. More than being well organized, friendly, funny, or fair. *Passion.*

With teachers, as with anyone else who has a goal in life to do great things—to create works of art or defend the environment or right social wrongs or create new technologies—passionate people are the ones who make a difference in our lives. By the intensity of their beliefs and actions, they connect us with a sense of value that is within—and beyond—ourselves.

Sometimes that passion burns with a quiet, refined intensity; sometimes it bellows forth with thunder and eloquence. But in whatever form or style a teacher's passion emerges, students know they are in the presence of someone whose devotion to learning is exceptional. Even when that devotion has an intensity that may make students uncomfortable, they still know it is something important. It's what makes a teacher unforgettable.

Of some of our teachers, we remember their foibles and mannerisms; of others, their kindness and encouragement, or their fierce devotion to standards of work that we probably did not share at the time. And of those who inspired us most, we remember what they cared about, and that they cared about us and the person we might become. It is this quality of caring about ideas and values—this fascination with the potential for growth within people, this depth and fervor about doing things well and striving for excellence—that comes closest to what I mean in describing a passionate teacher.

Here I can imagine an experienced teacher, someone with a pretty good reputation among colleagues and students, slamming this book shut and tossing it onto the teacher's room table: "What's this guy want from us now—blood? For eighteen years I've done my job, and done it pretty damn well. I not only teach them the stuff, but I take the time to try to get to know the kids in my classes. Isn't it enough to be a caring teacher who's got the students' interests at heart, who helps them learn each in their own way, who gives everybody a chance to succeed? What business does anybody have asking me to be 'passionate' on top of everything else?"

Obviously, no business at all. We should be more than grateful for each of the skilled, dedicated, caring teachers in our schools who do good enough work under conditions that are often demanding and stressful. I am tempted to say, "Oh, but this is not a book for you—it's for those other teachers, the ones who are just putting in their time and doing the minimum they need to get by."

But maybe it is part of my job in this book to make good teachers feel dissatisfied with being "good enough." Passion may just be the difference between being remembered as a "pretty good teacher" who made chemistry or algebra or tenth-grade English "sort of interesting"—or as the teacher who opened up a world of the mind to some students who had no one else to make them feel that they were capable of doing great things with test tubes, trumpets, trigonometry, or T. S. Eliot.

HOW IS A TEACHER "PASSIONATE"?

How, then, is a teacher "passionate"?

You can be passionate about your field of knowledge: in love with the poetry of Emily Dickinson or the prose of Marcus Garvey, dazzled by the spiral of DNA or the swirl of van Gogh's cypresses, intrigued by the origins of the Milky Way or the demise of the Soviet empire, delighted by the music of Mozart or the sonority of French vowels, crazy for health and fitness or wild about algebraic word problems.

You can be passionate about issues facing our world: active in the struggle for social justice or for the survival of the global environment and dedicated to the celebration of cultural diversity or to the search for a cure for cancer.

You can be passionate about children: about transforming underperformance among Black male students; about including children with disabilities in all school activities; about raising the low rate of high school graduation among Latino children; about the insidious effects of sexism, racism, and classism on the spirits of all children; about the neglect of "average" kids in schools where those at the "top" and "bottom" seem to get all the attention; about the decline of literacy in an age of instant electronic gratification; or about the wealth of hidden talent that goes unnoticed in so many children.

To be avowedly passionate about at least some of these things sets one apart from those who approach each day in a fog of fatigue, ritual, routine, or resignation, or who come to work wrapped in a self-protective cocoon. The passion that accompanies our attention to subjects, issues, and children is not just something we offer our students. It is also a gift we grant ourselves—a way of honoring our life's work, our profession. It says, "I know why I am devoting my life to these children."

I want to distinguish passionate teaching from mere idiosyncrasies or foibles. Lots of teachers have pet peeves or fixations: points of grammar, disciplinary practices, eccentricities of dress or diction. These may, indeed, make them memorable to their students (for better or worse). The passion I speak of conveys much more. It is their passions that help teachers and their students escape the slow death of "business as usual," the rituals of going through the motions, which in schools usually means checking that the homework was done, covering the curriculum, testing, grading, and quickly putting it all behind us. The example we set as passionate adults allows us to connect to young people's minds and spirits in a way that can have a lasting positive impact on their lives.

For me, passionate teachers include all those who ever entered the classroom because they loved kids, because they loved learning, because they wanted in some small way to change the world. Sadly, many who entered with high hopes have not been able to hold onto their passion for very long because of the conditions under which they work. Others nurse their passions quietly—almost embarrassed to care so much or to hold such high standards in a time when schools and society look for compromises and shortcuts. Still, others have become embittered by the whole scene: students who won't do any work, administrators who manipulate, colleagues who complain all the time, officials who won't provide adequate funds, parents who can't seem to be bothered, and a society that would rather blame its schools than fund them.

Many disillusioned teachers began their careers as passionate people, only to have their spirits dampened, depleted, ground to dust. The passion I talk about belongs as much to them as to the brightest-eyed newcomers or the cheeriest veterans. It is their struggle, too. Our nation of children, faced with the ever-changing demands of becoming citizens, family members, and breadwinners in a twenty-first-century world, cannot afford for any of their teachers' passions to be eroded or squelched.

WHO ARE SOME PASSIONATE TEACHERS?

What does passion look like when we see it at work in the classroom? Let's look briefly at some of the people whose stories appear in these pages.

We've just met Maria Ortiz. As I see it, her passion is to make sure that the students in her middle school, especially the girls, almost all of whom are African American or Latina, come to view science as a part of their lives and a part of their future. At a moment when so many forces around them are pushing these girls to abandon their education and their intellectual potential, Maria is determined to be that other voice—friendly and warm, but fiercely protective of the right of these young people to pursue a life of the mind.

For Tim Sullivan, the passion lies in a resolve that his fourth graders are going to be players on the field where classroom learning meets the real world: whether it's in lobbying for a seat-belt law, organizing and running a school store, or spray-painting "Stop, Look, Walk" on the sidewalk of every street corner near every elementary school in town.

David Ervin is a middle school music teacher in a middle-class college town who inspires the entire seventh grade to imagine, create, write, compose, organize, and stage an original musical play each year, with each of them playing a part.

Yvonne Griffin is passionately committed to teaching her students about making choices in their relationships with other people. She is determined that they become young people who make things happen, rather than people who things happen to.

Ed Clarke will not let any student he works with in his English classes write anything that is less than the best they can do. He flunks students in honors classes who try to slide by, while publishing the best poems and stories of even his least-skilled writers. Many of those who flunk come back the following year to work with him to get it right.

Alfredo Fuentes teaches math and wages a passionate struggle to convince everybody in the school that algebra is for *every* student, even those who have trouble with long division or don't yet know their multiplication tables.

When Dan Bisaccio was teaching science in a rural, working-class town in New Hampshire, his job was to show his students how to think and act like scientists, rather than simply to learn about science. The passion I witnessed in his teaching of evolution showed in his skill at coaching students to actively discover and debate Darwin's theories for themselves, not merely to read about and memorize them.

Susan Lukas teaches literature at an independent school with a diverse student body. She also writes poetry and fiction and edits manuscripts for other writers. Her passion as a teacher lies in assigning to her students works of literature that have great meaning for her and finding ways to encourage honest discussion about those works with all her students, even those who are hostile to the authors and their message.

Christine Sullivan teaches writing to students in all four academic levels of a traditional rural/suburban high school. Her passion about student portfolio writing has led her students to discover their own learning styles, to minimize concern for letter grades while adopting a performance-based approach to learning, and to advocate for their own individual approaches to assignments given by other teachers.

And, among the new teacher voices in this edition, Andrea Levin has, for twenty-four years brought her philosophy of empowering humanities to working-class high schoolers in Keene, New Hampshire; Joshua Chard works his magic with second graders in downtown Portland, Maine; Taylor Bussinger brings history and social studies to life; and Cory Lynn keeps the vision of that great and greatly underappreciated civil rights leader Bayard Rustin in the forefront of her middle school social studies units on "People who Changed the World Through Non-Violence."

Some of the most passionate teachers are quiet, intense, thoughtful people. They patiently insist on high standards of quality in a language or technology class. They talk with students in conferences about their work and where their talents and persistence might lead them. They stop to respond to a comment thrown out by a student that has more than a germ of truth in it. They bring in something from their current reading or their personal history that demonstrates the power of ideas.

On the other hand, a certain amount of abandon can also deliver the message. One teacher from Georgia announced at a workshop: "Ah intend this year to be jest a little bit *craaazy* about what Ah'm teaching!" What he wanted his fellow teachers to hear was that he was eager to break out of the competent but comfortable mold he had built around himself, and to break up the unimaginative complacency of his students.

What impresses me about such teachers is that no particular set of teaching tricks or topics, much less a common personality type, epitomizes them. As individual as they are, what unites them are some ways they approach the mission of teaching; they organize their curricula and their daily work with students in practical ways that play to those different strengths. These practical observations—the tools of the passionate craft of teaching—will emerge as the book progresses, but let's look at two of them here:

1. Passionate teachers organize and focus their passionate interests by getting to the heart of their subject and sharing with their students some of what lies there—the beauty and power that drew them to this field in the first place and that has deepened over time as they have learned and experienced more. They are not after a narrow or elitist perspective, but rather a depth of engagement that serves as a base for branching out to other interests and disciplines.
2. Passionate teachers convey their passion to novice learners—their students—by acting as partners in learning rather than as

> "experts" in the field. As partners, they invite less experienced learners to search for knowledge and insightful experiences, and they build confidence and competence among students who might otherwise choose to sit back and watch their teacher do and say interesting things.

But how do we make passionate teaching happen? How do we shove aside all the stuff we're supposed to do and make room in our lesson plans for things we feel especially strongly about?

GIVING OUR PASSIONS A FOCUS

Working within their disciplines, teachers best express their passions not only by what they celebrate but also by what they choose to ignore. "A man is rich," wrote Thoreau, "in proportion to the number of things which he can afford to let alone." Passionate teachers put it thus: Teachers are wise in proportion to those parts of the curriculum they conscientiously choose *not* to cover. Theodore Sizer, author of *Horace's Compromise* and *Horace's School*, calls this "the politics of subtraction" and says it is the toughest part of the reform agenda for schools.

Teachers, even in the face of new restrictions, can stop being the servants of a syllabus or curriculum produced somewhere else and take charge of a course or program of studies they have shaped out of their convictions of what is truly important and what they want students to remember and be able to use months and years later. We identify our passions within our subject area to separate what we care deeply about from what we are less excited about. We teach wholeheartedly those things that open up pathways to knowledge and engagement within our discipline for learners who have not yet come to appreciate them. We take courage from our deep interest in some things to pay less attention to other things, and we exercise a teacher's most solemn responsibility in choosing what to teach and what to ignore or pass over lightly.

We may want to ask our students to study the Cuban Missile Crisis in depth, rather than surveying the entire Cold War history. Or have them study the ecology of one small nearby pond instead of covering all the chapters in the biology text. Or learn a lot about Emily Dickinson's poetry and leave other nineteenth-century poets to be discovered later in the students' lives. Or, my own obsession, have students really get to know Hamlet (and the Hamlet within themselves) and let them approach Shakespeare through Hamlet's eyes. Language arts teachers in an urban middle school decided that learning how to write good, clear, convincing prose is so vital to students' future success that they want colleagues in science, social studies, and math to teach writing across the curriculum at the expense of some other things in the syllabus.

Unless, for example, we are teaching someone to operate a piece of dangerous machinery or to combine volatile chemicals in a laboratory, the act of teaching has more to do with preparing a learner to be an eager seeker of skills than with memorizing pertinent data. Helping young people engage in the ideas and issues *surrounding* content is crucial to their ability to make meaning out of what they are learning. If the subject seems unconnected to their own lives or seems unnecessarily tedious, they will soon forget all or most all of it and our teaching will have been for naught.

As teachers, we have only our passions to guard against students' inclination to dismiss what adults care about as boring or irrelevant. But it is not enough to focus on our passionate interests. We must show our students what it means to be passionate learners as well.

CONVEYING OUR PASSIONATE INTERESTS

Teachers are critically important role models because of what they are still learning, not just for what they already know but for their dedication to continue to learn. As experienced learners—with a high interest in and high standards for knowledge and skills—teachers are able to communicate the lasting value of these things to students. The obverse is also true: When we are no longer learning, we no longer teach effectively, because we have lost the power to exemplify for young people what it means to be intellectually active. Even though we may still be able to present them with information, we have become purveyors of subject matter—"deliverers of educational services," in the jargon of the field.

Passionate teachers share their commitment to active learning by showing, not just telling. Teachers are, after all, role models of adults who care about issues of the mind. We are readers, writers, researchers, and explorers of new knowledge, new ideas, new techniques and technologies, and new ways of appraising old facts and theories. Our very excitement about these things helps young people reach beyond their social preoccupations and self-centeredness. Teachers are people who manage to earn a living by doing intellectual work for the betterment of society. We have found a career that, for all its shortcomings, allows us to open up the world for young people. Our greatest gift to students is to engage them through passionate teaching in areas of intense concern to us—intellectual, aesthetic, cultural, spiritual, political, environmental—and, by the example we set, to help them accept themselves as vibrant and thoughtful people.

A key to such engagement is the learning partnership that passionate teachers create with students. It is not enough for us to possess these qualities in ourselves; we must bring our students on the journey with us. A high school history teacher I know in a rural New Hampshire town brought her intense interest in archaeology into the classroom by bringing her students out into the woods in search of a long-forgotten graveyard. After watching her example, they pitched in to clean and right fallen headstones and then, a week later, followed her into the local historical society to search for the records of the people whose graves they had tended. Each student, again following her example, became a two-hundred-year-old former town resident and shared their life story in a presentation for townspeople.

There are any number of ways in which passionate teachers convey, through their personalities, the devotion they give to their work. Here are a few of the characteristics that will emerge again throughout this book.

Passionate teachers love to work with young people, but they also care deeply about knowledge and ideas so that they try never to let their compassion for a student serve as a reason for excusing that student's ignorance or lack of skill. They can be hard taskmasters precisely because they care for kids so deeply. Passionate teachers are alive to what's happening in the classroom and in the world outside school, and they bring those perspectives together in their work with students. They are always relating—and helping their students relate—learning through their lived experiences, inviting students to forge their own meaning in the confrontation between life in school and life "out there in the real world."

Passionate teachers have the capacity for spontaneity and humor and for great seriousness, often at almost the same time. They join with kids in appreciating the abundant absurdity of human nature but are also sensitive to issues that deserve to be taken seriously, particularly fairness and decency in how people treat one another. They try to build a culture of mutual respect amid societal pressures to stigmatize and condemn unpopular persons and ideas and to dismiss young people and their concerns.

Passionate teachers are always taking risks, and they make at least as many mistakes as anybody else (probably more than most). What's different is how they react to their mistakes: They choose to acknowledge and learn from them, rather than to ignore or deny them. Thus, they help make the classroom a safer place for students to make their own mistakes and learn from them.

Finally, we know who passionate teachers are because they take their mission seriously and communicate their beliefs. They truly are passionate *teachers*, not just intense people who hide their passions behind a workaday mask and allow only the rare student to connect with them and benefit from their example.

STUDENT VULNERABILITY AND THE TEACHER'S ROLE

The greatest value of our passionate concerns is that they invite students to feel emotionally alive in our presence. Children are, after all, sensitive to the same emotional currents as those I've just attributed to passionate adults: intensity, vulnerability, immediacy, risk. They may not always want to feel these things, but they can hardly avoid it. School-age kids are emotionally "hanging out there" in all the physiological, social, and developmental stages they go through. They feel at times exposed, at risk, uncomfortable—anything but serene or self-satisfied.

It's so easy to forget this as we cope with children's often erratic personalities, especially in their teenage years. Even young teachers not many years removed from their own high school experience often forget what it was like to be a student. Even conscientious parents who recall their own rebelliousness expect their children to behave more consistently and more rationally. There is much pain in the loneliness, anxiety, and alienation that so many of us felt as teenagers: We want to put it out of our minds as soon as we can.

The reasons for a student's turmoil—family conflicts, worries about acceptance or sexuality, lack of meaning in life, lack of money, fears about violence—may be quite similar to, or different from, those of adults. But in most cases, what students seek from us is not that we identify with their problems (although they may seek our understanding and sympathy at times) but that we engage them on issues of importance and help them more easily accept themselves as vibrant and thoughtful people.

The pity is that we wear our successes so hesitantly and that our achievements are arrayed in such drab colors. The pity is that today's teachers are heroes to so few of the young people who file into our classrooms. Schools would be wonderful places if the depth of caring about children and their future, the desire to be helpful, and the reservoirs of good will that are so abundant within the teaching profession could more often connect with the longing that young people have for acceptance, power, and respect. That schools are not so wonderful is due to the climate created in them more by social ills, lack of resources, ineffective practices, and misguided policies than by any want of caring on the part of teachers.

Students *need* us, not because we have all the answers but because we can help them discover the right questions. We don't always know what's good for them, but we can try to protect them from having to face life's dilemmas in ignorance or despair—doing drugs, dropping out, drifting into a dead-end career or unplanned parenthood. Those adults whom young people look to for guidance know how important they are to kids' futures. For all teachers, the recovery of passion can mean a recovery of our influence—dynamic and positive influence—in the lives of children.

By modeling, examining, and explaining our values and our passionate concerns in a way that does not harangue or intimidate students, we adults—teachers, parents, coaches, and mentors—encourage children and adolescents to feel okay about believing in and aspiring to thoughtfulness.

This, I argue, is what education is. There simply is no education without a commitment to developing the mind and the character of learners. And in our time and culture, perhaps as never before, that commitment must be a passionate one if we want young people to hear and heed that calling.

4

THE CONTEXT OF PASSION

Our schools must be the labs for learning about learning. Only if schools are run as places of reflective experimentation can we teach both children and their teachers simultaneously.

—DEBORAH MEIER,
The Power of Their Ideas

So far we've been talking about the passionate individual, about passion from the internal perspective of the teacher. But passionate teaching, like all teaching, is necessarily a social process, not just an individual performance. It is grounded in the relationship between teacher and student. It aims at a goal outside itself—engaged, intense learning that changes the course of young people's lives and helps them realize their potential. A full view of the passionate teacher, therefore, comes only when we widen the lens and see teaching in context.

Passionate teaching can only take place in a certain setting. There's more to it than getting clear about what kind of impact one wants to have on students. Teachers should take aim at the heart of their subjects, as passionate learners in partnership with students. But to survive the daily grind of school life, teachers need an environment where their passionate beliefs and actions are allowed to bear fruit. As every teacher knows: "I could really be a terrific teacher, if only . . ." is an all-too-common and debilitating refrain.

YVONNE GRIFFIN'S PASSIONATE COMMITTMENT TO STUDENTS DEALING WITH THEIR SEXUALITY

The fact is that passionate teachers create the environments that make passionate teaching pay off. They can't often work in isolation (though some do), and a teacher's best efforts can be seriously undermined by a hostile school environment. But the passionate teachers I have observed are able to develop a culture that forges relationships of integrity and respect, in which people—adults and kids—know they are engaged in important work together. Yvonne Griffin is one such teacher.

The first thing you're likely to notice in Yvonne's classroom are twin posters on the wall. One of them reads, "I Expect My Students To," followed by a list of items you might find on the walls in almost any classroom (except, perhaps, for the final item in all-capital letters):

- Arrive to class on time
- Be prepared to learn
- Be eager to learn
- Respect each other
- Listen when another is talking
- Demonstrate mature, wise, and proud behavior
- Strive to earn good grades
- Never say "I can't"
- Never be afraid to say "I don't understand"
- Live up to my expectations
- EXPECT THE SAME OF ME AS I EXPECT OF YOU

Yvonne's other poster—rarely seen in classrooms—begins with "I Expect My Teacher To." This list has been compiled and added to, over the years, by her students:

- Make the class interesting
- Teach and be willing to help
- Treat everyone fairly
- Have an open mind

- Be understanding
- Hear my point of view
- Be human and personable
- Be polite
- Try to make sure everyone understands the material before tests
- Not bring personal problems to school
- Have a respect for me

At the time I observed her, Yvonne Griffin had taught for twenty-three years in the Life Management department (formerly Home Economics) of Hartford Public High School. She was selected as the city of Hartford's Teacher of the Year for 1993–94. Her favorite course is called Life Relationships.

> I invented the course a number of years ago, when the public wasn't ready for sex education but wanted someone to teach the kids about morality and values. Since then, public attitudes have shifted a bit—everyone wants you to talk about preventing AIDS and so on—but I find I like the title Life Relationships even more.
>
> I thought I was being creative by putting up on the board the chapter headings of the textbook we were using and letting my students decide which chapters to begin with. But this year I left the textbook in the closet. Instead, I asked my students: "What do you need from a course called Life Relationships?" Once they understood that it was their course to design, they went to work, made up lists in groups, prioritized them, and then decided how much of the twenty-three weeks of the semester to spend on each topic area: sexual issues, love, self-awareness, dating older adults, social problems, parental relationships, marriage. I'm even going to have the students, working in groups, design the tests for each topic.
>
> The students are very specific about what they want to know. They see the letters "OB-GYN" on the door of a doctor's office and wonder: "What's the 'OB' part stand for? What about 'GYN'?" They want to know what's wrong with high school girls dating older men, and how to talk to your mother about serious things your friends are getting into—without destroying trust among your peers. They ask, "If I'm pregnant, how should I tell my mom?" and I tell them, "Say a prayer, and then tell her the truth."

They are fascinated about the meaning of "love" in all its manifestations. And they are genuinely confused about what "marriage" means, since so many people are living together these days and having children without being married. It's not unusual for a student to ask, "If he's the father of my child, doesn't that mean he's my husband?" And they're very curious about my being married to a teacher in this school. They ask: "Don't you all ever argue?" and when I say, "Of course we do," they are baffled: "And you *still* love him? How does *that* work?"

Teaching is fascinating, but it can also get to you. One year, not too long ago, I felt my enthusiasm withering. Everything seemed all right, but I felt myself getting stale. So I did something absolutely crazy—I opened up the file cabinet and threw out all my files! All of them—the old lesson plans, the lectures, the course materials. I made myself start over. In a way, I'm doing that again this year, with the Life Relationships course. Only this time, it's the students who are putting the course back together, based on what *they* want to know.

Whenever the rigor is too fast-paced, or the frustrations creep in, I feel again how much it hurt to be told by my counselor, back in my high school in Waterbury, Connecticut, that "You're not college material; why don't you choose the Armed Services as a career?" And then I remember my math teacher, Mrs. Juanita Kent, one of only three Black teachers in the school, who would say to me, "Sweetheart, you can be anything you want to be, if you're willing to work for it!"[1]

LOVE AND SELF-AWARENESS: MY DIALOGUE WITH YVONNE GRIFFIN'S STUDENTS

Yvonne Griffin's students developed an agenda during the first week of classes. The kids decided to spend:

September 1–14 on LOVE: What is it? How to recognize it? Characteristics of good and bad relationships

September 16–29 on SELF-AWARENESS and SELF-ESTEEM, including dealing with stress, habits, and routines

October 1–13 on FRIENDSHIPS and TRUST

October 14–26 on DATING (including DATING OLDER ADULTS)

November 14–23 on CAREER PLANNING

November 28–December 8 on RELATIONSHIPS WITH PARENTS, including talking to parents about key issues

December 12–21 on MARRIAGE: What is it? Expectations & Realities

January 3–27 on SEXUAL ISSUES, SEXUAL PRESSURES, and how to cope with them

By beginning in this way and giving up a teacher's normal prerogative and duty to plan the course herself, Yvonne Griffin opened up whole new avenues of student engagement and collaboration. She then invited me to come in and speak with her students, most of whom were now taking another course with her. After briefly introducing me to the students, some eight or nine of whom had taken the Life Relationships course that had just ended, she excused herself so that the students and I could talk. All but two of the students were young women, African Americans and Latinas. She hadn't told them I was coming, but seemed to feel it wasn't necessary to prepare them in any way. We just started to talk.

RLF: Tell me what happened last semester in the Life Relationships course that was different from what normally happens.

CHRISSY: We had a chance to choose the subjects that we wanted to talk about in this class. We made a list of them on the board and then we voted on the ones that were most interesting to us. We set a time period for each—one subject was love and we used about four weeks for that. That was the longest. Everybody got to express their own views.

GINA: And we made up some of the questions for the tests that we took.

RLF: Why should students be doing this? Isn't it the teacher's job to come in and tell the class, "Here's what we have to learn; here's what the textbook says; here's what's going to be on the test"? Why should students be asked to do that stuff?

GINA: It made it more comfortable for us to decide what we want to learn and made it more interesting by seeing what we have to say about it.

RLF: Then what's the teacher's job?

GINA: To make sure we're learning something.

RLF: So you get to say what you want to learn, and how much time you want to spend on it, and she gets to help you learn it?

NIKI: And test you on it.

AMBER: So that you learn what you really want to learn.

RLF: Does that change how much you're able to remember?

NIKI: You're interested in it, so you remember it.

RLF: What do you remember about that class?

GINA: The "trust walk," where you had a partner and you were blindfolded, and your partner had to guide you through the halls. And we had to trust that they were not going to let us fall or bump into something.

NIKI: We were learning about building friendships.

AMBER: In a friendship, if there isn't any trust, it won't work.

RLF: What else did you take away from that course that you think is useful to you?

GINA: I liked the discussions. If someone had a question, you'd just sit down and talk about it. Or Ms. Griffin would ask us a question about how we felt about something, and we would just say what we thought.

RLF: Are your friendships or relationships going to be any different because of what happened in that course? Are you any different because of it—or was it just more interesting?

GINA: To me, it made me more aware. I'm the kind of person that doesn't listen to what my boyfriend has to say. I always want to have my own say first. And it made me more patient and less aggressive.

COOP: I learned the difference between love and infatuation, and so I don't think I'll fall into the same kind of stuff that I might have fallen into.

RLF: Can you tell me what the difference is?

AMBER: Infatuation is just the thought of being in love.

RLF: [to a boy who was not in the class last semester] If you met someone you liked, how would you know if it was something real, and not just a "WOW" thing?

ROC: Ain't never been different than "WOW."

AMBER: If there isn't much communication and trust and stuff, then you know you're not in love.

ANNA: If you're really in love, you have more emotion, and it's not just physical.

RLF: This is a different way of going about school, isn't it? You don't walk into other classes and have the teacher say to you, "What would you like to learn this semester? And how much time do you want to spend on it?" Do you?

SEVERAL: No.

RLF: Then why did it happen here?

CHRISSY: Because Ms. Griffin is a different kind of teacher.

RLF: And what makes her a different kind of teacher?

NIKI: She wants you to learn.

CHRISSY: She tries different things to make sure that everyone gets something out of it—

NIKI: Not just what the textbook says—

CHRISSY: So that we understand enough of it in order to teach one another.

RLF: What else, besides love, did you learn about?

TISHA: About abusive relationships. What the statistics are about it. Why they stay in it.

RLF: Why who stays?

COOP: Battered women—

ROC: Or men, sometimes—

TISHA: And it's not just physical abuse or hitting you. It can be someone calling you names all the time and making you feel worthless.

RLF: And what did you get from the class that you didn't already know about it?

CHRISSY: That when someone says they love you but they are watching you all the time and not trusting you—

AMBER: That's just control, that's not love.

RLF: But you knew that before you took this class, didn't you?

NIKI: Yeah, but we didn't think about it that much, didn't pay it much mind. You'd say, "That's an abusive relationship, but that's their business." Now we've learned to be more aware of it, so that if you see it going on, maybe you should say something. Because maybe the person that's involved in it is too scared to say something about it herself.

RLF: So you learned that it's not just getting out of it yourself, but how to help a friend?

SEVERAL: Yes.

RLF: But what happens if your friend says, "But I love him. And he always apologizes. And he's all I got." What do you say then?

CHRISSY: You say, "He doesn't love you, because if he loved you, he wouldn't put his hands on you. And there's nothing you could have done, or whatever, that justifies his hitting you."

GINA: You can be as angry as you want about something, but you should take it out on yourself. Don't take it out on someone else.

NIKI: Break a table, break a glass.

JOHN: Maybe the person is scared, because it's the first person they loved, and they're afraid. And sometimes people who abuse were abused themselves.

GINA: It could be that when they grew up in their family, they saw their mother and father abusing each other. And then they abuse their wives or girlfriends.

JOHN: What if your girl finds you've been cheating on her and the first time she sees you she slaps your face?

SEVERAL: Oh, that's different. That's something else.

AMBER: If she slaps you 'cause she's real angry, 'cause you got caught cheating . . . that's not abuse, that's just a slap. And you're lucky that's *all* you got. Abuse is if he asks you to be home at a certain time. And if you weren't there just then and when you walk in the door, he grabs you by your head and throws you around the room and smacks you up like that. Now, that's abuse! But to get one smack for cheating on somebody—you came out pretty good!

RLF: It sounds to me like you got a lot out of this class—

SEVERAL: Uh huh! Yes. Mmmm.

RLF: What I'm really interested in is what can we tell other teachers about how to run a class where students get to play a real part in deciding what we are to learn and how long we learn it? Where else might this idea work?

SEVERAL: English. Definitely.

NIKI: We could get a book list, and choose the books that we want to read—

CHRISSY: And how long we want to spend on it, and what kind of discussions we want to have about the book. 'Cause we don't do that in my English class. And I wish we did.

GINA: My English teacher makes it fun. He's always doing something to make us laugh and make it interesting.

RLF: It seems to me that we're talking about three things here: There can be a boring class (everybody has had one of those). Then, there's a teacher who makes things fun (we know that, too). But isn't this class different? Because what you said was not "She came in and she did this, and that was fun. . . . " You said—what did you say about Ms. Griffin's class?

NIKI: Ms. Griffin seems like she wants to relate to us. She makes us feel—

CHRISSY: She goes into everything—

AMBER: She takes us back to when she was our age. And then you get to compare—

NIKI: And see all the patterns—

CHRISSY: Yeah, see the patterns that have been changing.

RLF: But you also did something different. It wasn't "the teacher was boring" or "the teacher made it fun." You got to make some decisions, didn't you?

SEVERAL: Yes, uh huh.

GINA: We all got to help make up the exams.

RLF: Now, was that cheating?

SEVERAL: No. No.

AMBER: Because we still had to study. And she added some of her own questions to the ones we made up.

RLF: Supposing in almost every one of your classes, the teachers involved you in helping to decide things, in getting involved in projects and having discussions—would that make your education better? Or would that get boring after a while?

CHRISSY: It would make it better. Because in some other classes, when we have a test we don't make up the questions. And when we get the test, it's a whole different set of questions than what we were studying. And we fail it. But in Ms. Griffin's class, we know what's on the test. And even though she adds a few new things to it, we study and we score higher.

RLF: And you learn more, too?

SEVERAL: Yes, yeah. Because we know—

NIKI: We know what we've been talking about. Because we've discussed it all together.

COOP: It's respect. You have respect for her and she has respect for us.

CHRISSY: And you can go and talk to her, because you're there in the class and you feel close to her.

It didn't take a redesigned course for Yvonne Griffin to earn the trust and affection of her students. She has had that for many years. What was new is that her depth of caring, her skill and confidence as an experienced teacher were paying new dividends in terms of the quality of the learning partnership she is able to establish with her students. In her many years of teaching, Yvonne has learned a lot of things that "work" for her. Like other veteran teachers, she has her bag of tricks and keeps it tucked into an easily accessible part of her mind. But successful, inspired teaching, especially in a school where most of the students would be defined as "educationally disadvantaged," has to be more than a bag of tricks, more than a string of techniques or sure-fire lessons that can be drawn upon to enliven a class.

Passionate teachers like Yvonne Griffin are more than the sum of their lesson plans, anecdotes, and strategies for motivating kids. There is something about their personality that helps students engage and stay focused—but that something is not just a unique personality. It is, I believe, a blending of three elements—*respect*, *collaboration*, and a sense of the work's importance and *connection to the world* outside school—that combine in mutually reinforcing ways and enable teachers like Yvonne to sustain such a climate and culture. Let's look at these qualities in turn.

RESPECT

A high degree of mutual respect, a rare commodity in our society and in our schools, is critical to the success of learning. Only in a climate where people feel they can be themselves—without facing ridicule, prejudice, or alienation—can they take risks, make mistakes, and keep growing as persons. Without such respect, everyone's energies get diverted toward self-protection and survival—the very opposite of what is needed for learning to take place.

We can no longer simply assume, as many of our own teachers did, that students will come to school ready to respect us and the knowledge we offer them. We must earn the respect of young people. We must convince them that we know things of real value to them if we are to persuade them to work hard. We can't just throw the hard stuff at them and tell them, "I am your teacher, I know what you need, and you'll thank me later for making you learn this." Above all, we need to demonstrate respect in order to receive it.

Yvonne Griffin put it this way: "Twenty-three years ago, when I began to teach, I wanted most to prove to students that I could be somebody's friend. The part about respect seemed less important. But I've learned that it is by demanding and offering respect that I do get to be somebody's friend, rather than the other way around."

Respect must exist among students as well as between students and teacher. Nothing inhibits active learning in a class half so much as students' fears that they will embarrass themselves in front of other kids. Many students will accept a failing grade for class participation rather than expose themselves to potential ridicule by saying something awkward or unpopular. And if students are not participating, they are probably not learning much, either.

Most students understand school rules about not hitting or using their cell phones. They are also supposed to be taught something about respecting people of different cultures and backgrounds. But rarely do they learn how to be kind or act decently to classmates who've been labeled "unpopular." We must find a way to get students to join the conversation about mutual respect so that it won't always be our role to try to cut down on the teasing and bullying.

Developing a climate of mutual respect is part of teaching about science, music, or grammar. Such respect develops most readily among adults and young people who know they are doing important work together—not necessarily among groups that spend the most time talking about it.

COLLABORATION

When young people develop an awareness that teaching and learning are collaborative, not isolated, individual ventures, they see their own work as part of a team effort and are more inclined to give their best. This is particularly evident in neighborhoods where many families suffer from inadequate schooling. Many at-risk kids with high potential just won't perform if it means "showing up" their friends.

Teachers no longer really have the luxury of focusing on their students solely as individuals (although they will, of course, continue to acknowledge their students' individuality in any number of ways). And, just as important, students are no longer as likely to ignore their classmates and do their work in isolation. They must come to know, accept, and work with one another.

This presents some challenges, to say the least. Few of us who are now adults spent much time as children learning collaboratively. We got A's or B's precisely by doing our own work, and those among our classmates who could not work well under those conditions left school to find other places to grow up (in the army, on the job, raising a family, etc.). But things have changed: For more children these days, learning requires teamwork.

We have seen our middle schools transformed from the junior high school model to one where students are grouped in clusters, teams, or houses, and this trend appears to be extending to the "clustering" of ninth and tenth grades. Cooperative learning, the practice of forming temporary, interactive learning groups within the classroom, has spread even more widely. Teachers are being asked as never before to collaborate across disciplines and grade levels. The existence of national performance standards in the various curricula (though denounced by consevative groups), along with the movement toward new and more authentic forms of assessment, will hopefully accentuate that process.

CONNECTION TO THE WORLD

The notion that students work harder when they understand how their learning connects with their culture, family, neighborhood, and personal concerns is an idea that has been around since John Dewey first proposed this in the late 1800s. This doesn't mean that teachers have to pander to popular culture. It means that we search for ways to help students translate the real dilemmas of their time—about the quality of their lives and their neighborhood, about fairness and prejudice, opportunity and despair, friendship and betrayal—into the subject matter at hand.

Passionate teaching can only be recognized, ultimately, in terms of students engaging in productive learning that connects with real-world problems and events. If we are to succeed in our work with students, we must realize that what they produce and the habits of mind that allow them to be productive are essential. The old notion of "Well, I've laid it out there for them—whether they pick it up or not is *their* business" cannot serve us anymore (if indeed it ever could). We need to nurture the growth, not just scatter the seeds, of knowledge and skills among a great diversity of students. Mutual respect comes when teacher and students realize that the work is real and useful, has value in itself, and that acquiring certain skills and knowledge and attitudes allows them to accomplish something they recognize as important.

Education is, after all, about enabling students to know and do important things and to act as decent, responsible, and thoughtful people. Our preoccupation in schools should be with nurturing the capacity within students to learn while they attend school and to continue to learn on their own after they have left.

Not everything we teach must immediately become connected to the "real world"; nor should teachers be thwarted by their students' lukewarm reactions to subjects that we adults are passionate about. Part of what makes us important role models for young people is the patience we display when something (a book, a play, a scientific article) doesn't engage us immediately, the appreciation we show for hard work on difficult skills, and our faith that persistence and diligence pay off over time.

Whenever we can inspire young people to put to use the knowledge and skills they are trying to acquire by accomplishing some task that is respected in the world beyond school (e.g., tutoring younger kids, creating a nature trail, using math to help families with shopping or taxes, organizing an environmental action, writing for community audiences, rallying around a local issue), students are much more likely to understand why they need to acquire the basic skills that lead to success, and they are more willing to work hard to learn them. Students who employ their fledgling grasp of geometry to design a playground for a neighborhood preschool appreciate both what they know and do not yet know about the subject.

My argument, then, for passionate teaching and its connection to engaged and sustained learning can be summarized by three interwoven statements:

1. When students can appreciate their teacher as someone who is passionately committed to a field of study and to upholding high standards within it, it is much easier for them to take their work seriously. Getting them to learn, then, becomes a matter of inspiration by example, rather than by enforcement and obedience.
2. Without a trusting and respectful relationship among students and teachers, everyone's ability to work collaboratively and to take the kind of risks that learning requires is jeopardized.
3. Unless students are able to see the connection between what they are learning and how they might put such learning to work in a real-life context, their motivation to excel will remain uneven at best. The self-directed and the obedient ones will manage to get something out of their schooling, and the rest will fall by the wayside. When students know that their work has meaning in the world beyond school—and that other people are an audience for what the students can produce or perform—their sense of pride motivates them to do their best.

THE INDIVIDUAL TEACHER AND THE CULTURE OF SCHOOL

But how will the individual teacher attempt all this in the face of what the late Seymour Sarason called "the culture of the school"? How much can one person do, after all, in the midst of the stress and turmoil of contemporary school life? Am I not placing too much responsibility for passionate teaching and learning on the shoulders of the individual teacher?

Our society's economic and social traumas are familiar to all of us, as is the range of unmet needs and unfulfilled dreams students bring to school. Teachers who work in schools within neighborhoods plagued by poverty, violence, and family hardship face even greater obstacles in trying to create the right environment for learning.

There is much we can do to help kids get excited about learning, even amid today's constraints and hardships. Many teachers work small miracles with their students in the face of great obstacles and lack of support, and they rarely get the credit they deserve for the many acts of compassion, encouragement, and courage that their job demands. This book is for all who struggle to do their best for children under the tough conditions in our schools and neighborhoods and for those who seek inspiration and support for their work despite centuries of bad lessons in human dynamics that form the foundations of many school practices.

While much of what teachers now do in class represents caring, commitment, and experience, much of their vitality may be undermined by wrong-headed policies and bureaucratic humiliations. I think of a Spanish teacher who had finally managed to get her beginning students to take some pleasure in learning a new language and who helped them build a piñata. On the day that she brought them outside to break the piñata, her principal leaned out the window and ordered the class back inside, declaring that it was not an educational activity!

Though our entire nation may be crying for better schools, too many efforts for change come in a format that puts teachers off or never really touch the classroom. If the challenges of AI seem unnerving today, let's remember that, years ago "new paradigms" were all the rage, trumpeted by a superintendent who had just come back from a conference. By the next year, everyone was chasing around to implement "total quality management" because a school board member had been impressed with how it works in the company where she was employed. But if teachers don't feel that a new strategy or approach can be put to practical use, they won't bring it into their classrooms. And if it doesn't happen in the classroom, it isn't going to mean much to students.

Any worthwhile school change effort must be owned by teachers working together, or it is unlikely to take hold. Veteran teachers tell me that almost any innovation or change that teachers don't care for can be undermined or simply ignored; eventually it will just go away. They have seen it happen dozens of times.

And it's not enough, usually, for one or two or a few teachers to adopt a new initiative. A change has to be shared, fussed over, kicked around, and reshaped by enough teachers until it feels comfortable. This happened to cooperative learning which, after several years of awkwardness and experimentation, was adopted by a critical mass of teachers, and students today are not nearly as resistant as they once were to taking responsibility for working in diverse groups. This process is beginning to happen with performance-based graduation standards and with assessments of student learning in which the "tests" approximate situations in real life—although both changes have a long way to go to gain widespread acceptance. While most of the paths suggested in this book can be followed by individual teachers and their students, in the end it may just be too exhausting for most to sustain real change in the face of apathy, exhaustion, or resistance from others within and without the school. Lacking such support, a lot of good ideas atrophy and die.

Thus, like it or not, passionate teachers may need to become reformers as well. This is a very hard role to add to the enormous burdens that teachers already shoulder, and there may be resistance to the notion of reform among some passionate teachers who have managed to keep their idealism alive in tough situations mainly by isolating themselves from much of what goes on in school.

As teachers, parents, and adults from any walk of life who are devoted to young people, we often feel restrained in what we can offer to this, or any, new generation. Caring is certainly an essential part of what we can give. But however much we care for our students as people, we must also work with our colleagues to give them our love of learning, our commitment to both academic and ethical standards, and our passionate resolve to know the truth about things.

5

A PASSION FOR CONTENT

Surely we are incomplete as teachers if we are committed only to what we are teaching but not to our students, or only to our students but not to what we are teaching, or half-hearted in our commitment to both.

—PETER ELBOW, *Embracing Contraries: Explorations in Learning and Teaching*

DEPTH VS. BREADTH: DEBATE IN AN ELEVATOR

In an elevator filled with some of the nation's top high school biology teachers, at an invitational conference on how to integrate new biotechnologies into the school curriculum, a conference leader cornered one of the participants, Dan Bisaccio—whose school subscribed to the principles of Ted Sizer's Coalition of Essential Schools—and proceeded to tell him just what she thought of some of his ideas: "This less-is-more philosophy, which you Coalition people advocate, is doing real damage to biology content in our schools. It is helping to gut the biology curriculum."

Dan, always ready for a good debate, responded: "You've obviously been influenced by the myth that 'less is more' means that 'content doesn't matter.'" He proceeded to describe the work of several of his students whose self-designed projects had allowed them to work with content in much greater depth than if they had been required to assimilate great quantities of material from appropriate textbooks. One student had done original research on "Self-Recognition in Goldi's Monkeys" that led to her becoming the first high school student ever invited to present a paper at the annual meeting of the North American Zoological Association.

His antagonist wasn't satisfied: "Of course there are exceptions. But what are we doing for our brightest kids? Won't they be dragged down by a curriculum that appears to be focused on helping mid-level kids find relevance in their schoolwork? What about those who are eager for real content and don't want to be held back or forced to spend all their time teaching the slower kids in their 'learning group'?"

"I share your concern about academic rigor," Dan replied. "But you don't have to force content on kids in order to be rigorous. What you have to do is to think of them as amateur biologists, or amateur mathematicians, or whatever—throw a real problem at them and help them work through it."

And so it went, the elevator moving from floor to floor for more than ten minutes, but none of the dozen or so biology teachers inside moved to leave. Nobody wanted to risk missing any of the debate. It was an issue that hit home for every one of them, no matter whose side of the argument they favored.

The episode points to an apparent tension. On the one hand, I have been arguing for teachers to be passionately and openly engaged in celebrating the content of their field, serving as models for their students of what people are like who care about things of the mind. On the other, I plead that in order to focus students' energies on in-depth content, we need to cover fewer subjects; we get to the heart of our field of knowledge, in part, by teaching less material.

But people who are passionate about their subject will want to do it justice in all its scope. People who have spent years reading and thinking about history or literature, about the arts and sciences, keep finding new things they want to teach, as well as foundation knowledge that they are convinced students need to know in order to work within the field and to appreciate new developments in it. What a contradiction: Isn't a love of content in conflict with the injunction to teach less? Isn't it true that much of a teacher's worth lies in how much of the important subject matter of the discipline he or she is able to convey to students?

Before attempting to resolve this tension, let's push the argument a bit further. Passionate teachers who view themselves as thinkers, scholars, researchers, and critics—not just as coaches, facilitators, or managers of learning—are loath to imagine any shift in curriculum that results in reduced content. Indeed, they view lack of attention to a knowledge of the past as contributing to the failure of students to perform to world standards in the future and may make it even harder for disadvantaged students to find their way to college. Something is sorely lacking in the rhetoric about self-concept, self-motivation, and essential outcomes if academic standards keep focusing on what's minimal and if we continue to shield students from the rigor and the challenge of immersion in the content of the humanities and the sciences.

A number of our most concerned and influential parents—those who respect and even revere the education they received in schools where high standards and immersion in "the classics" were championed—share this view. They are unwilling to see any change in schooling that appears to "dumb down" the curriculum to make it easily accessible or "fun." They do not see this as an elitist view; to the contrary, they want to see classical, content-rich education broadened to involve more students, especially those kids whose families are not able to provide them with extracurricular opportunities in the face of school cutbacks and retrenchment.

Content, after all, is what defines a discipline, makes it unique and rich in meaning. By immersing themselves in the content of their disciplines, teachers and scholars participate in the survival of intellectual life in our culture and our age. If being a teacher means anything to them, it means holding that beacon aloft in a society awash in ignorance, prejudice, and a chronic devaluation of education.

But advocates of "less is more" plead just as passionately that forcing vast amounts of information on students only dulls most of them to the intellectual engagement that lovers of content ardently seek. Unless we restrict our teaching to the 10 percent of students eager for content-heavy Advanced Placement courses (and how many of even this group have enrolled because of love of transcript, as opposed to love of content?), the realities of the classroom work against the delivery of information via lecture and vast amounts of required reading. Even the most colorful and entertaining presenter wages a losing battle against a generation habituated to instantaneous electronic variety. By the time we are halfway through covering the essential background information that the typical syllabus demands as a prerequisite for classroom discussion, we have lost much of our audience. And only the threat of the grade book can keep most students in line once they realize they're bored. Advocates of the less-is-more argument say that we must be ready to sacrifice breadth of content in order to achieve the depth of engagement that passionate teachers seek to engender in their students.

So, which is it to be: a rich, traditional focus on content, or a commitment to in-depth student engagement in critical issues? As the historians and social studies scholars who worked over many years to define national standards are discovering, the battle can get pretty nasty.

For the passionate teacher, it's got to be *both*—students will experience a rich, content-filled curriculum; students will discover for themselves the excitement of in-depth study. But to want both requires sacrifices and changes.

Resolving this tension begins with a reexamination of what we mean by content. Educational content, after all, has no intrinsic value. A date or a naked fact is without significance. After all, what do 1066, E = mc2, and 98.6 degrees mean? Each gains meaning only from its context, from being surrounded by activities of thought, investigation, comparison, synthesis, and application. And, inconvenient and time-consuming though it may be, students must be part of developing that context, or else the factual content their teachers impart to them will quickly disappear from their minds and memories. If anything remains with them at all, it is likely to be a long-lasting distaste for the entire subject.

Witness the fate in our society of Shakespeare, of the classics, and of history in the wake of our traditional approach to content in our pedagogy. Are we not a nation of ex-students who were expected to imbibe content just as it came from our teachers' lectures and from our textbooks? Once out of school, too many of us never touch the stuff.

CONTENT KNOWLEDGE MUST HAVE A CONTEXT

Content knowledge must have its context: A degree of temperature is only a mark on a scale unless it is related to the boiling point of water; a line of poetry is just a string of words without the context of the poem and the voice of the poet. "Freedom" is simply one word out of a hundred thousand in the dictionary, until we hear it in the voices of the marchers from Selma to Montgomery as they faced police dogs and billy clubs during the civil rights struggle.

Thus teachers' passion for content serves them best when they draw upon it to help students understand and appreciate what the context is all about: what kind of world was scrutinizing Galileo as he peered through his telescope; what manner of society Columbus was barging in on when he "discovered" the "New" World.

All this seems to be—but is not—the age-old dialectic of "process versus content," that hypothetical choice between *how* we learn and *what* we learn. That is a false issue, a red herring, and we should remove the weight of its prejudice from our pedagogical inquiry. As adults who care deeply about learning, we must ensure that our passions for our discipline never leave us stranded between the "how" and the "what" of learning—in literature, physics, history, or other subject areas. Instead, our passions can build bridges over that supposed chasm and forge links between facts and their meaning and utilization. What musician, chef, trial lawyer, midwife, or landscape gardener would try to separate "process" from "content" in their work?

Even in the "hardest" of the hard sciences or the most linear and sequential of math courses, the successful teacher shows students that concepts are learned not to "get them down" but to put them to work—here and now, at higher levels of study, and in the workplace. Even in the "softest" of liberal arts, as in poetry and philosophy, the successful teacher helps students take pleasure in the tactile qualities of words, and then shows how to make language serve us in building powerful arguments or eloquent thoughts.

To engage students in content, we must change our pedagogy by limiting the amount of stuff we teach so that our students learn the important things well and dig deeply into the subject; by posing interesting questions, setting up a framework for inquiry; and then by getting out of the way to let the students do the work.

The truth is, we can't do any of these things if we try to "cover the curriculum" or to make sure students are "exposed" to everything of importance in the syllabus. We can't search for the heart of our subject if there is no heart—if it's *all* supposed to be important. We can't let students think their way through the course if we take responsibility for teaching it all. Students, being inexperienced, will—out of necessity—waste a lot of time, as do all discoverers, tinkerers, and inventors. In a sense, it is more economical for teachers to deliver the material by lecturing and writing notes on the board—it's just that by this method, students are almost guaranteed to forget it. Students cannot dig deeply when they are rushing to get through quantities of stuff.

WHEN CONTENT FAILS: CLASSICS AT A CLIP

Here is a typical example of how good teachers get trapped. In the middle school years, the study of classical civilizations is part of the curriculum. What do we include? What dare we leave out? Afraid to omit anything in this culturally diverse world, we race from ancient Egypt to the Ming Dynasty of China, then on to the glory that was Greece, with perhaps a side trip to Ghana's golden age, then on to the Aztecs, Incas, and Mayans, finishing up with the grandeur that was Rome—a kind of historical package tour. We offer young people little more than a CliffsNotes scan of major personages and events: Tutankhamen and the Sphinx, China's invention of gunpowder and printing, Spartans versus Athenians with a few Olympians thrown in, then on to more pyramids and bloody sacrifices in the New World.

What we get back from them are pat answers from the textbook; paragraphs copied from Wikipedia; cardboard posters of Egyptian or Mayan pyramids; out-of-scale Buddhist temples or lopsided Greek columns; Great Walls made from plastic Lego blocks—all capped off, perhaps, by a pre-teen toga party or a luncheon of Chinese or Mexican food. It's a microwave curriculum: food for anything but thought. By this point in the unit, the kids know it's just a game.

THE ALTERNATIVE: STUDENTS TAKING THE INITIATIVE

What should we do instead? Here are two alternatives similar to those I have seen in middle school classrooms. In the first option, we fill four or five boxes with raw materials, one for each civilization we've decided to address. Each box contains a textbook, one or two *National Geographic* issues, some digital images or slides from art museums, a book of stories or myths of that era, a modern and an ancient map, and anything else of interest that we can put our hands on.

Students are grouped into teams of four to six kids, and each group selects one of the civilizations to work on. Each group has to research and answer several questions:

- What made this civilization "great"?
- What was it like to be a child living at that time? A woman? A servant or slave?
- Which people were the most powerful? Which were the least?
- How did people earn their living?
- What did their towns and cities look like?
- Did these people invent anything that we still use?
- Why did this civilization fall from power?

We give them several weeks to discover the answers, using stuff from the boxes and from the school and town library, along with online sources, perhaps having some older students or interested parents come in to help them with their research. The students prepare to respond to the questions—both orally and with displays—and to share their findings with their classmates. As each group makes its presentation, their classmates take notes and evaluate each group on how well it has answered the questions. At the end of each presentation, we ask each group to answer a final question: "Why should we want to learn any more about this civilization? Why are they interesting to people like us?" Then the whole class votes to see which civilization we should all spend another week or two studying; the group that won the class vote can have the satisfaction of leading this final part of the unit.

A second option for this unit has the teacher select one, or at most two, civilizations to spend as much time on as is normally allotted for studying all of them. Using the same general list of questions, each group of students investigates two or three questions of their choice, including one that every group has to answer.

Simultaneously, the class is asked to come up with a few questions that they want their teacher to research (especially questions that aren't answered in the text), so that everyone in the room is engaged in discovering and sharing important information about the civilization being studied.

If several classes in the same grade adopt this approach, each class could choose one civilization and share their answers to common questions with other classes. In both of these options, students have some involvement with all of the civilizations via their schoolmates' research, while also doing their own in-depth research on one.

Units like these fit our criteria for engaging students. In choosing not to cover all of the civilizations for all of our students, we have limited the amount of stuff to be learned; students dig deeply into the subject and have the time to share and apply what they have learned. As we develop the questions, we are free to include issues that matter deeply to us—What kinds of freedoms did people enjoy? What was the role of women? What kind of education did common people receive?—and topics of long-standing personal interest: architecture, athletics, art, technology, and ecology. The content of the unit includes not only the information to be discovered in answering the unit questions but the intellectual and social skills that students will develop and practice as they conduct research and prepare to deliver their reports.

Finally, this unit allows us to set up a framework for inquiry and then let the students do the work, while we act as research adviser and coach, modeling how an adult learner investigates the questions that our students have posed to us.

SACRIFICES FOR PRODUCTIVE LEARNING

What have we sacrificed, as our students work on one or two ancient cultures instead of quickly running through all five? At worst, not every sixth grader's study would be alike or reflect the textbook. Teachers could not testify that they had "covered" Greece and Rome, the rise of the Pyramids, and the decline of the dynasties. We might be accused of crimes against cultural literacy in not "exposing" students to each of these civilizations—as though "coverage" and "exposure" had become synonyms, rather than opposites.

But in asking students to discover for themselves what the lecture or textbook would have more efficiently presented, we have helped them to honor the richness of historical content by doing the work that historians do: digging things up, asking questions, making comparisons, and presenting and debating findings that they think are interesting and worth knowing.

In fact, the traditional approach to covering the curriculum has little or no data to support it: We rarely retest kids a year later to find out how much of the covered information they have retained. I often ask teachers: "If the school board decreed that the final exam for any course had to be given a year after the course was completed, would that change how you teach?" The answer I get (after a guffaw or two that signifies the total absurdity of such a proposition) is that their entire pedagogy would have to be reinvented since it is now based on conveying information to students that they are likely to soon forget. As one veteran teacher put it: "Retest them in a year? It's all gone in three weeks!"

A FRAMEWORK FOR CONTENT

I'd like to propose a way to organize the content of a unit, a course, or an entire curriculum so that students experience a variety of ways to acquire subject matter knowledge, while also developing their capacity to work with information, to synthesize it, and—most crucially—to apply it to the world around them.

Here's my model:

1. INTRODUCE ⇨ READ ABOUT ⇨ EXPLAIN ⇨ IDENTIFY
⇧ ⇩
2. EXPLORE ⇨ DISCUSS ⇨ RELATE ⇨ UNDERSTAND
⇧ ⇩
3. RESEARCH ⇨ COMPARE/CONTRAST ⇨ SYNTHESIZE
⇧ ⇩
4. SELECT ⇨ SPECULATE ⇨ CREATE ⇨ APPLY

We might begin, in planning a course, with category 1: information we think students ought to gain some familiarity with, even if they will inevitably soon forget most of it. We then move on to category 2 and describe knowledge we want students to comprehend because it holds the conceptual keys to our discipline and contains ideas we want them to be able to use in a variety of contexts. On the other hand, we might start out in category 2, with an exploration and discussion of a subject or problem whose content students believe they know very little about and proceed to identify and introduce some of the category 1 information based on their questions and discoveries.

Category 3 is for aspects of the knowledge in category 2 that we want students to work with in depth—to research and become familiar with, to synthesize and report on—for example, the theory of evolution and the scientific method. Finally, in category 4, we see a more sharply defined area of content in which a student might choose to do original, creative work and apply such knowledge to life outside the classroom.

With this framework we can begin our engagement with content almost anywhere on the chart, according to our own pedagogy or approach to learning, and move up and down as the need for information, understanding, synthesis, or application of knowledge dictates. The challenge for teachers in making this work is to decide which areas of content belong in each category—distinguishing what is essential for students to learn from what students can access on their own when and if they need it. Here's more on what each category represents.

Content to Identify

In this framework, the first category consists of all those things that teachers want their students to be able to identify—to recognize and give some definition to. In a science course, it would include the particular terms relevant to that area of science; in French or Spanish, it would be the appropriate vocabulary for the first, second, or third year of the language—content for students to become familiar with so that they can participate in the readings and discussions of the classroom, but not necessarily to remember beyond the end of the course. One hopes that even after forgetting most of the definitions, students will be familiar enough with them to be easily reminded of their meaning when they appear again or to know where to look if they ever need to use them again.

Content to Understand

Here are some examples of important concepts and principles, themes, theories, movements, and issues that characterize a subject or discipline: irony in literature, what holds the solar system together, negative numbers in math, the imperfect tense in a language. We want students not only to identify such things (i.e., give the right definition on a multiple-choice test) but to investigate and become familiar enough with them to be able to put them in their own words, to connect them to similar concepts and ideas in this and other fields, and to understand what they mean and how they are used. Here, we want more than a surface or cursory identification: We want more depth of comprehension and, we hope, a longer memory of what these concepts mean.

Content to Synthesize

In this category, we have material that we expect students to really work with: to research to compare and contrast with related material, to evaluate the relevance of, and to communicate and show that they have carefully and systematically made that information their own. This is the stuff of research projects, of student-led investigations, leading to a synthesis wherein students put together what they have learned and convey what it means in a written report, an essay test, a class debate, or a multimedia presentation. Inevitably the content in this category is selected from the first two areas. Teachers assign topics for students to work on (or allow students to select them from a given list) with the expectation that each student will go into greater depth on a part of the content and will integrate ideas and data from a variety of sources.

In literature, students do not just define or discuss irony but show, for example, where irony may be found in the works of a poet whose poems may not at first appear to be ironic. A history teacher wants to see that the student has researched an important military battle or political struggle from a number of points of view and can offer a reasoned opinion as to why certain forces prevailed. In biology class, the teacher wants students to undertake projects that involve experimentation and research, even if each student studies in depth only one of the species that inhabit a bioregion. A foreign-language student might combine the vocabulary, verb tenses, and expressions that have been learned during preceding weeks or months into a dialogue or story.

Content for Creative Application

The final category of learning is one that passionate teachers yearn to see their students engage with but one that we find difficult to promote under current conditions of schooling. It is content that students actually create or extend, content that they put to work in unique contexts. A student may decide, for example, to write a group of poems with an ironic theme or develop and support with documentation a new hypothesis on why a historical event happened the way it did. Or a group of students may decide to teach the foreign language they're learning to younger kids in an elementary class or take action on a local environmental issue, based on the biological research they have done. Another student may take an idea from a vocational or technology course and turn it into a small business venture or organize a math Olympics for the school. In all these examples, students apply their knowledge to new or unpredictable circumstances.

Years after students have performed these projects, the experience and the pride remain for all involved. These are experiences that shape careers or engender a lifelong interest in an area of study. And to a passionate teacher, they are worth whatever sacrifice it takes in quantity of content introduced in order to bring them about.

Most teachers would rightly argue that you cannot base everyday teaching on an expectation of such peak experiences. Students need to learn their irregular verbs and their multiplication tables, after all. They need to understand how our government works and how good sentences and paragraphs are put together. They need to get their algebra straight if they want to do good work in physics or chemistry—as well as math.

True enough. Here is how all four categories might come together in a given unit of instruction. Let's take the US Constitution, which most of us agree students should know something about if they are to be active citizens in their communities and play a role in the political processes of their state and nation.

At the level of *identification*, we want all students to be able to know when the Constitution was written and adopted, who were some of the people who helped draft it, what its chief components are, and some of the rights guaranteed to us under it. We should expect, however, that while students may derive some benefit from being introduced to this information, we cannot be confident that they will remember these facts unless they are put into context, integrated into other content categories, where their use—not merely their identification—is important.

At the level of *understanding*, we expect students to understand the idea of a constitution in regulating governments of all sizes—along with concepts such as states' rights, separation of powers, judicial review, and the formal and informal processes by which laws are made under a constitution. Many teachers do this by having students draft a simple constitution for their school or class.

At the level of *synthesis*, we invite students to choose from a list of constitutional topics to research and report on, such as studying the Federalist debate and explain why it aroused such conflicting passions, investigating how slavery was handled in the Constitution and speculate about how it could have been better dealt with, researching the fate of a constitutional amendment and describing how and why it succeeded or failed.

At the level of *creative application*, students could opt to: develop a brief for eliminating one of the amendments in the Bill of Rights and replacing it with another one they think is more important; work with a local council member or legislator to propose a law they think would benefit society; organize a formal debate around a constitutional issue (like censorship, term limits, birthright citizenship, gun control, the death penalty, etc.) of interest in their school or community.

What we can see in this progression of categories of content is that as the breadth of data—facts, figures, and terms—gets concentrated and more narrowly focused, the depth of student engagement increases. Teachers (and ideally students too) get to choose which areas of content knowledge to focus on as the class moves to more in-depth engagement. What students need from their teachers is guidance in keeping the content in perspective: finding the right balance between the four categories described above so that the course material is not repetitive, tedious, or so limited and concentrated as to leave out knowledge that students will need in order to do further work in the subject.

The wrong way to interpret this framework is to think that it requires students to master content at the lower levels before they can address more complex content. I give examples throughout the book showing that when students are given lots of background content before they actively engage in concepts, they develop passivity and resistance. There are excellent reasons for introducing students to content at the higher category levels, where creativity and application help awaken their interest in the subject's facts, terms, key concepts, and historical figures.

TEACHERS MAKING CONTENT CHOICES

No matter which comes first, teachers should decide how much of any given instructional unit, course, or curriculum—measured in terms of class time and weight on final grades—should be devoted to each category of content learning:

> How much of the unit or course should be devoted to presenting or introducing students to information that they will only have to identify on quizzes or tests?
>
> How much should be devoted to helping students investigate, review, and understand the essential themes, ideas, and concepts?
>
> How much should be devoted to content that students will choose to research in some depth and that they will prepare a report or presentation on?
>
> How much should be devoted to students' creative application of what they learn to real situations, or to their original research on themes or issues that go beyond what's available in textbooks?

It may not be easy to answer these questions, to divide content into all these categories, but we should build the structure of each unit, course, or curriculum to allow students to study the content in sufficient depth and breadth to get the most long- and short-term benefit from it. This represents, in my view, the best way of honoring the content of a teacher's discipline and its ongoing importance to students.

Getting to the heart of one's subject means keeping a vigilant, scholarly eye on where the heart has wandered: what issues in our field are raised by new technology, where new theories and controversies are coming from, how changes in student demographics and their cultural heritage might suggest new points of view and require a revisiting of old formulations. It's a good bet that most teachers who opt to take control of the syllabus within their discipline are people who have remained active scholars by choice.

A passion for content can greatly enrich what teachers give to students, but only if we organize our passions well. Let us now see how to design a unit of instruction from a passionate teacher's perspective.

6

DETERMINING WHAT IS ESSENTIAL TO TEACH

There has been an incredibly high rate of administrative turnover in my district that has led to some pretty significant challenges, in terms of climate and morale, largely due to a lack of understanding of our established practices. But what then came with it were new curriculums which took away the autonomy that we had before. So even though I don't let this happen, now it truly feels like they want us to behave like robots, to read the manual and stand up there and go through slides. This is true for reading, for math, social studies, and science.

—DEIRDRE, second-grade teacher

THE CURSE OF "COVERAGE"

Teachers have always faced a tripartite dilemma: (1) What do I need and wish to teach? (2) What can I get away with *not* teaching? and, (3) How will I know if my students really learn what I have tried to teach them and will be able to apply their learning a day, a week, a month, or more after the unit or course is over?

For generations, educators of all stripes have relied on the word "coverage" to describe the information they feel responsible for conveying to their students: "What am I expected to cover in this course?" "Don't worry—we'll cover that topic by the end of the semester," and "I don't understand why only thirteen percent of eighth graders meet national standards for history—we covered all the material they were tested on." When a curriculum supervisor urges you to "make sure you cover" a topic or unit, I believe that person is tacitly admitting, "I have no idea what your students will know or be able to do as a result of your teaching. But at least we can rest assured that you covered it."

My friend and colleague, Tony Wagner, pushes the argument a few steps further. The author of groundbreaking books on education, like *The Global Achievement Gap*, *Most Likely to Succeed: Preparing Our Kids for the Innovation Era*, *Creating Innovators*, and the newly published *Mastery: Why Deeper Learning Is Essential in an Age of Distraction*, Wagner upends the entire conventional notion of what teaching and learning should be about. "We accept that conveying knowledge is important in the learning process. But in today's world, skills are more important than knowledge. And motivation is most important."

TONY WAGNER'S "FIVE BIG IDEAS"

Wagner has recently summarized his thinking about education into what he calls "five big ideas." I asked him about this:

> The first is that the goals of education must be to acquire the knowledge and skills needed for productive work, active and engaged citizenship, and personal health and well-being. I am convinced that our education system fails on all three because we've chosen the wrong goals. Decades of educational reform in the US have emphasized standardized tests, seat-time requirements, and content memorization without improving long-term student outcomes—and have increased student disengagement and teacher burnout.[1]

Second, he says that

> the focus of teaching must shift to development of character and cognitive skills and the ability to apply knowledge. Critical thinking, creativity, collaboration, communication, and character strengths like grit, curiosity, and empathy are far more important in the age of AI than the acquisition of content knowledge that is quickly forgotten and can be easily looked up.

Third, as a consequence of such a change in focus, "The role of the teacher moves from being a source of information to a source of inspiration: a mentor, facilitator, performance coach." Teachers, under Wagner's reform agenda, "offer critical feedback in an environment that encourages a growth mindset and deliberative practice."

Fourth, Wagner calls for a monumental shift in how we define "the unit of student learning" so that it is "no longer calculated based on seat-time served [e.g., Carnegie units, credit hours, weeks spent in a classroom] but on evidence of proficiency [the ability to apply skills and knowledge to real-life research and problem-solving]." For Wagner, this requires teachers to "individualize learning—varying the amount of time and support that individual students need to achieve such proficiency." Accordingly, rather than measure student achievement by their performance on standardized tests, student accountability will be based on "what people can do with what they know," as demonstrated through oral presentations, student portfolios, and other projects.

Fifth, for all this transformation to be achievable, Wagner believes it essential "to motivate students toward mastery through personalized learning, based on assuming that such motivation is intrinsic." To do this, he suggests emphasizing "student agency [i.e., their ownership of their learning process], voice [i.e., allowing them to articulate ideas and goals], and choice [i.e., giving them options, wherever possible—and it is almost always possible]."

Time was, we believed that teaching the "basic skills"—learning how to read and write and perform basic math calculations—should take place in elementary or middle grades. Skills have also been part of science and technical/vocational courses and, more obliquely perhaps, in the humanities. But although teachers have often promoted such skills, most schools leave it to individual students to actually learn how to understand a complex text, to separate opinion from fact, to anticipate where ideas or events may lead, to speak and listen well in a variety of real-life contexts, to make and test hypotheses, to design and pursue an independent study project, to make appropriate use of technology like AI, or to assess their strengths and shortcomings. There are, of course, talented and dedicated teachers who do teach and assess such skills, but too many do not. This is why some top inventors and innovators in technology and other fields abandoned formal schooling to pursue learning on their own or with friends. They just didn't find the freedom and inspiration they needed in school.

And motivation? We see it operate in every toddler struggling to walk or talk, every five-year-old trying to throw and catch a ball, every curious kid fiddling with our electronic devises when we weren't looking. We see it on our sports teams, led by inspiring coaches who exhort players to "practice every day and go out and do your best!" And in many of our music and arts programs, where getting really good at playing an instrument or creating a work of art is a goal shared by student and teacher alike. But how can anyone expect us to "teach" motivation to every child in every class? Isn't that really up to each learner?

So, the dilemma of having too much information that we're expected to "cover"—along with the pressure in many schools to have students practice endlessly for standardized tests—is compounded by the need for students to master essential skills and develop a zest for learning, goals that require a wholesale transformation of the teaching profession. And if we add to this a responsibility to help students motivate themselves as thoughtful, persisting learners, who among us isn't inclined to throw up our hands?

A POST-COVID DILEMMA, AND ITS CURE

Andrea Levin, who has taught humanities in New Hampshire's Keene High School, adds,

> There is also the issue of legislators, school boards, and superintendents being unaware of the actual state of most students, in this generation of young people who've spent their lives on screens and who, during COVID, were educated remotely during key educational years. Teachers at all levels are dealing with students who have lower verbal skills in comparison to past generations because they don't engage in as much conversation with adults and peers as they once did. Students are more anxious, less willing to experiment or playfully engage in activities that may not guarantee a "right answer," fighting constantly shifting attention stimuli, and demonstrating far less "grit" in the face of challenging tasks, such as doing word problems in mathematics and reading more complex or longer texts, such as novels.[2]

Fortunately, we have among us in this book talented teachers who have surmounted this dilemma. When Dan Bisaccio hands out the final exam in his biology course on the first day of class and promises that this will, indeed, be *the* final exam; when Tim Sullivan challenges his fourth graders to take on the state legislature over a seat-belt bill; when Christine Sullivan lets her English students know that her only job is to help them make themselves proficient writers; when Alfredo Fuentes says that algebra is really all about starting with what you know and using that to figure out what you don't know; when David Ervin announces to his middle school kids that eight weeks from today they will perform an original musical play in the auditorium—a play that nobody (including him) has the faintest idea what it will be about; when Yvonne Griffin invites her students to pose questions about sex and relationships that no other adult will talk to them about—each of these educators, as have so many others in these pages, has taken an exceptional leap of faith, saying in effect: "If I lead with passion, and with curiosity about my students, they will rise to the challenge of motivating themselves to learn important things." Interestingly, none of the teachers I observed and talked with in the first edition was teaching honors classes; in many cases, they were working with kids whom "the system" had designated as "slow" or indifferent learners.

Theirs is a faith that kids naturally want to become good at things they value (rather than having to be threatened or rewarded for memorizing stuff), that (as Deborah Meier reminds us) kids naturally want to become powerful in ways they see powerful adults behaving, that they want to own their learning, rather than submit to authoritarian agendas from the state, the district, the curriculum director, or their classroom teacher. What can easily get in the way of these natural appetites for learning are the habits of the Game of School, described in chapters 8–11.

Two caveats are perhaps in order. First, this is not a plea for a teacher to stand up every day and say, "Hey, kids, what do you want to learn?" Every one of the teachers in this book is passionate about knowledge, skills, and motivation, and they don't hide the rigor that underlies their passions. Rather, they work very hard to lead and inspire by example.

Second, I doubt that each of these teachers had the confidence (or, as my mom would say, the *chutzpah*) to begin their careers with such a bold stance (though some clearly had). They usually had to earn the right to take that leap of faith by performing up to the expectations of their supervisors. Yet I am reminded of the high school choral director who came to her first class and announced, "If nobody sings, I'm dead, out of a job. So let's figure out how to make singing something you really want to do." She had had the whole large class organized into singing groups, led by a student chosen by their peers, so when she had a sick day, the principal didn't bother hiring a substitute; the class went on as if the teacher were there.

SO, YOU'RE NOT READY TO TAKE THE LEAP?

Some of the readers of this book—whether veterans with decades of experience or teachers new to the profession—may feel ready to take that leap. For others, the best advice would be to find the most passionate teacher in your school or district and ask her or him to mentor you by allowing you to watch them teach and inviting them to your classroom.

It wouldn't hurt for a new teacher to address her elementary or middle school class with words like, "I've been trained to be a pretty good teacher. But I'm certain that I will be a better teacher by the end of my year with you. And do you know who will help me become a better teacher?" (If the kids don't call out "We will!" you might have to prompt them.)

I have long advocated that every teacher, from kindergarten through high school and beyond, spend the first two weeks of every class focused at least half the time on topics that their students know as much or more about than they do. Topics might include what students have learned from their parents, older siblings, friends, employers, coaches, and others. What students think about the world they inhabit—its treasures and its troubles; the people in their lives they most admire; the things they see as unfair or unjust; and the aspects of the curriculum they are most curious about—is as important as anything they learn in school.

At the end of those two weeks, while it may be true that your classes are "behind" others in plowing through the content, you will be far ahead in building a classroom environment of mutual respect, kindness and appreciation, curiosity and warmth. Your students will be convinced that you really do care about who they are, how they think, and what they value. Discipline issues will be greatly reduced because your students will see you as being "on their side." Parents will tell you that their children are more excited about coming to school than they've been before.

STUDENTS TURNING MATH FEELINGS INTO MATHEMATICAL EXPRESSIONS

Still skeptical? Here is a content-driven example of how this approach might work in a middle school math class for average or below-average math learners.

Hand out a scrap of paper to each student and ask them to write a number from 1 to 5, anonymously, depending on how they feel about math. You can write the following on the board to help them determine their number:

5 = I love math; it is one of my favorite subjects.
4 = Math is pretty good—I like it okay.
3 = Math is so-so. It's just like all the other subjects.
2 = Math is not so good. I do as little as I have to.
1 = I hate math. I avoid it whenever I can.

Then pick two of the most resistant-looking students and have the class pass their slips of paper to them to tabulate, while you write down your estimate of how many students selected each number. Then have the two tabulators pool and announce the actual results. It will probably demonstrate that your estimating skills are imperfect, showing your students that you don't have all the answers.

For the next part of the lesson, divide the class into five groups. Ask each group to take the actual results and turn them into one of the following: (1) percentages, (2) fractions, (3) a pie chart, (4) a bar graph, and (5) a chart of stick figures. The completed charts are placed on the wall. They allow students to see how "feelings about math" can be expressed mathematically. They also demonstrate that you *accept your students as they are* and respect the fact that not everyone wants to be a math teacher when they grow up. While they are working, you are drawing a visible timeline of how your class's feelings about math will progress over the coming weeks or months (in effect, you are doing the same work as they are—you are, as they say, "walking the walk").

Then, pass out three-by-five-inch index cards and ask each student to put their name on the top. Announce that by Halloween or some other upcoming holiday, your hope is that each student will move up one number (1s will become 2s, 2s become 3s, etc.) Of course, you tell them, you can't make that happen—all you can do is try your best. On the lined side of the index card, have each student tell you what you can do to make them move up a number. On the blank side, have each write what they can do to achieve that goal. Collect the cards and tell them you will present to the class some of the best ideas they have articulated for how their feelings about math can improve and perhaps let them vote on what they think are the best ideas. It's likely that some will ask, "What about those who are already 5s?" You can turn that question back to the class, and someone will soon suggest that the 5s (if there are any) might help others move up a number.

I will leave it to you to guess how such an approach might change the atmosphere in a math class and lead to a productive working partnership between teacher and students and among students helping one another move up a number. By surveying the class each month, your timeline can show any movement of "feelings" about math, and the class can discuss why things have or haven't changed.

FORMATIVE LEARNING AND PROFESSIONAL LEARNING COMMUNITIES

Andrea Levin examines the issue of "coverage" from two perspectives: (1) how coverage changes through the lens of formative learning and (2) the pang that teachers feel when, facing increased demands and ongoing pressures from all sides, they believe they must give up some of their favorite teaching units. Andrea says:

> In early 2019, I was drafted to attend workshops on formative assessment (also known as formative learning) with Margaret Heritage as part of Keene High School's state-mandated transition to competency-based education (CBE). I really didn't know much about CBE, but I trusted the administrator who sent me because she had a long track record as an amazing, award-winning teacher. The training totally changed the way that I teach: I started to have the students in all my classes spend time working with models of final products and the success criteria for assignments. The goal is that they will eventually be able to self-assess and more reliably provide constructive feedback to their peers. I discovered that shifting my focus from "getting through material" or "covering" to doing what is necessary for each student to be able to practice higher Depth of Knowledge skills as more independent learners significantly reduced what I could "cover." However, it didn't take long for me to see

> a genuine improvement in student learning that was verified by stronger final products in my class, as well as by higher standardized test results.
>
> I sympathize with teachers who don't want to embrace formative learning/assessment because it means cutting units they've been deeply invested in. (I think it has to be acknowledged that at a time in history when being a public-school teacher can seem like a thankless task because of the inadequate pay and the trend toward demonizing teachers and public education it is hard to give up teaching material that brings one joy). I've always loved my subject matter, but the shift to a formative-learning focus has made me love it even more. For me, part of a formative-learning approach is sharing my own reading, thinking, and writing with students. This has brought back levels of connection to students that I thought were long gone.[3]

A teacher of chemistry in a high school near where I live came into one of my coaching seminars for teachers and announced, "My God, I just realized that all of us in the sciences really want our students to master the same set of skills, you know—how to apply the scientific method, how to collect and analyze data, how to work with a challenging concept until they understand it. Yet we teach our subjects as though we each inhabit a separate kingdom of knowledge. So the opportunity to reinforce the skills we all agree are most important is lost."

Rather than leave all of this to each teacher to master alone, Andrea Levin says that such reinforcement may be aided by the availability of Professional Learning Communities (PLCs) for your school and your grade or subject: "PLCs in which we discuss what standards and skills are most important have been the single greatest factor in recreating among us a sense of community after the isolation of COVID teaching. In my ninth-grade PLC, we try to be honest about the extent to which we have 'watered' down our expectations in order to survive the past five years, and now we are working to realign ourselves with the expectations of Common Core State Standards."

The matter of the Common Core that Andrea refers to presents another interesting dilemma in the conversation about what's essential to teach. Often praised—and just as often reviled—the CCSS emerged in 2008–9 as a movement organized by the leaders of various state education departments to bring coherence and ease of student transfer across state lines, while also integrating a number of essential skills into the public-school curriculum. It has regularly been condemned by conservative pundits as an effort to weaken states' rights and local control. But unlike high-stakes standardized testing, CCSS does not impose exams that threaten to deny students their right to graduate.

As Andrea explains,

> Even though it has been popular to say that the Common Core State Standards are evil, I've found them useful in giving me an idea of what skills should be prioritized. Schools, especially rural schools or extremely underfunded schools, can become closed systems in which administration and teachers lose track of the larger picture—they overlook the skills that are necessary for future education and training in favor on focusing on less vital or complex skills that contribute to the illusion that significant learning is going on.

In the end, for teachers of all grades and subjects faced with pressures from all sides, the fundamental question of "what and how to teach important stuff" cannot be resolved by any one formula or approach. It must evolve through dialogue—first, inside your own head, based on your insights and passions; second, with trusted colleagues and inspiring leaders who can help you weave a path through conflicting mandates and competing priorities; and third, with your students as partners in the enterprise of productive learning.

7

DESIGNING A UNIT

All genuine learning is active, not passive. It involves the use of the mind, not just the memory. It is a process of discovery, in which the student is the main agent, not the teacher.

—MORTIMER J. ADLER, *The Paideia Proposal*

THE BLOODY FIGHT FOR FREEDOM

I have worked over the years with several schools where the faculty has decided to take more control over their curriculum in an effort to get all students to be more active and engaged learners. Our experiment begins with a typical unit of instruction.

The idea came from discussions with teachers at a middle school with a diverse immigrant population. They were frustrated trying to teach the Civil War because so few of the kids knew anything about US history (many had come from places like the Azores, Haiti, Yugoslavia, Jamaica, and the Dominican Republic). Yet by the time their teachers had provided them with the background needed to begin understanding the Civil War, the kids were bored, disengaged, and it was tough to get them to participate.

After puzzling out this dilemma for some time, we decided that we needed a way for all the kids to begin the unit in an active manner as players, rather than passively sitting back and watching their teachers present material. But how to begin? We came up, finally, with a question that seemed promising. Why not ask all students to begin the unit on the Civil War by writing a short essay on the question "How is a fight within my family different from a fight with strangers?" In this way every student, regardless of what culture he or she had been born into, could contribute an insight into the nature of a civil war. Every child is an expert in family feuds.

The next problem we faced was one of coverage—so many battles, so many issues, so many generals, and so little time. We decided to ask the students to go to the library and spend a period looking up different topics related to the Civil War and then bring a list of their findings back to class. From that exercise, each class developed a list of topics—and here the teacher could spend a moment or two explaining what each of those topics referred to. Rather than have the teacher cover each of these, students were asked to pair up, and each pair could select a topic to work on in depth for two weeks.

But this led to other problems. There was not much in the library on some of the topics the seventh graders were most interested in and on topics they and their teachers had developed through brainstorming exercises: the foods and medicines of the Civil War, the Andersonville prison, Harriet Tubman, Clara Barton, the kind of work that children did in the mills of that time, the battles of Gettysburg and Bull Run. What would the students do with the material they were able to discover? How would they be motivated to do in-depth work, not merely copy a few encyclopedia paragraphs? Also, how could teachers give tests to students who had studied so many different topics, and how would the unit be graded? In trying so hard to get students to become actively involved in a period of our history, hadn't we created more problems than teachers or students could reasonably cope with?

The solutions, it turned out, were imbedded in the problems themselves: the teachers decided that the students would compile a book of their own essays, written on their chosen topics, and contribute their book to the school library for use by other students in later years. Rather than a test, the quality of their essays would determine their grade. And by reading the essays of their classmates, students could gain a breadth of understanding about the Civil War without their teacher having to cover all these topics in class lectures.

I have a copy of the final result. It is called *The Bloody Fight for Freedom 1861–1865*, and it is a lively and interesting collection of seventh-grade student essays. The teachers tell me that the quality of the writing far exceeds what they had been used to getting from their students. It seems that knowing that the book would be presented to the library, and would be there for all students to read, was a far greater motivator of student effort and pride than the threat of any test or in-class assignment. The proof, say the teachers, is that every student wanted a copy of the book to take home. In the letter that accompanied my copy, one of the teachers wrote, "Our copy machine broke down while copying our book. Some of the children stayed after school and put the book together, all one hundred copies."

In a nutshell, this approach to a unit begins with one or more questions that have no single right answer but that all students are likely to have an opinion about. It ends with a performance, project, or demonstration—not a paper-and-pencil test—that students share with some audience beyond the classroom. In between its start and finish, the unit is designed to promote a high level of engagement, thinking, independent work, and problem-solving for each student.

DESIRED RESULTS, PERSONAL STAKE, HOOK QUESTIONS, PERFORMANCE ASSESSMENT

Here's an outline that evolved out of the approach that the seventh-grade teachers and I developed for the Civil War project. It can work across a variety of contexts. Why not take one unit—a small part of a course—and try an experiment, perhaps in collaboration with other teachers? Here's how it goes:

A. Unit Topic:

B. Unit Length: How many weeks.

C. Essential Results for Concepts and Skills: What you expect students to remember about this unit and be able to apply a year from now, when they've forgotten most of the details:

1. ______________________________

2. ______________________________

3. ______________________________

4. ______________________________

5. ______________________________

D. Your Personal Stake: What you would say to students about why this unit is personally meaningful to you:

____

____

____

____

____

____

____

E. "Hook Questions": Getting students to begin as players, not as spectators.

1. ____
2. ____
3. ____

F. Students Working Together and Making Choices: Ways all students can work in teams; ways the unit can be structured so that each student can contribute to the learning of others:

____

____

____

____

____

G. Performance Assessment: Ways students can show that they understand and can perform the "Desired Results for Concepts and Skills":

- What might students produce that will be useful to others?
- Who are some of the "natural audiences" for what the students will discover?

- What are ways that all students can be included in demonstrations?
- What kinds of demonstrations will encourage student pride?

Examples of possible student performances:

1. ______________________________
2. ______________________________
3. ______________________________

Here is a further fleshing out of this unit design:

A. Unit Topic. Pick any unit of instruction that you already plan to teach, something that is part of the curriculum and, importantly, that you are passionately interested in. It may be a unit that you wish to collaborate on with a colleague or one that you teach by yourself. It helps if this unit is one that you have some discretion over, not one whose parameters are strictly prescribed by your curriculum leader or department chairperson.

B. Unit Length. Choose a unit that will last for two to three weeks or longer. Since this unit may require lots of planning for you and some new behaviors for your students, allot a good amount of time for it. Some teachers plan one unit like this each season or semester so they don't get overwhelmed with extra work while getting themselves and their students used to working in this way.

C. Essential Results for Concepts and Skills. Here's where your challenges really begin, and you start to exercise a passionate discretion over content. You must distinguish what is *truly* essential from other, less useful material. Ask yourself what it is that you expect your students to remember about this unit and be able to apply elsewhere a year from now, after they have forgotten most of the details. What do you want to stick with them? Using the content framework of chapter 5, it should be material from categories 3 and 4, where students aim to synthesize and apply what they have learned.

This material now becomes the *only* thing you will teach. You may, for your own sense of security, have students skim over other chapters in the text or ask them if there is anything related to, or in addition to, your reduced content for the unit that they want you to touch upon. But do not undermine the experiment by trying to cover everything you might normally spend time on, or by letting students know they are responsible for all the other material on the final exam for the course.

D. Your Personal Stake. Most teachers have a hard time telling students why they themselves care about a unit. The key is to tell them why *you* are interested in the content as a learner. If you are not passionately involved with this material, choose another unit topic that you do feel strongly about. But once you have reflected on why this topic fascinates you, tell your students. How does it connect with what's important in your life and theirs? If you can't give them an inspiring and personal reason why this stuff is really worth learning, you've lost half the battle already—the whole thing may well seem to students more a matter of obedience than of inspiration. Here are some of the "personal stake" arguments that teachers who developed and taught units like these in Sturbridge, Massachusetts, offered their students:

From a middle school, multidisciplinary unit called Harmony in Diversity:

> Almost daily I observe someone being singled out for being different. At this age, that difference is style of dress, physical appearance, personality, intelligence, family financial status, or even the town a student lives in. I was a fat seventh grader, and I remember what it was like not to blend in. Your generation needs to realize that the real world is made up of all kinds of people. We all contribute to the whole. Sameness is boring. Diversity encourages growth.

From a semester-long film studies course taught by a history teacher:

> I developed an interest in American history solely through my fascination with the Hollywood film. The history books didn't do it, the history teachers didn't do it, the history lessons didn't do it. The movies did it! My love for classic movies (and the classics are what you

> will get in this course) bridged a gap between me and people twice my age. Now, more than ever, students need to reassociate themselves with America's past and with the lives of their elders.

From a month-long unit focusing on the human search for identity from cross-cultural and developmental perspectives:

> My "personal stake"? To get me out of my "academic rut" and present information using a variety of new and different teaching strategies; to have the opportunity to share ideas and teaching with a colleague in a different discipline; to help students re-establish a sense of "generativity" (using Erikson's term) with some future point in their life.

From a unit titled "Ghosts of Brick and Wood" in which middle school students create an activity book on "buildings that were once the center of bustling activity in our towns, but no longer exist," for students in grades 4 to 6:

> I love to produce an excellent product. I enjoy history, especially when tinged with drama, a good tale, or mystery. I would do this kind of reading for recreation, myself.

From a unit on *Cyrano de Bergerac* for British literature and French students:

> I think the story of Cyrano is profoundly rich, especially for teenagers, regarding its "beauty versus character" theme. I would like to permanently convince you that all word choices, either in your own writing or in works of art and poetry, are fundamentally important and rich, and to have you see that true "vocabulary mastery" means learning subtleties of meaning, not "big words," and that emotion can help unlock meaning.

From a unit on the Development of the Constant Pi and the Relationship of Circumference and Diameter as a Linear Function:

> The topic of linear functions has always been an intangible concept for students and a frustration for us to teach. I think by using this

> "hands-on" approach, the students will have a better understanding of and deeper insight into the concept, thus making it a lot more fun for us to teach.

From a unit on Propaganda and Gender-Role Stereotyping designed by three teachers for English classes:

> How has gender-role stereotyping affected me? And how is my thinking manipulated or shaped by propaganda? How much of the traditional role stuff do I have to buy into?

These statements speak to me in many voices of the passion of teaching. They are the voices of people in love with words, ideas, problems; people excited about tragedies of the environment and of the stage; people who have learned powerful lessons from history and from life and are avid about wanting young people to learn them, too. These are the voices students need to hear. They are the voices of teachers.

E. Hook Questions. Rather than starting out by giving students a lot of background to the unit, it is crucial that you get them actively involved from the beginning. Once they have grown passive listening to you present or read the background, it may be difficult for them to believe that they can perform the intellectual work of the unit on their own.

The best technique I know to start things off actively is to ask one or more questions (Ted Sizer calls these "essential questions") that allow students to form and express opinions even if they know little or nothing about the unit, such as with the seventh-grade Civil War project. Let me give some examples for each aspect of these hook questions from two units, one on America's future, and the second on the environment. These units could be offered as early as the fourth or fifth grade or up into high school. The best hook questions have several of the following features:

- It has no one right answer—students know that neither the teacher nor any one of them has *the* answer:
  1. How long will the USA remain a first-class world power?
  2. Can the movement to save our planet from climate change survive the current politics of "climate denial"?

- It lies at the heart of the subject or unit and is central to whatever it is that students will be learning:
  1. What does it mean for a society or a nation to be strong or weak?
  2. Are humans the masters of the earth or only one species on our planet?
- It is phrased in simple, direct language students understand—not in jargon or terms that students think are meant for adults:
  1. How do people feel when their country loses respect in the world?
  2. Is our world becoming a healthier or a sicker place to live?
- It deals with issues that students have direct access to—ideas that they can relate to in their own lives:
  1. In what ways is a nation like a person?
  2. How "natural" is my environment?
- It offers students choices in how to respond and invites kids to find lots of ways to use their intelligence:
  1. How can you show without words what America means to you?
  2. What creature can you design that could live in a world grown too hot for human habitation?
- It encourages students to become investigators, to go out and seek knowledge that isn't easily available from textbooks:
  1. What issues do people in your family think are vital to a more just and healthy America?"
  2. What environmental problems are here in our neighborhood?
- It involves thinking and speculating—not just answering—about questions that challenge students to use their minds well:
  1. How will life in the US differ for your grandchildren?
  2. What should Americans give up to ensure a safer environment now that global warming is becoming a greater threat?
- It provides a sense of fun and adventure, allowing teacher and students to enjoy exploring ideas and issues informally and without pressure:
  1. What would it take to make life perfect in our society?
  2. What are some things kids can do right now to save our planet?

These questions invite students to become an active part of the lesson and to use their experiences, opinions, and creativity to join you in examining the content. Such questions, and the students' tentative answers, should come *before* you present the content so that they develop a stake in the unit. As you introduce new content, students can relate it to things they have already alluded to, discussed, or debated.

F. Students Working Together and Making Choices. Students can make choices about what aspects of the unit to specialize in. Many teachers know how working in small groups helps students learn from each other and address issues from several vantage points. In a unit based on this structure, you can promote individual and group excellence. The units for studying ancient civilizations and the unit described here are but two of the many ways that subject matter can be broken down and rebuilt through student synthesis and demonstration.

At a time when the movement toward mixed-ability grouping has caused concern among advocates of programs for faster learners, this unit permits students to reach as high as they can without dividing the teacher's time between helping them and keeping the rest of the class "on task." Different learning styles can be accommodated without sacrificing the needs of the class as a whole.

G. Performance Assessment. Figuring out how students can demonstrate what they have learned and how teachers will assess that work may loom as big obstacles to experimentation. Reliance on one big demonstration may challenge traditional grading practices. But in designing a unit to foster in-depth student engagement, our energies are directed less at monitoring and more at promoting and coaching student efforts. Here are some questions to help guide students toward achieving high-quality results:

- What learning activities, whether inside or outside of school, do you take pride in?
- Who, outside the class, might be interested in what you produce or discover?
- What problems or needs exist in the community that your learning in this unit can help people deal with?

- How many of the skills and content outcomes (see heading "C" above) might be combined in one big product or demonstration?

Here are some demonstrations that have been devised by teachers who have developed experimental units using this outline. Per the content framework in the previous chapter, these are category 4 demonstrations; they require students to *select*, *speculate*, *create*, and *apply* what they have learned:

- Students teach their unit to kids in another class or grade. When students take a large area of study and have to reduce it to its essentials in order to develop a lesson plan to teach it, they practice the very intellectual skills that teachers (or textbooks) use in curriculum design. And when they actually teach those classes to other kids, they remember the content much better.
- Students prepare materials for their school library. They can make books from collections of student articles and online resources and add them to the library's permanent collection.
- Students connect with businesses in the community to design a display for their front windows on the unit they have explored.
- Students design and conduct surveys for local government or nonprofit agencies on questions relating to the unit and then tabulate and present the data to them.

As far as an assessment of student work is concerned, the important thing to keep in mind is that assessment is not the end of the learning process—it is an essential and ongoing part of it. Students do much of their memorable learning as they prepare and produce such demonstrations. By giving them only one or two grades for the unit (e.g., one for their performance and one for their preparation and group collaboration), we let them know we expect high levels of performance and that inferior work will not be accepted. And the more public the performance, the more likely students will rise to the occasion.

Our assessment message to students should be: "What we care about is the quality of your engagement and of what you produce. So choose what interests you most, and show everyone the best you can do!"

PASSIONATE TEACHING AND VULNERABILITY: A CONVERSATION WITH SUSAN LUKAS

When I interviewed her for the first edition, Susan Lukas taught English at Watkinson School, an independent school in Hartford, Connecticut, that attracts a broad spectrum of students. She writes poetry and does professional editing, along with teaching full-time. Our dialogue took place in a break between classes.

RLF: Where does your understanding of your passion as a teacher begin?

SL: It has to do with how engaged I feel in the teaching process, how connected I feel to the content, to the teaching of it, and to self. I believe the best teachers have a real understanding of self; they're the ones who can get the kids to pay attention.

RLF: Do you see any risks involved in teaching the way you do?

SL: In my advanced literature class, we're working on some questions that I don't even have a clue what the answers are, like: "Is there such a thing as 'male' and 'female' language?" Part of the risk is kids not being comfortable with such open-ended questions. A lot of them don't know what to do when they see their teacher, too, uncertain of where things are going, and that makes some kids insecure. The risk is that I might lose some of them. The risk is greatest when I'm unaware that my passion is not being shared, or when it looks like kids are buying into something, but they're really not. And occasionally I'm surprised by the "good student" syndrome—the kid who's so used to "doing the right thing," so tuned-in to what I want or what I care about that she or he doesn't even know if the interest is real. I've learned over the years that not everybody's going to love this or that book the way I love it.

The experienced passionate teacher, who's already known what it means to get too far beyond the students, understands that there's more to it than just being excited about the discipline. There are people who are passionate about their discipline but less so about the teaching of it. My struggle, at times, has been between those two things—passion for the work itself and passion for kids really engaging with it.

For one thing, I keep part of what's important to me as mine. I don't have to share it all or put all of it into the lesson. I'm a writer and a reader outside of school, so I feed that passion in other ways. If I expected to get all of it from my students, it just wouldn't work. That's not at all to say my students never have anything to give to me. But for my own needs, as a writer and as someone interested in language, it's obviously more than they can offer.

RLF: But you don't say to yourself: "Well, I can't really be intense here, because I'm worried about the kids not keeping up with me." You do something else.

SL: I think my expectations—and my vision—become more precise so that instead of being excited in that big way about some work of art or the issues it raises, I can bring it down to a piece that we can look at and decide about. That focus can allow kids to get hooked on what I'm passionate about in a smaller way. And then it radiates out, and they go much further than when we come clunking in with our passions blaring, "Isn't this wonderful!"

RLF: I've used the metaphor of the class as a playing field. If a teacher defines the playing field as the world of his or her enthusiasm and expertise, with all its intensity and magnitude, then kids are going to tread very gingerly on that field. They'll think, "I don't want to play on a field whose dimensions I can't see, whose rules I don't know."

SL: That's right. We're about to begin reading *Beloved* by Toni Morrison, who is in my mind probably the finest writer in America at this time. And I could talk about that till the cows come home. But if I do that, it becomes intimidating to students, who then feel they cannot disagree. Maybe they don't even like that book, much less love it. There has to be a way for their responses to be heard. Passionate teachers are big presences; we can take up too much space in a room.

RLF: How do you take a book like *Beloved* into the classroom without overwhelming your students?

SL: First, I try to figure out the kids. Last year, I had two twelfth-grade classes of not very good readers. One had kids who were highly motivated and willing to plug through

Beloved. But in the other class, I knew we were lost three pages into it, so I made the decision—for the first time since teaching here—to stop the book and bring in something else. The struggle was too great. They didn't have the sheer stick-to-it-iveness to get through it.

They felt better about it when we changed books. It wasn't a judgment on them—like "Oh, you guys don't want to do this? The heck with it; we're just not going to read it, then!"—but more a sense of "You know what? This isn't working. Why don't we put this away and try something else?"

RLF: What did you try?

SL: We did *This Boy's Life* by Tobias Wolff. This was an instance where I really had to pay attention—a group of kids who were very resistant to all they'd been hearing around them about feminism and multiculturalism and diversity and tolerance. And there was some real anger being expressed in this class.

There were some boys who were very hard to deal with because of the rampant homophobia and sexism in their point of view. They were responding to *Beloved* as, "Here we go—another Black woman writer!" I knew that if I hit them over the head with it, it wasn't going to get me anywhere.

RLF: So you knew you had to be in tune with their level of receptivity, as a matter of empathy, not just pedagogy? You could feel that the struggle they were having with *Beloved* was too great; they felt unequal to it and resentful of being in that place?

SL: It made them feel stupid.

RLF: What happened with *This Boy's Life*?

SL: They loved it. It was much more accessible. But I didn't choose a book that was merely accessible. I didn't want to shortchange them by giving them something of less quality. It was simply a better match for this group, and we could talk about issues and language.

RLF: The other twelfth-grade class continued with *Beloved*?

SL: Even though they initially also found it very difficult. At first, they thought that the other class had had it easy. But by the time they got to the end, they were very glad that they had finished the book. And they *got* it.

RLF: Every teacher feels vulnerable, of course, and runs the risk each day of having some student say, "This is no fun. This is boring, and I just don't want to do it." Is that vulnerability any different for you?

SL: Because I love some things—because the field of writing and language and literature is so big in my life, and I have so much respect for it and for those who work at it—the risk of being hurt by those who will trample on it is great. And so, for me, as someone who is deeply connected to that piece, it's a greater risk to put it out there and hope that I can protect it by setting the tone of respect to begin with. I know I can't expect them all to engage in what I think is wonderful.

Lots of kids respond, initially, with "This is stupid!" And I expect that, too. It's when there's another level of resistance, and I recognize fear and anger and a willingness to slash at something. It doesn't happen often. It's not a lack of respect for me but for the ideas and the person who's done this work. If the student reads the work and *then* responds in a hostile way, that's different. I don't feel dismissed by that response.

RLF: So your passion becomes a desire for students to be open to an experience that they may well end up being critical of. It's about the importance of students having that experience and then forming their own judgment of it.

SL: Right. The best things I've done at those times is to create a way of looking at the situation apart from the book, to create exercises where everybody can explore difficult or controversial ideas, usually in small groups, and then hopefully connect what they come up with to the literature we're reading.[1]

PART TWO

THE GAME

8

THE GREATEST OBSTACLE WE FACE

The agreement between teacher and students to exhibit a facade of orderly purposefulness is a Conspiracy for the Least, the least hassle for anyone.

—TED SIZER, *Horace's Compromise*

FAMILIAR OBSTACLES TO GOOD TEACHING

The desire for any new vision of teaching and learning is bound to run into the apparently immutable facts of life in our schools and communities. Passionate teaching, however enticing, can seem unreasonable in the face of the daily realities of school life. It can sound like pie-in-the-sky or head-in-the-clouds stuff. It's as if I'm not talking about real schools that real teachers work in, with the 1,001 obstacles to good teaching and learning that are every teacher's lot in life.

Let's examine some of these obstacles, put them out on the table, and see if there is any underlying theme or quality about them that, once recognized, allows us to diminish some of their awful impact on our work with students. Where do teachers hit the wall in their struggle to become or to remain enthusiastic about their profession? Who or what is undermining our passions and our ideals?

- Authoritarian administrators who try to run classrooms from the main office?
- Disruptive students who spoil learning for others and make teachers act like police?

- Cynical colleagues who always find a reason to kill a worthwhile idea?
- Parents who are either overzealous or under-involved in their children's education?
- Students who come to class unprepared, unmotivated, or unwilling to work?
- Class sizes that are too large to allow for personal instruction?
- Little time in the school day to meet with colleagues and plan together?
- Lack of adequate staffing and specialists, which requires teachers to do other people's work at the expense of their own?
- Standardized tests that determine who succeeds and who fails, without regard for individual differences or learning styles?
- Outmoded, unattractive, or unsafe school buildings and a lack of sufficient texts, materials, or technology?
- Outdated curricula, inadequate time for planning, a school schedule that carves up the day into forty-five-minute spasms of instruction?

We cannot minimize the impact of these afflictions on good teaching and learning. Far too many teachers suffer daily frustration and hardship from them. In poorly funded school districts, and in many of our neighborhoods, the lack of basic staffing and supplies and the appalling host of societal problems that wind up on a teacher's doorstep are much too serious to overlook in any discussion about improving teaching and learning. Even in affluent communities, teachers experienced many of these obstacles.

THE GREATEST OBSTACLE IS ONE WE OFTEN MISS

But yet another obstacle, often missed and rarely articulated is, in its way, actually more destructive. It hangs around in the background; it's a mood, a mindset that makes the other problems and obstacles we've listed even more difficult than they already are. This obstacle occurs whenever nobody cares what's going on intellectually in the classroom or in the school, when the idea of learning is treated as a mindless duty—something to "get through any way you can." It's what I call having to play the "Game of School."

Here's how it starts. Or, rather, here's how soon it starts.

A friend of mine, then in her early twenties, got her bachelor's degree with a secondary teaching certificate in English. She was living in New York City and, after trying for a while to find a teaching position in her field, took a job that she very much enjoyed in an after-school program for primary school kids, located in a diverse West Side neighborhood. The program was run by the YMCA but operated out of the same public elementary school that most of the kids attended during the day.

> We have a homework hour every evening, from five to six o'clock. Wednesday is usually our night for Reading Homework. The kids have a story or chapter to read—it's in a really good anthology that includes *Winnie the Pooh, Stuart Little, Mouse House*, as well as some traditional tales and poetry—and then they're supposed to write out one question on a special question form and hand it in to their teacher the next day.
>
> But the kids have become so adept at figuring out what they're supposed to do that on Wednesdays they get into groups and pick the best reader among them to begin reading the story aloud (even though most of them are quite capable of reading on their own). The process usually stops after the reader has finished the first page or so, at which time the kids go off and write down their questions.
>
> What's weird is that they seem to pick the dumbest things to ask about, questions I'm sure they don't even want to know the answers to, like "How did Pooh know Eeyore's tail was missing?" or "Why doesn't the Country Mouse like city food?"
>
> They're clever enough to pick questions they think won't be answered somewhere later on in the story (so their teacher won't know that they only got through the first page). They also check with each other to make sure their questions are all a bit different because they're aware their teacher knows that these kids are in the same after-school program. And having written down their questions and checked them out to avoid the appearance of collusion, they stop reading and go off and play games.
>
> The contrast is so amazing between how they respond to these homework assignments and how they react when I read to them. *Then* they're full of questions—real questions, like "How old is Pooh, and why doesn't he have to go to school like we do?" or "Why is Eeyore so sad when he's got friends like Pooh and Piglet?" And they're always making connections

> between the stories and their lives, saying things like "The Country Mouse is dumb! I hate the country! The city has got everything. The only thing I don't like about living in the city is the cockroaches." All this convinces me that they do, in fact, take the stories seriously.
>
> It's as though by the middle of first grade they've already figured out that school—or at least homework—is a trick, something to learn how to get around. It's not as though they've got some horrible teacher who forces them to do tons of busywork. She's trying to do it right, asking them to invent questions of their own instead of answering the ones at the end of the chapter.

DISENGAGING OUR INTELLECT AND FEELINGS FROM REAL LEARNING

A game is both a microcosm and a parody of life. It is like life: It brings forth the same energies and the same feelings, but, in the end, it is not real. It is a charade of something real. We may be absorbed by it and be willing to play along. But a voice within us is there to say, "Take it easy. It doesn't really matter. It's only a game."

The particular offense of playing the Game of School lies in the disengagement of our intellect and our feelings from tasks that deserve to be taken seriously—tasks like writing, reading, thinking, planning, listening, researching, analyzing, performing, applying, and evaluating. We do harm when we reduce these acts of intellect, creativity, and judgment to rote exercises, perfunctory deeds, or meaningless gestures. Faced with the stresses of daily life in school, it can seem easier, at times, to pretend to believe rather than to truly believe in the value of what we are about. Despite the positive aspects of going to school, which many children and adults experience, the temptation is always there to cope with school by going through the motions.

I focus on the Game of School because the impact of the other obstacles on that list could be significantly lessened, even overcome, if students and teachers were united as allies in a struggle against ignorance, oppression, and poverty of the spirit. What prevents people in schools from joining together to rescue learning from at least some of these obstacles is that too many of us are caught up in the Game of School.

The way our schools do business unknowingly makes it easy for students and teachers to play the Game of School, by loading us up with things to do that help everybody avoid confronting issues about meaning and motivation and choice in our work. By their own account, teachers spend far too much class time taking the roll, giving directions, assigning homework, checking homework, monitoring seat work, giving quizzes and tests, marking those tests, giving grades, and, more than anything else, talking their way through textbook chapters and lesson plans that may have precious little to do with what excites anybody in the class. Martin Haberman calls this "the Pedagogy of Poverty," which he describes as "certain ritualistic acts that, much like the ceremonies performed by religious functionaries, have come to be conducted for their intrinsic value rather than to foster learning."[1]

WE ALL PLAY THIS GAME

Lest we be tempted to see crusty administrators, uncooperative students, or cynical teachers as the only players in the Game of School, let me say that almost every single student I have talked with admits to playing it almost all of the time. And most teachers also grudgingly admit to playing it during some part of every school day. We're all players, as the following examples illustrate:

- "A" students who are ready to do anything asked of them to earn that A—except take risks, share their true feelings, or think for themselves
- "B" students who believe that writing down a bunch of platitudes in neat, regulation-style paragraphs and handing them in on time is a substitute for pursuing a topic with critical imagination
- "C" students who are interested in keeping out of trouble academically but do only as much work as they need to in order to avoid getting thrown off the football team
- Anybody who gives or accepts a grade of D, an acknowledgment that the student doesn't know enough of the material but has somehow convinced the teacher that he or she doesn't deserve to be flunked
- Any student who opts not to ask a question or disagree with someone else's ideas so as not to give the impression that he or she really cares about what's going on

- Teachers who cover the curriculum without stopping to ask if it even makes sense to kids and who give short-answer tests because it is too time-consuming to grade essays
- Teachers who base more than 20 percent of a student's grade on short-answer recall or on obedience to deadlines, thus restricting the percentage that students earn for acquiring and demonstrating essential skills and knowledge
- Teachers, parents, and administrators who try not to frustrate students by asking more of them than their "innate potential" appears to warrant
- Administrators who are content when students are quiet, when litter, graffiti, and fighting are reduced, and when nobody throws food in the lunchroom, regardless of how much students are actually learning
- Administrators who spend more time making sure that teachers have filled in their lesson plans than visiting classes to see these lessons taking place
- Guidance counselors who schedule poor or minority kids into low-level courses because they think the kids probably won't be going to college and because their parents are unlikely to complain
- Parents who complain about the grades their kids are getting but who don't try to find out what their kids' teachers are expecting them to learn
- Parents who push their children into courses or activities because "it'll look good on your transcript for college"—whether or not the children are interested in those activities

We can think of a host of other players waiting on the bench. Waiting, in fact, is a major part of playing the Game of School: waiting for someone else to answer the question, waiting for someone else to take the initiative, waiting for the bell to ring, waiting for the day to end, waiting to graduate, and waiting to retire.

We're not talking about bad students or bad teachers—people who are mean, insulting, or vengeful, or who cheat, lie, or commit acts of violence or vandalism. The types of students, teachers, parents, and administrators listed here—virtually all of us at some time in our academic careers—are not criminals or miscreants. They have merely made a personal decision or accepted the common view of their peers that there is little intrinsic value in learning in this course, this class, this school or college program, and moreover, that they don't intend to do anything about it. They act as though getting along, getting by, and getting out is what school really is about.

THEY PRETEND TO TEACH US—AND WE PRETEND TO LEARN

"Hey, we're all stuck in here together," the teacher explains to his ninth-grade general math class. "Let's try to be reasonable with each other and we'll get along fine. Just obey the rules, come to class prepared, hand things in when they're due, and you're guaranteed a passing grade."

What student hasn't been offered this deal from one or more teachers? Who hasn't felt grateful to some teacher for not acting as though their work was so terribly important that we'd all have to make believe we were interested, just so the teacher wouldn't be offended?

When the Game of School is played frequently enough and by enough people, the Game *becomes* school. The artificial and superficial replaces what's authentic and purposeful in a lesson or curriculum. The pursuit of learning turns into the avoidance of conflict or extra work. A powerful feeling of unreality takes over. Passion, idealism, self-respect, the search for knowledge, and the pursuit of excellence give way to a pervasive, mind- and spirit-numbing mediocrity. We go along to get along.

Under their former Communist system where money was almost without value (there was nothing worthwhile to buy) and production was without quality (the only standard set was a numerical quota to be filled, however shoddily), Polish workers used to say, "We pretend to work, and they pretend to pay us." Where school is a game, students act as if to say, "We pretend to learn, and they pretend to teach us." And some teachers actually do say, "Hey, I get my paycheck whether you kids learn anything or not."

In those places where the Game has become school, there is little competition based on true quality, little accountability based on real performance. You get good grades or advancement by adhering to the rules, by being obedient to those in control. Quality is incidental: Some teachers continue to demand it, some students continue to strive for it, but the system mostly expects and rewards perfunctory compliance. Too many students get their diplomas by being there, by putting up with it all, by serving their time. Too many teachers spend their time controlling the noise, covering the syllabus, and getting grades in on time.

WHEN EXCELLENCE BECOMES EMBARRASSING

In the unspoken canons of the Game of School, real excellence may be an embarrassment. The truly outstanding teacher is honored by being patronized: "She's so great with kids! I wish I had a hundred more like her." Or they're seen as a threat to colleagues: "Take it easy! You're making the rest of us look bad." And truly outstanding teachers are even shunned as oddballs: "There he goes—the Mad Scientist of Central High." The outstanding student may also be ostracized by peers: "She's a real brain. I would never want to be that smart." A member of the football team whispers to a teammate in class: "Put your hand down! What are you trying to do—make us other guys look stupid?"

Few schools have a system that allows them to profit from those teachers who exude excellence or to sanction those who manifest mediocrity. We don't seem to be able to say: "She's so great with kids. Let's learn what she does well and see how more of us can do it, too," or "Students always complain that your classes are boring. What plans do you have to change that?" We so rarely ask our students: "Tell us what has to happen around here in order for you to be willing to study hard, think deeply, and take real pride in your work?" Teachers who do the minimum get the same salary increases and seniority rights as those who knock themselves out for their students. Students who do the minimum, or less than minimum, get promoted along with everyone else.

Whenever and wherever the Game of School prospers, passionate teaching subsides and intense and purposeful learning diminishes. It can happen to the best of people, in the best of schools. In a lot of schools, it happens to almost everybody almost all the time.

In citing the Game as an obstacle to good teaching and learning, I am not envisioning some educational utopia where learners and their mentors float along on clouds of diligence and good will, where honesty, integrity, and mutual respect stream from the intercom and everyone sings a chorus of "learning for learning's sake." I won't deny that part of my case for passionate teaching and my critique of the Game stem from a kind of idealism and from the fact that I am the parent of two public-school graduates. What's more, I spent seven years teaching experienced educators who are preparing themselves for new roles in educational leadership. And I won't pretend that conditions in most schools favor a renaissance of passionate teaching and engaged learning. Anyone who wants to be cynical about the prospects of substantive improvement in teaching and learning in American classrooms can find plenty of evidence to support the bleakest views.

INSPIRING PICTURES FROM THE GALLERY OF SCHOOL

But allow me to paint another picture and offer an exhibition of images that come from every school, along with scrapbooks from the past and examples of learning from around the home and community. My gallery includes:

- Creative and careful schoolwork that some students seem able to produce almost all the time and that most kids can do when they put their minds to it
- Digital recordings of rehearsals for school plays and concerts; practice sessions for sports teams, with coaches helping students get ready to perform before live audiences; activities where pride, teamwork, and excellence are unselfconsciously championed
- Notes from student/teacher conferences where, away from the noise and glare of the classroom, they talk together about what the teacher's standards mean and how the student's strengths and weaknesses can be addressed
- Photo albums of parents and kids working together on their hobbies—building a tree house, planting a garden, redecorating a room, or mastering the skills of the family sewing machine or table saw
- Sketches from the best of one-room schoolhouses, where mutual respect was assumed, where older children taught younger children, and where pupils worked in small groups or alone while the teacher moved around, helping them stay focused on where each of them (not the class as a whole) was headed
- Records from teacher cluster-team meetings, where four or five teachers who share the same eighty to one hundred students

meet daily to plan interdisciplinary curricula, establish consistent standards, review student progress, confer with parents, and support one another in their work to promote learning for all

- Exhibits from science fairs, inventors' conventions, art shows, and young authors' events, where student individuality and creativity are celebrated (the very same characteristics they might suppress in the classroom)
- Notes from student/teacher advisory groups, where fifteen kids meet regularly with an adult—whether a teacher, principal, librarian, guidance person, or nurse—to talk informally about school issues, personal concerns, and career goals
- Snatches from an informal class debate, where students engaged in a controversial topic have temporarily forgotten that it's not cool to show they care about ideas
- Videos from community and church projects that involve urban youth with neighbors of all ages, working to enhance community life
- Accounts of kids who volunteer in hospitals, coach Little League teams, teach Sunday school, help in daycare centers, and take part in charity drives or political campaigns
- Dossiers from apprenticeship programs, where students work with adult masters, absorbing from them both the content and the ethos of what it takes to do a job well
- Home videos of students working hard at their hobbies (computers, crafts, athletics and fitness, animal care, music, and dance), where connections between what they're doing and why they're learning are obvious and unquestionable

There are certainly counterarguments to these images: There were plenty of lousy one-room schoolhouses, some student hobbies have little educational value, and lots of teacher/student conferences are perfunctory. Voluntary pursuits and associations—teams, plays, fairs, family projects, hobbies, and the like—more easily inspire student interest than required classroom activities. And any normal teacher who tried to foster individualized learning for 125 students and five classes a day would be an emotional basket case by Thanksgiving. The reason so many teachers feel compelled to cover the curriculum is that the system won't pay for small classes and the more personalized instruction that small classes would permit.

Why do we play the Game of School? Many will argue that it's the only game most of us—students and teachers—can afford to play, under the conditions of a compulsory education system that is underfunded, undermined, and overwhelmed.

But is it? Just how much of what students and teachers do in school is compulsory? What factors are indisputably beyond our influence or control? Aside from taking the roll, keeping reasonable order, relating in some way to the curriculum, and coaching students in taking standardized tests, can't teachers do pretty much what they think makes sense in most of their classes? Aren't there a lot more options open to us than we are in the habit of exercising? In the most depressed city neighborhood or on the most affluent suburban campus, don't we find lots of eager minds and high aspirations once we seriously begin to look for and nurture them? Let us reconsider our customary resistance to hearing about great things going on somewhere else and open up to the possibilities that surround us.

The point about the images in this collage is that they also are part of the reality of school, even schools that operate under deprived conditions. Of course they are not found everywhere in schools, present or past. Of course they demand a level of energy and commitment very hard to sustain. And of course such positive examples shine all the more brightly against the background of generalized apathy and business as usual.

HOW "NORMAL" SCHOOL CONDITIONS BRING US DOWN

It is also unquestionably true that the combined effects of a heavy teaching load, insufficient planning time, increased nonteaching responsibilities, lack of collegiality, lack of recognition of success, the harmful effects of social media on students, and the demands that needy students place upon teachers' energies and emotions—the whole list of afflictions this chapter began with—sap our vitality and hinder us from looking for, nurturing, and appreciating what these images suggest. Teachers simply cannot go on blaming themselves, or accepting censure, for trying to be "good enough" workers in a demoralized or dysfunctional system.

But these positive images and others like them offer hope that learning need not be held hostage to the Game, that there is nothing predestined or natural about the lack of intensity in most classrooms. Teachers must find ways to harness hope and make it work for them, their students, and their colleagues.

The Game of School is pervasive, and its rituals are deeply entrenched in the actions and expectations of students and teachers. But it is not immutable. It can and must be changed.

9

OPENING UP THE DIALOGUE

All study of human thought must begin by positing an individual who is attempting to make sense of the world.

—HOWARD GARDNER, *Frames of Mind*

I WANT TO CHANGE THE DAMN GAME—I'M TIRED OF PLAYING THIS ONE

Some time ago in a New Jersey high school that I had been working with on curriculum reform, a group of teachers became animated when one of them voiced what she felt was a central issue. "I can't be the kind of teacher I want to be," she said, "because of the atmosphere in the class and the lousy attitude of too many kids." There was a chorus of "Amen to that!"

Their complaints were that too many students come to class unprepared, unmotivated, disrespectful, and indifferent to the challenge of learning. This attitude, they said, turns the teacher into a disciplinarian, a curmudgeon trying to force reluctant kids to do a minimum of work. The excitement of being a teacher is gone, they said. What's left is a constant battle.

"No, not a battle," said another teacher. "It's more like a con game. We do all the hard work while the kids sit back waiting to be entertained." A third spoke up: "Those students who do want to learn are hindered by those who fool around and waste everybody's time." And a colleague added, "Most of them want to do as little as possible, and then they put up a big argument if they don't get a good grade." "What

I want," the first teacher continued, "is to change the damn game. I'm tired of playing this one."

"What would it look like," I asked, "if the Game of School were changed?" Without hesitation, the teachers told me they want to see

- kids coming into class prepared to work
- kids attentive and enjoying learning
- kids asking good questions, being thoughtfully engaged
- kids helping each other and respecting one another
- kids feeling good about themselves and proud of their accomplishments

The Game of School, as I have been discussing it, is a complex pattern of habits, avoidances, and defenses, creating an atmosphere in which serious learning falls victim to the everyone's goal of getting through the day, the week, the year with as little hassle as possible. The complaints these New Jersey teachers directed at kids' attitudes are ones almost all teachers have acknowledged at one time or another and that many teachers suffer from daily. Yet teachers play a tremendous role in shaping kids' attitudes, even when we allow that the mindset many students bring with them into the classroom can make that job challenging indeed.

But let's continue our discussion of the Game as these teachers have defined it and see what it might take to turn the situation around. Of course, once the classroom has become clogged with adversarial relationships and bad habits of learning—typified by the teachers' list—digging our way out may seem next to impossible. The trick is to change the Game before we get caught up in it to the point where it seems normal and inevitable. And to help our students realize that there's more to learning than this Game.

HARTFORD'S STUDENT SUCCESS CORPS: ASKING THE KIDS ABOUT LEARNING

One way is to turn the question around and ask it from the students' perspective, to find out from them what's getting in the way of the kind of learning that they, like all of us, are naturally predisposed to seek out and respond to. It's a perspective that assumes it's in our students' interests every bit as much as in our own to change the Game of School.

Thirty years ago, I reported on a group of educators in Hartford, Connecticut, testing a theory that teachers can build a new relationship with students by assuming that students know why schools aren't working for them—and that students haven't bothered to tell us why for a very good reason: We haven't taken the time to ask them. Through a series of conversations with eighth-grade students in each of Hartford's three middle schools, we formed the Student Success Corps, coordinated by area college students who are graduates of these same Hartford public schools.

The Student Success Corps was a gamble. We were betting on the notion that when students became part of the process of making meaning and saw themselves—and were recognized by the adults around them—as experts in what students think really goes on in school, they would be able to shoulder their share of responsibility for overcoming apathy, disrespect, and poor academic performance, and they'd work with their teachers to change these conditions.

The hardest job for adults may be to put aside our inclination to preach to kids about what's good for them, and instead ask them: What has to change—in your school, your community, among your peers, and within yourself—for you to be willing to work hard and do well in school? Taking students' views seriously, in dialogues such as this, is one way to change the Game of School.

In June 1994, as the school year was coming to a close, we invited sixty seventh-grade students from Hartford middle schools to the University of Hartford to tell us, and each other, what they think. After some initial exercises and role-playing, we put them to work. It was their job to identify

1. things adults in school do that help kids like me want to do my best
2. things adults in school do that make kids like me feel discouraged and not want to try hard
3. things other kids in school do that help kids like me feel it's okay to be smart and do good work
4. things other kids in school do that make kids like me feel put down and not want to show that I am smart

After each school's Corps members had responded, with their answers listed on newsprint sheets, we all took a look at what they had said. The picture they painted pointed to the subtle pathways that can lead into—and out of—the Game of School. Kids' responses to the question about how adults bring out their best work featured statements like: "When the teacher talks to me as a friend and encourages me" and "Teachers who make us feel like we can do something" and "Teachers who encourage us to work hard and tell us not to be with the wrong crowd." By contrast, students reported that they get discouraged "When they show favoritism," "When they don't try to understand why kids do bad things but just punish us," "When they say: 'That is a dumb question,'" or "When they give so much attention to the bad kids, it makes you want to goof off, too."

With respect to things that other kids do that make them feel it's okay to be smart, students said it is "When they encourage you and help you do your work," "When they do their work, they make me want to do it, too," "When we work together in groups," and "When other kids stop me from making the wrong decisions." And the students feel put down by other kids "When they call us a 'nerd' and rank on us," "When they call you 'stupid' and say you can't do the work," "When they cheat by copying your paper and lying about it," and "When they use peer pressure on you to try to get you suspended or to do drugs."

"POPULAR?" "SMART?" WHICH WOULD *YOU* CHOOSE?

One advantage of listening to students' voices is that we're reminded of things we might otherwise overlook when we're caught up in the routines of school life: handing out assignments, checking for homework, getting students ready for the next test. As an example, I spoke at that time with eighth-grade students and their teacher from Fox Middle School in Hartford. The students represented four classes in a cluster of about one hundred kids. At the center, they said, is the predominant teenage issue of "being popular" versus "being smart." (They defined smart as being willing to work hard at school tasks and get good grades.) Right now, they said, only a small segment of kids are both popular and smart.

We made a graph on the board with four categories, and the students estimated how many kids in their cluster belong in each category.

1. Popular and smart—18 kids
2. Smart (but not popular)—28 kids
3. Popular (but not smart)—24 kids
4. Neither popular nor smart—30 kids

They then reasoned that everyone in the first category, about half in the second, only a few in the third, and none of the kids in the fourth are satisfied with being where they are now. That leaves about sixty-four kids out of the hundred who wish they didn't have to choose between being popular or being smart (or who wish they were more of both).

We talked for a while about what has to happen, and who is responsible, for improving things in their school. Among the points they raised is that, for some kids, being smart is enough—they don't care if they are popular or not; they already have their sights set on leaving their neighborhood and going to college. The kids also theorized that many of those who are in the "popular (but not smart)" category are afraid of working hard and being successful academically because they might lose status. A colleague says the same is true in a rural town where she works: Among boys, flunking at least one course is an important status symbol. The students at Fox Middle agreed that kids in school have a huge influence—for good or ill—on one another.

BUT NOBODY EVER TALKS ABOUT IT!

But the most astounding thing we discovered was that nobody ever talks about this in class! It's only in the lunchroom or outside of school, the kids said, that talk about doing well in school or being popular with peers ever occurs; their teachers don't initiate, and rarely get to participate in, the conversation. It seemed evident to me that this is one of the most critical issues in deciding whether teenagers feel free to apply themselves to the tasks of learning in school. It's an issue that they can speak eloquently about. Yet, typical of areas that kids feel expert in—style, friendship, fairness, loyalty, powerlessness, and hypocrisy—the issue of "popular versus smart" is not normally part of the curriculum.

Their teacher offered a hypothesis: "Maybe it's because so many of us teachers were in the 'smart but not popular' category when we were in school. Maybe we have a hard time dealing with the kids who are popular, so we don't bring it up." Her students seemed to enjoy imagining their teacher as a teenager, who had her own social survival issues to contend with. "That's why we got to get in here some people who were popular and also did good," said one of the students.

We must discover areas where students are already "smart" (or are convinced they are) so that they, in turn, will feel confident enough to acquire the knowledge and skills that they don't yet possess. Since school curricula are predicated on what students don't know, an approach to learning that emphasizes student expertise may be difficult to sell to professional educators. But it may well be that a lot of kids—particularly those without strong family traditions of educational success—will only begin to respond thoughtfully to school-based learning when teachers work with students at the frontier of their own individual and collective experiences, feelings, and opinions. Kids withhold their expertise—both from us and each other—much of the time because for them school is not a place where they trust that their true feelings will be respected. Finding a way out of the Game of School may require that we commit ourselves to learning from our students, not just teaching them—even, or especially, when we're convinced that these students lack basic background information and skills.

CREATIVE TROUBLEMAKING: A CONVERSATION WITH TIM SULLIVAN

During his seventeen years of teaching in Concord, New Hampshire, elementary schools, Tim Sullivan gained a reputation as a creative and respected "troublemaker"—in the best sense of the word. Whether it is having his fourth-grade students challenge the state legislature over the seat-belt law (and opposing a governor in the process), or inviting them to open a school store and sell shares of stock to finance the venture (and raising the ire of the director of food services), or having them design a twelve-foot-high, twenty-foot-long bridge out of rolled-up newspaper triangles (using up the year's supply of masking tape), Sullivan's class projects tend to spill out over the lines that normally define learning in school.

I first met Tim when my oldest son was in his fourth-grade class, happily engaged in a school store that turned his $2.50 investment into $29.70 by the project's end, a venture that required him and his classmates to make almost all the marketing decisions. We talked about the risks and rewards of his style of teaching.

RLF: How does a teacher like you get into trouble? So much in my book argues that teachers should just "go for it—go where your passions are leading you." Am I being irresponsible in advising teachers to rely more on their passions than on following the curriculum?

TS: I think the question should be: "How are you going to stay *out* of trouble?" For me it's a matter of trying to look ahead and say, "Here's my idea. Is it feasible? What could possibly go wrong?" If I plan a project that may be outside the realm of the "normal" curriculum, I go to my colleagues in a teachers' meeting, or go to the administrator first, and ask, "Can I fit this in with what else is happening around here?" That diffuses a lot. I realize I may possibly offend some people, but I try and put those fears to the side and ask myself, "What's the goal?" When I know that the goal is educating the kids, and this is the avenue that I have to take to do it—then, fine. I work cooperatively with two other teachers, and they feel quite comfortable either joining me on a project or deciding not to.

RLF: What would your advice be to a teacher who was coming right out of college?

TS: Never grow up! I think that's the definition of a passionate teacher. In a lot of the things I do, I as a child am trying to teach another child about a concept that that child may not yet understand. The standard "adult" way may not get the point across, so I break it down to a kid level. I lecture sometimes, but I do a lot of hands-on project stuff that's more relaxed. So my advice would be: "Maintain your level of enthusiasm. Stay young. Grow young with the kids." I've been in teaching for twenty years, but it doesn't feel like twenty years. I'm still growing, I'm still learning.

RLF: Some argue that passionate teachers come into the profession with a level of zest, with a willingness to take risks and a playfulness that other teachers don't have.

TS: I disagree. I don't think you can just label people that way. I'm complimented that you want to include me in that designation, as a "passionate teacher." How did I get that way? I think everyone brings some sort of passion to whatever they do in life—

RLF: They should? Or they do—?

TS: Everybody does. That's my opinion about it. . . . But maybe after a number of years, they become less passionate. And then they need to do something about that so that they are challenging themselves as learners in order to be better as teachers.

RLF: Some people say that the history of formal schooling is the history of boredom, with rare moments of enlightenment. For most of us growing up, if you weren't especially smart, or talented, or a great athlete, school was a place where you played the Game and coasted along until you found something else to do.

TS: The reason why I became a teacher was because of my dissatisfaction with my education. I asked myself, "Can I do a better job?" And my answer was, "Yes, I can." Because I was not one of those people who had the qualities you just talked about. I was not particularly intelligent or talented in sports. I got by on my smile. I coasted on my personality.

That changed when I met my supervising teacher during my student teaching days in a fifth grade in Pittsfield, Massachusetts. Mrs. Johnston, who was certainly a passionate teacher by your definition, told me, "Sullivan—you've got to go through fifth grade again. And you're not going to get through on your smile like you did the last time." I would wake up with nightmares, in which this woman was standing on top of this mountain, throwing boulders—labeled "behavioral objectives"—down at me.

I also remember my college faculty mentor critiquing one of my math lessons, asking, "What are they going to get out of that? What was the purpose of the lesson?" And I couldn't answer him, because there was no purpose, no life-skill in what I was doing. It was experiences like those that turned me around. Their comments bothered me so much that from that point on I resolved that everything I do should have the bigger picture in mind.

RLF: How have you tried to put that philosophy into practice?

TS: The store was one of the greatest things I've done—the kids made money! In one month, we grossed $3,000. It was incredible! We had people coming to us asking if we could carry their line of potato chips, and the kids had to deal with these salesmen. The students became department heads; they had to write business letters on a daily basis; we had our own bank to deal with the finances, and they also had to open up an account at a local bank and balance the sheets. Then the principal started to charge us rent, on behalf of the school, since we were using their space. And the assistant superintendent started to charge us taxes, because he wanted to make it a real-world experience. You should have heard the kids complain about that!

We had to do our own marketing analysis. The kids asked students what they brought for snacks so we could carry the right items. We offended some teachers because the space we were using was a common hallway area and there was some noise. So we tried to solve the problem by operating during recess time or before and after school. And we made the school lunch director nervous because he thought we were competing with his lunch program. Then there was the time that a kid tried to cash his check from home for school lunch tickets in order to buy snacks instead. But we made a bar graph on the number of lunch tickets sold, which we followed for a month, and we were able to prove that as many or more kids were buying lunch tickets as previously and that they weren't spending their lunch money on snack items.

I had a teacher who was very concerned about the nutritional quality of our snacks. So we started carrying fresh fruit and cheese 'n' crackers in addition to pretzels, chips, and popcorn. We dealt with those objections by incorporating them as lessons: "Here's a problem—how are we going to solve it? Here's a legitimate complaint from a customer. How can we comply with the person's wishes, while still satisfying our business needs?"

RLF: You're describing a partnership where instead of absorbing the criticism or concern as the adult—thinking, "It's *my* job as the person in charge to resolve this"—you brought the concerns to the kids in a way that respected their capacity, as fourth graders, to deal with adult concerns. My guess is that the people who brought you those concerns did not expect you to take them right to the kids.

TS: Including the kids in all the thought processes just seemed the right thing to do, even though I didn't analyze it that way at the time.

RLF: So the passionate teacher communicates honestly with kids about adult concerns that are normally passed from teacher to teacher?

TS: I don't want you to misunderstand me. In many ways, I'm very conservative about kids, and sometimes I feel kids are given too many choices. There are times when a kid should just do something because "I told you to do it," and to trust me. But there are other times when I want the children to help solve the problem. And since this was a group activity, it seemed right for the class to deal with the issues.

After the first week, it became routine for us to ask, "How did we do today?" For the kids, it was a question about money: "Did we sell everything? How much profit did we make?" But I wanted to broaden the question to deal not just with profit but with customer satisfaction. So it wasn't a matter of "Mrs. So-and-So doesn't like this," but "I heard a customer say . . ." And then we would brainstorm what to do.

And I learned from this that one of the greatest pitfalls a teacher can blunder into is to assume that we know better than the kids—I mean, of course we know some things they don't—but we've got to give them credit for what they do know, for what they are bringing into the lesson, and show them the respect they deserve.[1]

10

MORE WAYS TO CHANGE THE GAME OF SCHOOL

I try to never stop dreaming when I'm with them. You would think that, as processes unfold, and the dreams never work out in exactly the ways you imagine them, they would get discouraged. But every time we dare to dream, the students dare to dream with us.

—DAVID ERVIN, music teacher

"WHAT IF?" DAVID ERVIN'S STRATEGY FOR COLLECTIVE CREATIVITY

David Ervin, who teaches music and directs drama at Oyster River Middle School in Durham, New Hampshire, comes from a family of engineers. Although he majored in music at college, he saw himself spending at most a year or two teaching music in school before heading back to graduate school to study physics and become an engineer like his father and brothers. "I thought of it as doing my own Peace Corps stint," he told me. That was years ago. Now he is busy helping his students produce a new play that they are going to write, compose, act in, design sets and costumes for, and perform. David says,

> My basic premise is that I want every moment to be important enough to engage kids spiritually, emotionally, intellectually, even physically. When I create such an environment and keep it going, that's when education

is happening. The way I do that is to create "arenas." So I set a deadline. When the kids walk into the class I tell them that in three months we will be in front of an audience of seven hundred people, sharing what it is that we have gone through, the process we're about to start with.

I've been teaming with a colleague who teaches language arts, and we look for a theme that is something we absolutely know the kids will be able to envision more than one side of. One of our recent themes was a musical that had something to do with the way the kids feel about how they look. From that they wrote a work called *In the Mirror*. Last year, they wrote a musical based on what they'd learned from interviewing someone who had lived through the Great Depression. Their musical was called *Backspace*: a couple of kids get zapped backward through their computer into the exact place they'd have been during the thirties. For their set, they reconstructed what our town looked like at that time. Another year, we took the kids to the mills in Lowell, Massachusetts, and told them to draw their idea from the life of children their age in the 1800s who worked in the fabric mills. It was called *The Thread of Life*.

When I was in college, we studied about Alexander the Great, and I learned that he had been in command of an army when he was eighteen years old. As soon as the enemy was in sight, he would run ahead of all his troops into battle. His army thought he was crazy, and they would run after him to save him from what they thought was certain doom, and the enemy would take flight. That's the way I teach—I take that as my role, to run out ahead and show the kids how excited I am to go through the process and write and perform a musical for all the people. There are a lot of kids who say, "I can't believe we're doing this," but they don't get a lot of time to worry because by that time, we're moving too fast to think about it. What makes them do it is a combination of forward momentum and almost a reckless belief in success.

I have some kids whom I stay in touch with all the way through their senior year in high school. They always talk about the incredible forward direction. I try to never stop dreaming when I'm with them. You would think that, as processes unfold, and the dreams never work out in exactly the ways you imagine them, the kids would get discouraged. But every time we dare to dream, the students dare to dream with us.

To me the real power in teaching is that what we create is created by all the kids together. I try to help kids show themselves how society might be. When we write and perform something together, kids gain a lot of respect for one another, despite the possibility of conflict and division. We define the common bonds that allow them to create and perform.

The first thing that happens when I spring the challenge of writing and performing a musical play of their own is that one group of kids comes forth that wants to make the whole thing pure slapstick. After a bit, another group emerges that wants to make the play a really strong moral statement about how the world ought to be. I find that humor and morality are really big pieces of what it's like to be a teenager. We use humor as a way to release the tension created when we don't understand someone or something (hence, also, its destructive potential, as with ethnic or sexist jokes).

So, we've got these two groups, and we ultimately find a direction that everyone can agree with morally and aesthetically. That takes incredible work. Coming to consensus is not something that kids do easily, especially when they get really interested in a project. They're much more likely to argue and try to put down each other's ideas.

To cope with this, I've invented something I call the *What if?* process. It works like this: When we're working out the idea of the play—a process that can take three or four weeks—I tell the kids that this has to be a period of time when evaluation or judgment is not allowed. Every statement they make, every suggestion they offer has to begin with the words "what if." So one kid begins with "What if we did a play about saving the rain forest?" and maybe the next kid pipes up with "What if we did it on a nun who goes crazy and shoots everybody at McDonald's?" And the next kid, after a period of awkward silence, offers "What if we did it about the rain forest and it dealt with poachers?" and immediately another kid says, "What if these poachers were after a rare and endangered animal and we had to stop them?"

And then somebody comes in with "What if we did it on poachers in a fast-food restaurant?" and everybody laughs and the tension is relieved. But then we realize that we have two themes going: violence and rain forests. And that kind of tension between themes is very rich with dramatic potential. An amazing thing about the *What if?* process is that the room, at times, is full of silence—for as long as thirty seconds (which for seventh graders is a very large amount of silence). At such times, the only power within the room is the power of a connecting idea.

> The moment we allow any evaluation or judging, it stops the creative process cold. The first response of "Oh, I'm sick of worrying about the damn rain forest" would lead, in turn, to "There's already too much violence on TV to make me want to produce any more of it." And the kids would stop inventing. It's not just negative comments, either. For kids in the beginning of the creative process, positive feedback can be as much of a killer as the negative stuff. They both stop the creativity.[1]

As David spoke, it seemed he was applying Newton's third law of motion to teaching: *Students in motion tend to stay in motion*—in contrast to the passivity of *Students at rest* . . . , an inertia that is often so difficult to overcome. So perhaps his family's scientific heritage is in there working for him as he remains a teacher.

FIND SOMETHING IN EVERY STUDENT WORTHY OF OUR RESPECT

We have to find a way to let students know that they count for something. Many of them just won't be motivated to work hard until they know that their teachers are genuinely interested in who they are. It may be as simple as admiring how they choose their clothes, appreciating their sense of humor, taking their questions seriously, or finding out about their brothers and sisters, or comparing stories about pets. But engaging them in our work begins with our finding something special about each of them. Students wait for their teachers to set the tone of that relationship.

When young people see that we are interested in hearing their ideas, opinions, and experiences, they become more open to what we want to share with them. The fabled "generation gap" is always a good place to begin. Teenagers love to point out ways that their culture has examined and rejected or superseded our own.

Elementary school classrooms are filled with family photos, birthday calendars, butcher-paper outlines of the kids themselves, displays that answer the challenge: "Tell me who you are!" We don't do "show and tell" for teenagers. They sit there, many of them, plagued by insecurities and self-doubt, afraid that the spotlight of classroom attention will be turned on them at precisely the point where they will be seen as inept, inarticulate, uncool, or inappropriate. The teacher who can break through that defense and encourage the students behind the masks to show themselves is the teacher who has the best chance of inviting students into the subject matter and getting more than a perfunctory, "getting through it" response.

Often a teacher's life story contains the clue. When I ask teachers, "What's the thing that your students find curious about you?" I get answers like, "Whether I'm ever going to get married," "What my kids are like," "Why I drive such a beat-up old car," "Why I wear such weird ties," or "What I look like without my beard." Teachers are examples to students of successful, caring adults who are not their parents (with whom they may or may not be in conflict). Kids are naturally curious about their teachers' beliefs, histories, families, hobbies, pets, and idiosyncrasies. How do teachers get along with their own teenage kids? What were they like when they were in high school? Learning about their teachers make them more individual and more accessible. The Game of School begins to change when we acknowledge one another's uniqueness.

STUDENTS AS PLAYERS—NOT SPECTATORS

The world of school is a world we adults tend to feel comfortable in. We may have decided to be teachers, in part, because we liked school even when most of our classmates, back in "the good old days," didn't. As teachers, school is a world in which we have most of the control. We are the active and important ones, more or less. Too many of our less comfortable students are content to sit back and watch us.

What makes them uncomfortable? We stand and they sit. We talk as often and as long as we want, and they must listen or raise their hands before speaking. We move around the room; they must stay in their chairs. We drink coffee; they can't chew gum. We wear funny-looking sandals; they can't wear baseball hats in class. We know what's coming next (at least some of the time), and they must wait to hear from us what's for homework, what's on the test, and when the assignment is due. We are the judges; they are the ones who get graded. The alternative does not mean turning over control to the students and abandoning our responsibilities. It means helping them begin each course, each unit, each class as players, not as spectators.

A spectator is a student who sits while the teacher or another student performs. A spectator is passive, able to drift off or daydream while the teacher gives their version of what the learning task is all about. By contrast, a player is engaged at the start with a clearly active role in the discovery of knowledge. Once in the game, players naturally want to keep playing.

One of the best ways to induce students to become active at the start is to ask the right questions, such as the "hook questions" discussed in the unit outline in chapter 7. It must be a question capable of engaging students' imaginations and getting them to bring out and share expertise they already possess. It has to be a question that all students can offer an opinion on, regardless of how little they may know. It's important that the questions—and the answers that students give—come *before* we present the content so that students develop a stake in what's happening in class and so that, when introduced, content can relate to many of the things that the students have already alluded to, discussed, or debated.

Thus, the true background to a unit of study is the stimulation of students' imaginations and mental energy to the point where they are ready to connect with ideas that require content knowledge to become understood. What we normally call "background" data (facts, terms, historical references, key concepts, and important persons) are reserved until students are ready for them and can relate to the larger picture.

This reversal of common pedagogical sequence is critical if we want students to act like budding scientists, historians, writers, mathematicians—people who can sustain an eagerness to absorb ever more sophisticated content—as opposed to acting like passive and temporary receivers of instructional commodities, forgetting content as soon as the final exam is over.

Below are more examples of initial questions to help students to begin as players:

- When dissecting frogs, we might ask, "Do humans have a right to kill animals in order to study them?"
- A class in Spanish might begin with "What will life be like when America is a truly bilingual nation?"
- In English class, we could speculate: "How would our language be different if Africans had come to this continent as masters and Europeans had come as slaves?"

Such questions not only coax reluctant students onto the intellectual playing field but also promote in-depth study. Sixth graders in one school began their study on the Incas, Aztecs, and Mayans with the question: "If you were creating a mythical society based on nature, and you were its leader, what force of nature would you be?" Follow-up questions included: "How would you convince people to believe in you?" "What would your mythical family be like?" "What other aspects of nature would be your allies, or your foes?" Suddenly, ancient civilizations became as close to the students as the weather, and as real to them as their imaginations and fantasies.

KEEPING UP THE MOMENTUM

The goal of opening questions is to whet students' appetite for the hard stuff that follows, for in-depth content and essential knowledge. But how do we sustain such interest beyond the hook question? How do we avoid returning to business as usual once the novelty to the question has worn off? Here are some ideas:

IN THE EARLY CONVERSATIONS, FOCUS AT LEAST HALF OF THE DISCUSSION ON TOPICS THAT KIDS KNOW AS MUCH OR MORE ABOUT AS TEACHERS DO. That allows them to impress you with what they already know, while it gives you insight into how they think and what they think about. When we introduce new material, we should tie it into the students' frame of reference. Fads, TV programs, and teenage life are apt vehicles for students to translate core content material into their own idioms and experiences and then, with our help, to transpose their ideas and opinions back again to the course curriculum. Far from pandering to kids' tastes, such translation acknowledges students for their knowledge and thereby opens them to ours. As one teacher put it, "If we want to teach them, we must learn from them. It's as simple—and as difficult—as that."

DO OURSELVES WHAT WE ASSIGN THE KIDS TO DO. Teachers are role models who've got opinions, ideas, and feelings. Especially when assigning research and writing tasks, a teacher's own performance of those same tasks gives students a chance to assess their teacher's writing and offer some suggestions, even as they edit their own and one another's compositions. When I was at Northeastern University, I was asked to teach a graduate seminar on educational theory to fifteen students. On day one I told them the truth: "Not only have I never taught ed theory, I never ever took such a course. But beyond that, I'm not sure there is any such thing as 'educational theory'—maybe we all just make it up as we go along. So, here's what I offer you: Anyone who thinks my lack of experience here means I'm wasting their time is free to leave, and I'll make sure you get your tuition back. But if you stay, I will do every assignment that I give to you, and together we'll try to find out if there is such a thing as educational theory." One student left; the others and I had a pretty good time of it.

When teachers write about their childhood experiences, they help students identify with them as people who have survived some critical challenges. A colleague, Jay Shapiro, who teaches social studies and was working with a class in summer school, assigned the class to write about an experience that changed their life. He then wrote about flunking out of college the first time he attended. This gained instant attention from his students because they, too, had flunked some courses. When his students learned that Jay had gone on to graduate from college and to get two master's degrees, they got to see what it's like to come back from failure and succeed.

Author and educator Deborah Meier has often reminded me, in our conversations, that children want to do what they see powerful adults around them doing. If we want kids to reflect, to ponder, to argue without putting other people down, to keep trying until they do it right, their best example may be our own ability to make mistakes and then think aloud about how to do it better the second time around.

HONOR THEIR QUESTIONS—THE TOUGHER, THE BETTER. Every teacher awaits with dread the student who asks, "Why do we have to learn this stuff—it's boring!" and most reply with some version of, "It's part of the curriculum; it'll get you ready for high school (or college)." We should perhaps respond: "Let's figure out why we are learning this—because if we can't find a good reason, we probably should be doing something else."

A special education teacher complained, "Kids with learning disabilities know that I can't legally flunk them, so they say, 'Why do we have to work?'" One response might be: "That's a very good question; if we don't know the answer, we're *both* in trouble. Why should you work? Let's find out." A white social studies teacher in a school with mostly African American and Hispanic students notes, "The kids keep asking me if I'm a racist because I grew up in an all-white community. I don't know what to say, without offending my students or labeling myself." An honest and self-respecting response might be: "I don't feel as though I am one, but maybe your point is that living in our society makes us all somewhat racist. We'd better find out if that's true, and if so, what we can do here in this class to deal with that fact."

Often the best way to respond to a challenging question from a student is to celebrate it, to help others see its complexity, to list it on the board and keep referring to it—and thus to encourage other kids to become good, tough questioners. We also have the option of posing the question, "Why does this class seem less interesting—for you and for me—than it was at the beginning of the year?" or "How can we deal with this material so that you will enjoy learning it and I will enjoy teaching it?"

No matter who does the asking, the most productive answer is the discussion generated around these questions. If the climate is right, people will soon find themselves talking about meaning, worth, choices, and consequences. Until the climate is such that mutual respect is pretty well assured, some teachers fear—legitimately so, I believe—that they will be ridiculed and spurned for their innovations, that their students will walk all over them. The fear of humiliation keeps students from sharing their most wonderfully creative or controversial ideas in class; it keeps teachers from expressing too openly their love for learning; it keeps most classes from having much fun and striving for great things that are only achieved in a spirit of adventure and in a climate of caring.

My strong hunch is that breaking out of this bind happens only when teachers can simultaneously break *in* to their students' world and find some place where they can talk reasonably and respectfully together, as David Ervin so beautifully demonstrates. Unless both take risks, nobody will be willing to risk much. If teachers suddenly drop their defenses and start acting on their passions, students will wrinkle their noses and think their teachers are weird. Or if a teacher manages to coax a few students to behave in an intellectually less-inhibited way, such kids will probably fail to bring other students along. It has to happen together. We have to find a way to talk our way through the process so that we limit our vulnerability even as we take those essential risks together.

The Game of School—the mind-numbing routine that is business as usual in most of our schools and classrooms—won't be transformed by pronouncements, condemnation, or curricular revision. It can only be changed by sensitivity and candor and guts. And the utmost humanity we can muster.

11

NURTURING A RESPECT FOR TRUTH AND A DEFENSE AGAINST FALSEHOOD

Our students are already chronically online, and many of their conversations are centered around what they are watching on YouTube and what video game they're going to go home and play and chat with each other. The danger is already there, beginning when they're seven and eight years old.

—DEIRDRE, second-grade teacher

THE POWER TO DETERMINE THE TRUTH FOR THEMSELVES

Questions of truth and falsehood are with us from early childhood through adulthood and into old age. And invariably, those questions become part of school conversations, both formal and casual.

If our nation wasn't in such a precarious position based on lies being repeatedly put forth at the highest levels of government, we might better appreciate the irony of an anecdote about a father and son who live near a prison. Whenever they drive by it, the son asks, "Who gets put in there?" The father says, "That place is for kids who don't eat their vegetables, kids who don't brush their teeth, and kids who lie to their parents." Lying to your kids while warning them of the consequences of lying is perhaps not the best way to nurture in them an appreciation of the truth.

A CHILD'S FIRST LIES ARE AN ESSENTIAL STAGE OF MENTAL DEVELOPMENT

According to psychiatrists who've studied the emergence of what they refer to as a Theory of Mind in children, a child's first lies are not only normal but may well be an essential stage of their mental development, allowing the child to realize that other people have different thoughts and beliefs. This typically takes place between two and four years of age and is a sign that children recognize that they are distinct individuals with their own thoughts.

Joshua Chard, Maine's 2024 Teacher of the Year, offers an experienced elementary educator's perspective:

> Sometimes, when young children lie, we personalize and attach a moral judgment to it. After all, we reinforce the idea that lying is wrong from a young age. We hammer home the idea that we always need to tell the truth. For young children, however, it isn't so black and white. They are navigating a world where they are learning how to be humans, and experimenting with the truth, telling stories, is a part of that development.
>
> Indeed, lying can be a way for children to avoid getting into trouble. Wanting to please adults is a regular part of this stage of development, so avoiding disappointment is natural. However, this is only a small part of why children experiment with the truth.
>
> Many children invent stories for attention or approval. Your classmate shared about their trip to the beach over the weekend during Morning Meeting. You want to share about your equally exciting weekend; what can you make up that will get the reaction that your friend got? You can make your life sound as enjoyable as theirs. These scenarios are especially true for students with low self-esteem. They cannot imagine their stories interesting enough, so they embellish.
>
> In second grade, I must be a gentle guide when helping students understand why lying is wrong. Shaming a student for lying will only result in them digging in. Instead, I create an environment where the payoff for telling true stories and taking responsibility for one's actions is greater than for lying.
>
> In the end, my goal isn't to catch kids in a lie but to help them see the value of honesty in a safe and supportive way. When truth-telling is met with understanding and care, students learn that their real stories are

> worth telling. Over time, they begin to trust that who they are—and what they have to share—is enough.[1]

But as children develop, we hope they will embrace a more critical posture regarding issues of truth, especially with respect to the social media that bombards their world. We want them to begin to question the truthfulness of what they see and hear as they begin developing critical-thinking skills and engaging with the world they live in. This gives parents and teachers an opening to explain how media works and how facts are distinguished from opinions and deliberate falsehoods.

We live in an era when many of our political and cultural leaders show little respect for the truth, and when radio, cable TV, and online platforms clamor with voices that defy or deny many of the truths that long have held our society together despite our differences. So, what's a teacher to do when students come to class chatting about social media nonsense they've ingested, kids whose parents have not helped them understand how media works?

WHAT'S REQUIRED? TRUST, SINCERITY, AND MUTUAL RESPECT

Talking openly about this issue requires trust, sincerity, and mutual respect among students and also between students and their teacher. Otherwise, it's easy for children with unpopular opinions to face humiliation or for teachers to silence students by using their positions of authority to preempt honest dialogue—or for teachers themselves to fear parent or community complaints. It might be tempting to avoid the issue or cover it over with platitudes and move on with the lesson. "Truth," after all, has dimensions that are philosophical, political, social, personal and, for many, spiritual and religious, and these can be minefields for a teacher who has not already earned that trust and helped create mutual respect, which allow for candid and enlightening talk.

Yet there is arguably no more essential purpose of education than to help learners discern truth from falsehood. So, an essential role of being a teacher is to find ways to create a space where students can develop agency and facility in seeking what's true—while contending with the universe of falsehoods and distortions surrounding them. Often, classroom or lunchroom incidents can be fodder for informal discussions about truth. The trick is to do so without imposing our own viewpoints on our students, however tempting that might be. For an imposed truth is, by its nature, undemocratic; it's what dictators and autocrats try to do. Hitler's "big lie" was an imposed "truth." There are plenty of instances of this phenomenon in today's political landscape. We might worry that we engage questions of truth and falsehood at our peril. But we ignore them, likewise, at the peril of losing our democracy by failing to educate future citizens to distinguish truth from falsehood.

TO BECOME WILLING SEEKERS OF TRUTH IN ALL ASPECTS OF THEIR LIVES

So how to begin—and how to remain true to your own passions and values without appearing to tip the scales toward your philosophical, political, social, or personal preferences? The most important thing is to nurture in the classroom a zest for exploration and discovery so that students come to realize that they are beginning a journey as learners, which has no specific destination but that has great impact. They are not in school to "find *the* truth," much less to be told what truth is. They are here to become willing seekers of truth in all aspects of their lives. This can seem intimidating or liberating or both at the same time.

I remember a high school principal in rural Maine telling me he'd been roundly criticized by a parent and school board member, who had demanded, "What business do you have teaching my daughter to think? You're supposed to teach her, not to make her think!"

Here are some guidelines that may be useful:

- You might begin by having your class (grades 4–12) think about truth as presented in the Declaration of Independence. What does it mean for a "truth" to be "self-evident"? Ask the class questions like, "Can you think of truths that your family considers to be self-evident?" "Can you imagine how a truth becomes 'self-evident' or how a truth you once thought self-evident (e.g., Santa Claus and the Tooth Fairy) turned out to be not so?"
- Karen Ball, who teaches high school English in Indiana, tells me that "the *New York Times* publishes a provocative photo once a week in 'What's Going On in This Picture?' In their journals, my students write ten concrete things they believe are true in what they see in the photo. Then they make a one-sentence

claim about what they think is happening. As we share what we have found with one another, I can challenge their assumptions and push back on their observations, which increases their level of interest and participation. During this activity, no one can play the 'guess-what-the-teacher-is-thinking' game, because I don't know the answer, either. Later in the week, the *Times* offers a link to the original article. They also provide a chat feed where students from across the world can share their guesses about what is happening."[2] This seems like a delightful way of introducing students both to the issue of truth in the media and to their own ability to perceive truth. You might encourage students to bring you images or opinions they encounter in the media or elsewhere that raise questions in their minds about truthfulness. You could then use those artifacts (without revealing who brought them to you, if the student prefers) to provoke class discussions. This, in turn, might encourage students to take pride in their growing ability to navigate the "brave new world" of falsehoods and distortions that we live in.

- It's fine to emphasize the importance of truth, as long as you help students understand that not all people will agree about what is true and what is, or might be, false. You might ask students to make a list of the truths they once believed but that they now are skeptical about or have found to be false. Inevitably, items listed as "former truths" by some students will be seen by others as still true, which will give you an opening to help students develop tolerance and respect for people with differing opinions.
- It's also worthwhile to point out that while it is up to each of us to determine the truth, when people can agree on basic truths—and here would be a great opportunity to have students discuss, debate, and define what "basic truths" are—people are more likely to get along and accomplish things together, as they build upon those truths and work out compromises. Again, there are wonderful lessons in the history of our nation to refer to.
- It can be both liberating and intimidating for students, especially in grades 5–8, to realize that they have the power to determine the truth for themselves. Some students may resist

> this, especially if they come from families that adhere strictly to a religious or politically imposed doctrine, but it may also be an opening for them to begin to have the courage and confidence to think for themselves. Here is where Karen Bell's exercise with the *New York Times* picture of the week might provide a low-risk opening. By helping students learn to feel comfortable about exploring questions not easily answered, you make room for your students to become responsible consumers of information. Students should be made to feel that your classroom is a safe place to begin or to continue this quest, through conversations, journaling, and reading. You will have helped them on the way to becoming agents of their own well-being and citizens who can help us live together in harmony.

There is a biblical phrase, often quoted, that comes to mind: "Ye shall know the truth, and the truth shall make you free." We have an opportunity to tap into the wellspring of great discussion that surrounds that quote. In such discussions, freely engaged upon and respectfully considered by students of almost any age, we achieve one of our most exalted purposes as educators.

PART THREE

THE STANCE

12

DISCOVERING A STANCE

The fastest way to ignite passion is to reflect on those moments that make you smile. Think about all the times when you saw your students' faces light up as they got those "aha" moments, as they sat on the edge of their seats just hanging on to your every word. Reflect on how amazing it is to see their minds absorb everything like little sponges. Think about your special calling as an educator and always remember to lead and teach with your heart. It takes a big heart to shape little minds!

—ASTRAL BATTISTE,
US Virgin Islands 2024 Teacher of the Year

When I first stood before my freshman English classes back in the mid-1960s, I had some typical attitudes of a new teacher. I tended to talk too much and listen too little. I was frustrated with what I saw as my students' ineptness and incoherence. I had wanted them to become "thoughtful" and "literate" writers and readers, and most of them stubbornly refused to meet my expectations. While I strove to be seen as clever and inspiring, I came across more as eccentric and obtuse. The truth is that I didn't know beans about teaching. And nobody thought it worthwhile to show me.

Since then, my work has taken me into a great variety of schools as a curriculum consultant with veteran teachers and, more recently, as an education professor and then as the head of an innovative educator training institution. With many years of hard lessons from a variety of educational jobs behind me, and many images of successful teachers in mind, I look at teaching very differently from the way I did back in my days of teaching freshman English. I have seen other teachers, and occasionally myself, get very different results from kids. Here's an example of what has happened in my own experience.

THE STARSHIP *ENTERPRISE* EXERCISE: "YOU'LL BE THE ONES IN CHARGE"

Back in the 1990s, when I visited sixth- and seventh-grade classrooms as part of my work with the school staff, I sometimes asked students to pretend they were—right at that moment—crew members on the Starship *Enterprise* of *Star Trek* fame. "And where does this spaceship go?" I'd ask them. Of course, they'd tell me, where no one has ever gone before. "You are really on this ship, right now," I explained. "And when it lands, you will be the ones in charge. Where exactly will the spaceship land?" I wrote on the board, "The 21st Century," and turned to them, "Am I right? Is this somewhere where nobody has gone before? And will you really be in charge there?" "Yes!" they responded. Even the tough guys found the idea hard to resist. So I had their attention, at least for the moment. Sometimes their teacher watched the kids a little nervously, not quite sure what I was up to or fearful they might lose control.

But that's when I put their minds to work. "I'm going to ask you two questions about the future that nobody but you can answer. I don't know the answer and neither does your teacher. Not even the principal. These are your questions, as crew members on the *Enterprise*. The first one is [and I write it on the board]: "What problems will you face when the ship lands back on Earth?"

"What kinds of things are you going to have to deal with when you arrive in the twenty-first century?" I asked. "I want an answer from everybody—because you know there will be plenty of problems to go around."

The answers came tumbling forth: "AIDS, crime, pollution, the ozone layer, no jobs, homeless people, wars, cancer, people being abused, people getting divorced, UFOs, hunger in Africa . . ."

The tough kids conjured up gory scenes of global mayhem; quieter kids talked about destruction of the rain forest; the erudite mention economic struggles or changing family patterns. And I wrote them all down on a newsprint flip-chart in bold magic marker colors, asking each student what color he or she prefers. As the sheets filled with their thoughts, I taped them up on the walls.

When they had almost—but not quite—run out of calamities, I asked them the second question: "What do you have to learn now, in this century so that you can deal with all these problems when you take over?"

The responses came a little more slowly now, but I kept the pressure on. "If you came up with a problem, you'd better try to come up with an answer," I told them. "Remember, you're the ones who will be in charge."

The kids started with the usual stuff: reading, writing, math, science, computers. But eventually someone said: "Working with different kinds of people" and when I asked why, the student explained, "Global warming is happening everywhere, so if we want people to stop polluting the air, we have to work things out with them so they'll stop, too." Their teacher smiled at them, proud of how well they were doing.

In this exercise, as opposed to my earlier teaching experiences, getting students to think and to talk seems so much less of a problem. As most experienced teachers have long ago discovered, if the atmosphere in the class is right, and students get in the right spirit and don't have to worry about being judged by their teacher or their peers, they tend to relax their natural resistance to taking part in a serious discussion.

In such circumstances, the teacher, too, can relax the fear that things will degenerate into chaos, or that some kid will say something one can't handle, or that the students will just stare ahead blankly, waiting for the answers to come from the front of the room. A big part of what makes this Starship *Enterprise* example work is that—like Yvonne Griffin's asking her high schoolers to define what they want to know about life relationships, or David Ervin's challenge to his seventh-grade students to invent a musical play—I began here by posing a serious question that assumes intelligence on their part, a question that doesn't make them feel that I already know what the right answer is. In such an atmosphere, most teachers can get pretty good responses from a broad spectrum of kids. The resistance, disdain, or apathetic silence that I used to fear as an inexperienced English teacher, and that kept me from taking risks, didn't occur here. The kids have risen to the occasion.

The list of what they think they'll need to know to solve problems in the twenty-first century begins to grow. By now the newsprint sheets have begun to line the front and sides of the room. The classroom decor changes: Displays crafted and mounted by the teacher are covered temporarily by lists of ideas and opinions generated by the students. The proof of their ability to think—and of their sensitivity to the world and its problems—surrounds them visually as well as in the sounds of their responses. I turn the question yet again: "Which of you will have to learn this stuff? Who are the leaders and decision-makers going to be?"

When most of the hands go up, I decide to provoke them a little: "You mean this voyage of the Starship *Enterprise* is filled with the leaders of the twenty-first century?" There is some giggling and some of the kids puff out their chests. Here, their teacher is likely to come into the conversation with a question like: "What kind of a world will it be if everybody thinks they'll be leaders? If everyone's a leader, who's going to follow?"

At first there is some uneasiness. The kids look at us cautiously, wondering if we're leading them down the garden path. Will they have to face, after all, the message that the adults around here don't think most of them really are "leadership material"?

After a moment, their teacher steps in to help: "Mr. Fried doesn't know what's going to happen in the twenty-first century, and neither do I. What kind of leaders do you think we'll need to deal with all these problems you've come up with?" There is a bit of nervous shuffling. The kids know they've left the familiar behind and are truly out in deep space. Nobody's even heard this issue discussed before, so there are no ready-made answers.

"This one's tough, huh?" I acknowledge, as the teacher and I exchange glances. "Your teacher must think you're pretty smart or he wouldn't have asked you such a difficult question."

When, in due course, their answers come, they are often enchantingly creative. In a typical classroom, filled with a mixture of kids from different ethnic backgrounds and so-called "ability groups," we will get answers like: "Well, everybody will have to be a leader at some things and a follower in others," or "People will have to learn first to be good followers and then they can be leaders," or "There won't be 'leaders' and 'followers' like we know them now. Everybody will have to cooperate more."

IDENTIFYING A STANCE

What just happened? How were we able to get such a breadth and depth of responsiveness from these seventh graders—students I'd never met before—when I could never seem to get, let alone maintain, that level of engagement when I started teaching back in the mid-1960s?

My initial success here is no proof by itself that this spirit of willing and widespread engagement can last. As seasoned teachers well know, starting with a good opener is no guarantee you can sustain students' interest, participation, and thoughtfulness over several months. All too often, a class begins well in September, only to bog down by Thanksgiving. Somehow or other, the mundane and the routine conspire to overwhelm our enthusiastic beginnings. And no doubt some of the kids' interest and participation in the Starship *Enterprise* lesson came from the break in routine and from my being a stranger, someone who wasn't there to check on their homework or grade their exams.

But while I don't want to attach too much significance to this exercise, I also don't want to dismiss it as merely a chance occurrence, a temporary detour from typical classroom activity. Something *did* happen, something in the nature of "critical thinking" took place, and it surprised us all, the students, their teacher, and me, with its vividness.

The Starship *Enterprise* exercise was for me both a happy accident and the outgrowth of something I'd been working on in my imagination for years. When I first tried it, I had been asked to help some middle school teachers utilize "brainstorming" in presenting a new unit to their students. Their principal was worried because he had overheard a teacher say, "My students aren't ready to brainstorm. We haven't covered that." I agreed to do what I could and walked into the room, hoping I could invent something to do so I wouldn't look completely foolish.

This happened again, two decades later, when I was working with five high school principals from rural, working-class schools in New Hampshire and Vermont. The principals were concerned that too many students were not taking their learning seriously. I asked them to bring a carload of their students, good talkers but with varying abilities, to meet on a mid-winter school day in a summer camp facility I had borrowed for the occasion. I placed the students into mixed groups with kids they didn't know and assigned one principal to act as scribe for each group.

"WHAT DO YOU KIDS NEED TO KNOW THAT YOU WON'T LEARN IN SCHOOL?"

The question this time was: "What do you need to know—that you probably won't learn in school—in order to have a happy life?" The result was an immediate and enthusiastic outpouring of ideas, which the principals scrambled to record. The idea of a question—essential to their lives—which had no apparent "right answer" was both inspiring and intoxicating. And being with "strangers" their own age liberated them to be themselves.

What I—and so many of the other teachers I talked with while putting this book together—*didn't* have to invent was a point of view on how to engage kids on a topic of importance. I already knew I wanted to approach them as active learners, as young people potentially able to become a part of a discussion on almost any topic I might raise that connected with their experience in some way. By starting off with this attitude—instead of assuming that we have to overcome their ignorance first and give them a lot of background information before they could participate meaningfully—we increase the likelihood that students will get into the spirit of the discussion.

What we have going for us is a philosophy, an attitude, a bearing, a way of encountering students based on a set of core values about kids and their learning potential.

What we have is a *stance.*

STANCE AS A PHYSICAL POSTURE

It starts in a physical way. There is a posture, a way we hold our bodies, that can communicate to students a sense of acceptance, respect, and expectation: how we greet them when they arrive (like Mrs. Betancourt in Puerto Rico, with her hugs and her hot chocolate), where we stand or sit when we talk to them, and how we move about the room. And, of course, there is the emotional or intellectual sense of the word "stance": the way we prepare ourselves for what students will bring with them into the classroom and what we want them to leave with. Who are these kids? How great is their potential? What are the talents they've got that nobody has yet discovered? What's holding some of them back from using their minds creatively in school? How can we help them get their act together academically? How important is this work we're doing, anyhow? What do we expect them to achieve?

Thinking about such questions is a crucial step in making us more able to help our students grow intellectually, for such thought allows us to link our devotion to a subject or discipline with our hopes for their development as thinking persons. This is not a debate about the relative merits of "affective" versus "cognitive" learning; it's not a call to stop teaching knowledge and start teaching personal growth. To be interested in how we can influence a young person's openness to learning is to concern ourselves with the whole person—but with particular emphasis on the development of the student's mind. That doesn't mean we have to try to act as psychologists or pastors or parents to our students (although, in the three decades since this book was first published, teachers have become more aware of the need to work with students who bring unmet emotional needs with them, as some of the new contributors to this book point out). It means that the way we present ourselves to them—the way we look at them when they enter the classroom and continue to engage them once they find their seats—has everything to do with how much they are going to learn from us.

Being passionate about our fields of study, or about issues alive in our community and in the world, cannot in itself make us teachers capable of transmitting a love of learning and ideas to students. We need something more. When I started teaching, I didn't know what that "something more" was, and I certainly didn't have it. It has been my great fortune, over the years, to get to know a number of teachers, like those we've met in this book, who do have that "something more," and who manifest it in a quality that I am calling a "stance." One such teacher is Ed Clarke, who had taught English for twenty-seven years when I was introduced to him.

ED CLARKE'S STANCE WITH UNDERPERFORMING STUDENTS

I met Ed because Nicola Riley, one of his former students (then studying nursing in college), told me that I had to talk to Mr. Clarke, because he was the best English teacher she'd ever had. She didn't tell me that she had failed his course the first time she took it. He was to tell me that on average one-third to one-half of his honors level freshman English class in this predominantly African American and Hispanic school fail each year.

It's not difficult to make an appointment with Ed Clarke, so long as you're an early riser. He regularly gets to school at 6 a.m. We settled for the relatively civilized hour of 7 a.m.; when I reached his office, it was clear from his animated personality and volubility that at least one of us was wide awake.

> I have enough seniority to teach any course I want in this school, but I choose to teach only freshmen because I want them to get off to a good start. If you can point them in the right direction, the rest takes care of itself. It's an advantage working with students who don't know what high school is like, since they haven't gotten used to the system yet, and you have a chance to inspire them to work up to their potential—not just to the level that got them through middle school.
>
> Why should we accept low standards? Better to start high, with the assumption that the kids can do things. Kids do what you expect them to do. If you expect them to do garbage, they do garbage. If you expect them to do gold, they do gold, or maybe some of them don't do gold, but they do silver. At the honors level, that means you assume that they have a strong background and you can just help them smooth out the rough spots. With students at the remedial level, working with them means filling in a lot of the blanks—but that doesn't mean assuming that they're stupid.
>
> They're not stupid. What we teachers often mistake as their being stupid is that kids tend to compartmentalize knowledge, and if this is English class, they figure they don't need to use their brain to deal with anything they may know in any other subject. They don't yet see the connections between math and science and history. But once you draw on their sources of information and experience, tap into what they *do* know and have opinions about (such as movies, music, neighborhood issues), it validates them and helps them draw things together.
>
> For example, when I do vocabulary with kids, we try to use sentences that have pieces of information that kids know from different contexts, like TV, and then use that as spinoffs for discussion. Kids say, "Hey, I know that!" and then they're ready to take part in the real work. It doesn't help to piss and moan about what kids don't know or what their teachers should have taught them in elementary or middle school.
>
> I think, to be frank, kids become used to a level of working and thinking that that's their role, to do as little as they think they can get away

with. They think that if they can get a B in a general class, why should they risk taking an academic-level course and getting only a D for the same work that gets them a B at a lower level? They know a B—at whatever level—looks good, whereas a D gets their mothers and counselors on their back.

Let's face the facts: Schools are overwhelming. Kids need to find a niche where they feel comfortable. But I don't think that this attitude should hold us back, as teachers. Hopefully we can explain our challenge to the kids. The way I look at it, you're a salesman, selling knowledge, selling yourself. Kids learn mostly for what are probably the wrong reasons. You want them to learn because they have realized that the knowledge or skills you offer them are important in themselves, or are essential to their future, or whatever. But if they do learn, it's because they like you, because they think you're funny, because they think you're different or cool or sincere.

Everybody who's ever taught has heard some kid say: "I'll do the work for you, but I can't stand to do the stuff that Mr. —— makes me do," even when you know that the other teacher is not asking them to do any more or harder work than you are.

So, in the end, you realize you're up there selling something. If it's writing that you want them to buy this week, you have to sell writing. And if you are excited about the product you are selling, then the kids will buy.

You can't underestimate how important the interpersonal factors are between adults and kids. You can be a genius, have the highest and most noble, grail-searching motives, but if kids don't like you, then they're not going to buy. Often kids will tell me: "You know, so-and-so [a teacher] said something disrespectful to me." And I answer, "But I say much worse things to you all the time," and they respond, "Yes, but you don't mean it," which means that if they know I like them, I can tell them what I really think, but it doesn't hurt.

And what they see in all that is the honesty. The kids respond to the kind of honesty that shows you're not afraid of them. They know when you're putting them on, when you're trying to build up their self-esteem by telling them something they did is "good" when they know and you know it's not. Kids are so much smarter than we give them credit for.

What I always try to do is to ask them to write about themselves. My hook is: I don't know who you are, and I want to know. It may be a short biography poem, in which they tell me about themselves. It's not

> threatening because they don't need to have any background, any prior information, to do the work. And then I print their poems in a booklet and they're thrilled to see their poems in print. The key is that I really want to know about these kids. I try to speak personally to each kid before class every day. And they will tell you amazing things—even kids I've never had in class but just talk to in the hall. They tell me because they think I'm different.[1]

Ed showed me some of these initial poems he had printed from a remedial-level class this year. They all start with the student's first name, which is the title of the poem. The first line will comprise two or three adjectives that describe themselves, then a line about what they like, another about what they fear, a third about what they hope for in the future, and finally, their last name. A typical example:

> MAURICE—
> talented, funny
> who loves rapping, dancing, art
> who fears getting shot, not passing a grade, seeing my mother getting killed for somebody else
> who would like to see myself graduating on stage, myself getting a car, myself bringing in a lot of money
> —ALLEN

Ed continued:

> If you teach a freshman, you get to see someone grow. You plant a seed and you get to see that seed take root and thrive over the next four years and beyond. Teaching freshmen, I can see them in a wider pattern, over a longer range than if I only got to meet them as juniors or seniors. I can see kids who failed during their freshman year pick themselves up and move on. Success is important, to be sure. But not instant success. Maybe, at first, they're not ready to play the game, the game of literacy—writing and speaking and learning how to think. But if you take a longer view, you see the changes, and most of them are positive.
>
> Nicola Riley took my honors freshman English course and she failed it. No, I didn't fail her—she failed herself! Like a lot of kids who come

here, she thought she could get away with doing the things she had done in middle school—do the same amount of work and get a B or better. I wanted her to do more. She didn't do more, so she failed. She just wasn't conscientious, she wasn't thorough, and she wasn't motivated to put in the work to do her best, to be what she could be.

Once she realized that I wouldn't take any less than her best, she began to produce great stuff. And she kept on doing it, right through high school and into college. On one of her college applications, she had to respond to the question: "If you had to spend a year in prison and could take three things with you, what would you take?" She listed deodorant, Tic Tacs, and a Bible. And then in wonderful Jamaican dialect, she described why she had chosen these items. When it came to the Bible, she said she knew there was a story in it claiming if you march around a city's walls seven times, they would crumble.

It takes some kids a whole semester, or even a whole year, to learn that what got them by before doesn't work with me. They let themselves fail because they're so used to grown-ups issuing threats that they don't follow through with that it takes them a while to realize that I'm serious about facing the consequences. When I offer them what's on the menu, it's up to them to take it. I never flunk a kid—when they fail, they fail themselves. But I never give up on a kid, and, more than likely, I'll have that same kid the next year, repeating the course. And most of them do much, much better. It's often the kids who fail my course the first time around who stay friends with me for years afterwards.

When you break the mold a little bit, it opens up their minds. But they have to be convinced that you are sincerely interested in them. You can't fake that; the kids see right through it. There has to be some sort of mutual recognition of worth. They have to know that you are really interested in them. Every teacher has to use their own personality, their own style. With me, it's mostly informal conversing, lighthearted teasing, and certain little rituals that may seem goofy but have a serious purpose. For example, at the end of every period I tell them: "Say 'good-bye,'" and they all say "good-bye"; "Say 'Have a nice day,'" and they do that, too; "Say 'See you tomorrow,'" and they do it—in chorus! It's corny, but it works. It lets them practice having good manners and—who knows?—they'll need those manners when they try to find a job. If I forget to do it, the kids start saying these things themselves.

> If someone does something wrong, goofs up, I work hard to keep them in the conversation with me, to not give them a chance to give up on me or on themselves. I use myself, my own vulnerability. I'm losing my hair, so I'm constantly poking fun at myself. If kids point out that my shoes look scruffy, I tell them, "I'm saving my money for a hair weave." I love to joke around with the kids. In my remedial English classes, we turn our little quips into a lesson: We collect funny gibes about everybody and everything, and the students write them down on note cards, organize them into categories, and type them up and print them. They get to practice collecting, organizing, and applying information.
>
> I always save two major projects for the end of the year, and I give them heavy marking weight. Every one of my kids, from remedial to honors, writes fifteen poems. I have specific rules. I tell them, "Give me three verbs, three prepositional phrases," and so on. All the grammar of the year is synthesized in these poems and incorporated into something meaningful. We illustrate them, edit them, publish them—and they all want copies. They end up with this great keepsake of their freshman year.
>
> When kids are busy doing things, your job is easy. I have no discipline problems during the last three weeks of the year, when other teachers are tearing their hair out, trying to get in those last few chapters on conjunctive adjectives.
>
> I can still say, after twenty-seven years, that I love coming in every day. I never get bored. I laugh every day. I look forward to the kids. And I make sure I have a good time. I figure that if I'm having a good time, the kids are getting something out of it, too. They are learning that school is not terrifying, formidable, or boring. I mean, how many other people can say that about their work?
>
> If for nothing else, I teach the way I teach to make the world a better place for me when I retire. I know I'm going to run into a lot of my former students on the streets of Hartford. I want them to be better people because of their experience with me.

This is what I mean by a "stance."

13

HOW A STANCE EVOLVES

Although I never learn exactly where to stand in relation to my students, I develop a reliable sense of what is too close and what is too far. Within these limits, I craft a workable relationship for the moment—now here, now there. I tune my stance continually to the values that seize me.

—JOE MCDONALD,
Teaching: Making Sense of an Uncertain Craft

THE BEFORE AND AFTER OF MY OWN STANCE

In the *Starship* example of the last chapter, my stance prepared me for what I wanted to see happen in the exercise on brainstorming, and it also told me what I'd have to do to try to get a good response from students. I wanted all or most of the kids in that class to be

- curious, attentive, and intrigued with what was taking place
- assured that I am very interested in who they are and what they think
- willing to talk, debate, and share ideas as players, not spectators
- open to the complexity of the issue
- curious about ideas and events that shape their lives
- thinking about and choosing what things are more important than others
- drawing on expertise they possess that might contribute to their classmates and tie school learning to life experience

- reflecting, assessing, and evaluating their own and others' thoughts
- ready to change their minds if it seems to make sense to do so
- willing to contribute the power of their thoughts and feelings in creating something of value to society

I certainly didn't go into the classroom with this list as a lesson plan. It is only now, as I sit down to write about it, that these wishes collect themselves into a list. The advantage of having a stance about students and their learning is that once we've taken the time to really work it out—to get clear about how much potential students have and how much we want to encourage their individuality and creativity—we're able to react more spontaneously to the energy they bring to whatever challenge, problem, or idea is before us. The examples of both Yvonne Griffin and Ed Clarke illustrate this beautifully. Although their styles of teaching are very different, their stances allow them the leeway to show delight in their students' originality and spunk, not just in their compliance. Their stances make them unafraid of losing control.

I don't want to imply that developing a stance comes easily. What we may later be able to do by instinct takes years of practice and confidence building. Maintaining a high level of student engagement is hard work and takes lots of planning. A stance can be tough to hold onto amid the wear and tear of daily life in school. Any of us, when we're nervous or when things threaten to get out of control, is likely to revert to a more controlling or defensive posture.

The value of having cultivated a stance is that it allows us to focus most of our energy, most of the time, on what we think learning is all about, on what's really important, instead of getting caught up in the details of the lesson plan or the formalities of classroom management. It lets us respond to kids' own spontaneity and good humor. It decreases the awkwardness between the generations and allows students to believe in us as advocates for their becoming powerful persons.

Needless to say, I had a different stance when I began teaching freshman English in the mid-sixties. My locus of concern then was less on my students and much more on myself. If I had been forced to create a similar list of objectives back then, they would have looked somewhat different.

THEN I WANTED STUDENTS TO BE	NOW I WANT STUDENTS TO BE
• curious, attentive, and interested in what I was talking about	• curious, attentive, and intrigued with learning about life
• assured that I was interested in who they were and how well they could write	• assured that I am very interested in who they are and what they think
• willing to talk, debate, and share ideas after I had provided them with the background I thought necessary for them to be able to contribute	• willing to talk, debate, and share ideas as players, not spectators, getting right into an issue from the start
• open to the complexity of the subjects that we were covering in the course	• open to the complexity of the issue and curious about ideas and events that may shape their lives
• making choices from topics I had prepared and presented them with	• thinking about and choosing what things are more important than others
• drawing on personal experiences to make their class participation and their written papers more interesting	• drawing on their own expertise to tie school learning to life experience
• able to accept, understand, practice, and adopt the suggestions I made on how to make their papers more literate	• reflecting upon and assessing their own and others' thoughts; ready to change their minds if it seems to make sense to do so
• willing to complete their assignments on time, to be ready for quizzes or tests (both planned and surprise), and to work within the class rules and grading system that I had worked out and presented	• willing to contribute the power of their thoughts and feelings to create something of value to society

These two sets of expectations have much in common, and many on the old list still seem worthwhile to me. The differences all have to do with whose performance I am chiefly concerned with. As a beginning teacher, I worried about myself most of all—a common enough phenomenon, but especially hard to overcome when we try to hide our inexperience and self-doubt from our students (who usually sense it anyway). I know now, upon reflection, that being as focused as I was on my performance got in the way of my students' ability to engage with me and to perform well.

It was baffling. I would prepare introductory lectures on "the value of literature in your life" or "what it means to write well" and deliver them with all the verve and polish I could muster, only to find my students browbeaten into silence by my own articulateness. I wanted to impress. I wanted to inspire. What I got, when I finally stopped talking, was silence and a resentful fidgeting. I would push and prod them to say something, refusing to go on unless they gave some response, and then I would get questions like: "Is it okay to use 'I' in a theme? Our high school English teacher told us we couldn't" or "How many papers do we have to write this term?" or—and this one paid me back for all the tricks of literary criticism that previous English teachers had abused them with—"Do we have to worry about the hidden meaning in this course?" In the English department, I would listen to my equally befuddled colleagues boast, with pained humility, "If I can reach two or three students in a class of twenty-five, I feel I'm doing well." And I would think to myself, "What about the other 90 percent?"

HOW I FINALLY FIGURED OUT HOW TO ENGAGE RELUCTANT STUDENTS

Some five years later, in the early 1970s, having decided to pursue educational reform as a career, I was working on a research project on the same campus. I wanted to see whether students who came from the same small towns were still friendly with one another now that they were at the state university. So I drafted a letter inviting about eighty of them from three New Hampshire towns to come to a meeting to talk about small-town life and campus life. I was about to send it off when I decided first to test this letter on a bunch of students. An acquaintance who was teaching freshman English agreed to let me borrow her class for a period.

I entered the class and, without any fanfare, asked the students to do me a favor. I told them I had written a letter to students like themselves, and I wanted to know if I'd worded it right. Handing them each a copy, I asked how they would react if they got a letter like this one, and how I might improve the letter so that more of the recipients would agree to come to my meeting.

At first they were awkward, skeptical: Is this guy for real? Does he really want us to criticize his letter? After a few minutes of explaining why I needed their help and was turning to them, the reactions began to come. Within half an hour, the letter had been totally rewritten, collectively and enthusiastically, by the class of thirty or so students, who delighted in tearing into my sometimes stilted, sometimes corny prose and who showed themselves to be experts in matters of both style and substance.

Their teacher was flabbergasted. Where had this responsiveness, this acuity on their part come from? She had certainly not seen anything like it from them before; nor had I in my own classes. But never before had I treated my students as partners. Though I didn't realize it at the time, I had the beginning of a different stance toward teaching.

WHAT IS YOUR STANCE?

Your stance is built on hunches and convictions, part reason and part faith, relying on both intuition and experience. It plays out in the way you build a working relationship with students.

Imagine you have been assigned to a classroom in a poor community. As you arrive at school, whom will you be expecting to find? Disadvantaged kids who had better have the basics drilled into them so they can at least get a job and keep themselves off welfare? Students harmed by racism and poverty who must be given heavy doses of self-esteem even if it comes at the expense of critical skills and knowledge? Or young people full of potential—for creativity and accomplishment or for violence and disorganization—who should be inspired with high standards and coached with patience and understanding? However you answer this question—whatever qualities you imbue them with in your mind, whatever makes them intriguing or ordinary—this is how your stance begins. A teacher who anticipates creativity and hidden talents in her students will greet a class quite differently from one who looks for shortcomings and defects.

But that isn't the whole of your stance—it's just the first half. The other half has to do with your expectations of their performance. Are you and your students here to get through the course, to cover the material, and to test their recall and assign a grade? Or are you here to help your students produce work of high quality, evidence of their understanding and application of skills and knowledge?

Your stance, then, is the attitude you take that communicates who you think your students are and how much you believe they can produce.

Some educators are famous for the transforming qualities of their stance. I think back to Deborah Meier and her staff at Central Park East Secondary School in Harlem and of Dennis Littky and the teachers of Thayer Junior-Senior High School in a rural, working-class New Hampshire town. Each looked out at a bunch of kids that others had previously defined as "losers" and saw not their deficits but their potential. Each based their educational approach on a stance that views real-world challenges and group solidarity as the foundation for students' intellectual diligence and high standards of performance. Their stance is based not only on a keen assessment of their students' true potential but also on a core value—a faith that, given the right conditions, these kids can perform quite adequately, if not superbly. Their job as educators is to try to create the "right conditions." That in itself is a tough challenge. Few of us have full control over the conditions we work under. But their stance at least makes it possible for their students to experience that faith, grow with it, and experience levels of success that far exceed what happens when we expect less of students and show it in the way we present ourselves to them.

"YOU COMPLETELY DISGUSTING ANIMAL!"

Other educators I have known have possessed a stance that has also taught me much. I think of Janice Weisberg, a math teacher I knew when I was principal of a rural elementary school. Janice never used the blackboard but wrote with a grease pencil and an overhead projector, so her eyes were always focused on her students. She was convinced that the way to get twelve- to fourteen-year-olds interested in math was to banter with them and tease them. That was her stance: Math has to be fun and kids have to be relaxed—or they won't be willing to think in class.

Janice would ask students to reason aloud while she translated their deductions into numbers on the overhead (her eyes fixed upon them in a friendly embrace). When a kid did well, she would murmur, "You *animal*! Keep going!" and when the kid struggled and reached further than expected, she would exclaim, "You complete, disgusting *animal*!" The kids were charmed, their shyness disappeared, and they basked in the good-natured classroom laughter that these impossible utterances produced. The monster of math had been tamed. Her stance allowed kids to be "smart" in front of their peers without the risk of being seen as the teacher's pet or an obnoxious know-it-all. Inexperienced or insecure teachers recoil at this story, not grasping that it was Janice's prior relationship of mutual trust that allowed her to be playful while pushing her students to reach beyond their comfort zone in math.

"HERE COME THE WHITE BITCH NOW!"

And there's Bette Chamberlain, formerly an assistant principal in a middle school, who, newly married, found herself in Rockford, Illinois, during the late 1960s. Her husband got drafted and went off to basic training in Texas so she looked around for her first teaching job. She was hired to work in an urban junior high school classroom for kids who had been labeled "mentally retarded," the standard jargon of the time. The class was large, with forty or more students aged twelve to sixteen, and she had them for the full day. There were supposed to be two or three aides working there, too, but the aides had never shown up, and, during the first two days of the school year, two previous teachers had quit. When Bette arrived on day three, the assistant principal brought her upstairs and pointed down the hall to her room. "I should have known something when he declined to accompany me to my class," she told me. Walking on ahead, she was met by a volley of insults from students lounging in the hallway ("Here come the m-f white bitch"), no doubt expecting that this teacher would likewise be chased out of there in a day or so.

Within a month Bette had most of the class working with her, or at least reasonably attentive, and she remained on the job for the entire year. How did she survive? I believe it was her stance. She walked into the classroom and sat down at her desk, facing the class to be able to see if objects flying about the room might be headed her way. Bette said, "I glanced under the teacher's desk and there was Carl, huddled in the well of the desk and looking up at me from the darkness. 'Are you going to be our teacher?' he asked. I knew then that I had to stay."

Bette made no attempt to bring the class to order or to otherwise challenge them, knowing that she would have been easily overpowered and defeated. In fact, she did nothing at all except introduce herself to Carl and to the two other students whose desks were close to hers and who seemed interested in who she was. They talked informally (while the rest of the students did whatever they felt like doing) until the day ended. The next day she repeated the pattern—guarding against the possibility of flying spitballs, being friendly but never challenging the disruptive kids, and never asserting authority—and by day's end several more students had joined the quiet conversation. And so it went. "I realized that the only thing I had that they could possibly want was my attention. So I decided that the only people who would get my attention were those who came and sat down," she said.

Every few days one or two more students would pull their desks up to hers, and she would get to know them, include them in the general conversation and, eventually, ask them what they wanted to learn. She read to them, and later they read to her and to each other. "I made up the curriculum as I went along, based on what the students were curious about. Many of the kids were not 'retarded' at all. They had just been put in that class because other people couldn't handle them."

What so impresses me in Bette's story is not only her clear-headedness in a situation that had paralyzed others but her ability to gain the attentiveness and later the participation of a group of students whom others had written off as hopeless. It's also the naturalness of her approach—the blend of realism, humility, and humanity—that allowed her to make a powerful connection with these kids. I speak of her approach as a stance because it involved a physical posture—a way of placing herself in that impossible classroom so that she could protect herself while reaching out, however tentatively, to the first few students—but also her unpatronizing belief in their value as potential learners, despite their tough exteriors.

YOUR STANCE MAKES PASSIONATE TEACHING POSSIBLE

Not all applications of stance are so dramatic or untraditional. We all know people who are able to reach out to young people (not only to "problem kids") and draw them into a learning partnership that produces results far beyond what is ordinarily expected of them. This quality of a teacher's believing and behaving—what I call a stance—makes passionate teaching possible. In each of the teachers highlighted in this book, a deep commitment to their subject is matched by a respect, just as deep, for students as people.

I can remember several instances in my own early teaching when I was able to achieve different results by breaking my pattern. Although they were few and far between (and much more modest than the examples I've cited above)—and although I did not yet recognize in them what I am now calling a "stance"—I remember them vividly. Pushed a little by my refusal to give up on his potential as a writer, James, a student who'd written grammatically correct but utterly colorless prose, finally wrote an essay about growing up Black in Kentucky and standing outside for hours on winter days, believing that cold weather would make his skin lighter. It was heartbreakingly beautiful. Flunking three football players in another freshman English class, but only after inviting them into my office to tell them myself, created relationships that continued throughout their college years. They later told me that my personally explaining my action to them had made them feel respected, which helped them accept responsibility for what they had failed to do. They re-registered for freshman English the following term with another teacher, did their work, and passed the course.

Again, these examples do not indicate a stance. They were isolated cases, such as every teacher can point to, when, based on our respect for kids' ability, we are able to move beyond the usual boundaries that school culture imposes, and see our students respond in ways that surprise us. In my case, it was only years later that I realized the significance beyond the particular students. When we reflect on why things work for a few students, we can begin to formulate a stance toward *all* students, a stance based on our commitment to respect the depth of their potential and the dignity of their person.

14

PUTTING YOUR STANCE INTO PRACTICE

> *High schools must respect adolescents more and patronize them less. The best respect is high expectations for them, and a level of accountability more adult in its demands than childlike.*
>
> —TED SIZER, *Horace's Compromise*

ALFREDO FUENTES' STANCE: ALGEBRA FOR EVERYONE

Alfredo Fuentes also teaches in Hartford. I met him when I went looking for someone who believed that all students can be taught algebra, not just those who have already mastered arithmetic. Alfredo is such a person. As we talked, he told me how he became a math teacher.

> When I was in eighth grade, in Luquillo, Puerto Rico, I discovered that I was very good in math. Luquillo is a very beautiful place, and my high school was right across from the beach, so from our second-floor window we could see the whales migrating. Anyway, I would sometimes notice that the way our teacher, Mrs. Quinones, was explaining math problems was not the easiest way to solve them, and other kids were not following her. So one time, when she seemed frustrated that they couldn't understand, I raised my hand and said, "Can I help explain it?" And Mrs. Quinones said, "Fine, Alfredo, go ahead." Since she worked from an overhead projector, the blackboards were nice and clean, and I went up to them and worked out the problem.

After that time, whenever Mrs. Quinones would run into a wall, she would say, "Alfredo, do you have another way of explaining this?" And I would try to do it not by using the formal mathematical concepts but using analogies or common examples we all understood that contained the same math ideas. I began to develop a habit, whenever there was a new topic or concept presented, of trying to develop easier ways to present that concept, so I'd be ready just in case our teacher would ask me.

I wasn't arrogant about it, but I prided myself that I could help all my friends, all my classmates, pass math. I became their tutor. In Puerto Rico, the school schedule is much more flexible than here. Lunch period was an hour long, and we only had five classes to take out of an eight-period day. During many of our free times, I would get together with my friends to help them. I didn't want anybody to be held back a grade in math—I wanted to keep the family intact.

This is a trait that I now bring into my teaching. When I am preparing my lessons, I always try to have three or four different approaches—visual forms, abstract forms, hands-on forms—to find some way of connecting with each child, just like when I was helping out in eighth grade. To me, the principles of mathematics apply very much to the principles of life. When we are solving problems and equations, we often already have the answers in the back of the book. So the challenge is not just to have the children get the right answer, it's for them to figure out *how to get there*. In math, as in life, there are many avenues to get to the right answer. I had learned, back in eighth grade, that this was true of math. Now I know it is also true of life.

I often use the social problems that surround the children I work with here in Hartford as ways of explaining math. For example, when discussing an equation, like $x + 7 = 12$, I make the equals sign represent a street between two neighborhoods, or turfs. I tell the class that the variable, Mr. X, is the stranger that you've been warned about because you never know who he is or what he's up to. "So," I tell them, "when you're on the stranger's side of the turf and he asks you to add a number like 7, you had better do just the opposite of what he says (subtract 7), because he only wants to get you into trouble. But you can't confront him on his turf, so you go back over to your side, with the person you already know, Mrs. 12, and *then* subtract 7. And that's how you figure out who the stranger is, without doing his bidding. Mrs. 12 tells you that Mr. X is really just a 5, not the mysterious guy he's pretending to be."

Back in Puerto Rico, Mrs. Quinones told me that I should be a math teacher, but that was not in my plans at all. Since the sixth grade, I had wanted to become a civil or mechanical engineer and design cars or build bridges. To me, an engineer was a person who has the right knowledge and tools and is a master at solving problems.

But as I began engineering college, I was also exploring the spiritual side of my life to see what my real role would be on this planet. Even though I had been raised as a Catholic, I began examining other religions, and I found what I was looking for in the Seventh-Day Adventist Church. I then decided to become a minister. When I told my father that I was going to apply to the seminary, he said, "I'll pay for you to go to engineering college, but if you want to go to the seminary, you'd better remember that money doesn't come from heaven." And I told him, "Money *will* come from heaven." The next day, I packed my suitcase and went to the seminary. I said to the dean, "I want to become a minister. I have no money but I'm willing to work."

In the beginning of my senior year, I spoke to the person in charge of hiring ministers and he said that there weren't any positions open for ministers next year. So I decided to concentrate on getting thirty-six credits of education courses into my program and to get certified as a teacher. As I saw it then, becoming certified as a teacher was only a stepping-stone to becoming a minister. But in my first year of teaching, I fell in love with the teaching profession and realized that instead of ministering to a congregation once a week on the weekend, I could minister to 180 students on a daily basis.

The driving force of my teaching ministry, back then in Puerto Rico and now here in Hartford, is my faith. As I work to ease the walls of tension in a classroom setting, children not only open their minds, they open their hearts. It makes students eager to know what I know and to find their own path. I tell them that learning math is only the tip of an iceberg—that it gives you doors and windows that open onto all kinds of opportunities. I say, "The more you understand math, the more power you have to understand music, painting, writing. Math is involved in everything."

Many inner-city kids come to school with the notion that school is their babysitting place while their parents are at work. If they had a choice, many of them would be elsewhere. I try to create an atmosphere in my classroom that makes them want to be here. First of all, I have to bond with them as a person, not as a teacher. I have to use all my skills to make math different, to make math fun, as they say, "user friendly."

I'm not a moviegoer, but after I had won an award as a Teacher of the Year in 1989, a reporter came to me to see my style of teaching and told me, "You are doing just what Jaime Escalante is doing in *Stand and Deliver*" and I said, "Who is he?" So I went to see the movie. As I saw the movie, I kept saying to myself, "That's what *I* do. Escalante is copying me!" Escalante did make an impression on me, because at that time I was working mainly with honors classes, but since I saw the movie, I have made it my goal to work more with low-achieving students.

Seeing myself, still, as a minister doesn't mean that I consider myself a holy man. Like Escalante, I know a teacher has to reach children at their level. Yesterday, for example, we were working on inequalities, and a student who wasn't trying very hard said, "I don't like to do this!" Immediately, I said, "Do you think I like to clean my child's bottom? But I do it because I know that if I don't do it now and don't do it right, her problems and my problems will only get worse. She will develop a rash, I will have to take her to the doctor. . . ." By this time, the whole class was laughing, including the girl who had been complaining. And I said, "You can't just ignore something because you don't like it. Like a baby's rear end, math won't go away. It will continue to stink and you will have to deal with that. You think that when you become a mother you can just order a self-cleaning child, like a self-cleaning oven?"

The whole class kept laughing at that idea, the tension was relieved, and students began to focus better. After that, the student picked up her pencil and started taking notes. After the class, she came up and said, "Well, I'll try my best to learn it—but I still hate math." And I said, "That's fine. I don't want you to love math, I want you to master its tools."[1]

I imagine some teachers, like those skeptical about passion, asking why they need this additional, mysterious trait called a stance. Isn't it enough to know your subject and come to class well prepared, to try to be fair to all students, to pull your share of the department or grade-level workload and get along with the people in your building? Why do you need a stance?

SO, WHAT *IS* YOUR STANCE?

In one important sense, a stance, like a personality, is something everyone already *has*, whether they acknowledge it or not. My asking "Do you know what your stance is?" is not the same as asking "Who are you in relation to everyone else in your life?" but rather "How do you come across to students and fellow teachers?" To say, "I come to class well prepared" is itself an expression of a certain stance. It says that an essential part of what it means for you to be a teacher is to come to class prepared to do your job as a professional, to engage students in the work at hand.

Like all stances, this one is open to analysis, reflection, and conversation. For instance, I'd ask my skeptic, "You come to class 'well prepared' for *what* exactly?"

- Prepared to tell the kids what you think they need to listen to and take notes on?
- Prepared to lead them through the next chapter in the text?
- Prepared to help students decide how best to connect the lesson to their lives?
- Prepared to challenge students to work collaboratively on a problem?
- Prepared to join them in making inquiries into a dilemma that nobody has yet resolved, and then begin to find their own answers?
- Prepared to coach students as they develop projects or demonstrations of what they have learned in this area?

There's a great story about a third grade teacher who placed two bags of little candies on her desk and invited her students to pick one candy on their way out of class. She praised one bag over the other but, from time to time, ate a candy out of the less-favored bag. You can guess which bag most of the students chose.

Each definition of what it means to be "well prepared" as a teacher may produce very different results in terms of what students learn and how they are able to grow under our influence. While each of us may select more than one of these definitions from time to time, the essential issue for teachers is: What is the real work of the class and how do I prepare myself to engage all of my students in that work? Your stance, in large part, is what you think it really means to be well prepared.

To say "I try to be fair to all my students" can mean anything from "I grade them all exactly according to the system I told them about at the beginning of the class" to "I make sure I learn enough about each of my students to be able to challenge them to do the best work they can do." We may take great pains to make our grading system "fair," only to end up being grossly unfair to our students by encouraging them to focus so much attention on grades that they forget about learning things and acquiring skills for a lifetime.

Does a school that sends 125 or more students into your classroom every day even allow you to be "fair" to each by recognizing individual learning styles and keys to helping each of them get motivated? If not, what might be done so that you can really be fair and get to know each of them? (Ted Sizer has a lot to say about this in his *Horace* books.)

Saying "I get along with most people in my building" can mean anything from "I keep pretty much to myself but try to be pleasant to fellow staff members when I meet them in the teachers' room" all the way to "I see myself as part of a team of professionals working together to improve conditions for teaching and learning in the building." In some schools, faculty "get along" by avoiding all but minimal contact with one another: hurried lunches, casual conversation in the parking lot, war stories shared in the staff room, or an hourly staff meeting once or twice a month where little of substance is discussed.

HOW A FOURTH-GRADE TEACHER PUTS STANCE TO WORK

Imagine the kind of climate created in a fourth-grade class by a teacher whose stance emerges from the sincere expression of things like:

- You are my students and I respect each and every one of you. I'm going to work very hard to help you respect yourselves, respect one another, and respect me.
- I care too much about you to let you get away with doing anything but your best. So when I ask you to redo something, it's my way of expressing my faith that you have it in you to do really great work.

- You kids have talents that no one has uncovered yet. Let's discover those talents—and then we'll find a way to let the whole community know about them.
- I bet each of you is a leader in your family in some way. I wonder what kind of a leader you are. Let's find out and talk about it because we need all kinds of leaders in today's world.
- The other fourth-grade teachers and I have been meeting to talk about what books we're going to use for reading next year. I'd like you to look over some of them and tell me which ones you think would be most interesting, and why.
- Your job today is to work with your group to solve this problem for the rest of us. But first, you need to make sure that everyone in your group understands the problem and expresses their opinion on how to solve it.
- I don't want to see you putting each other down. We have important work to accomplish here, and meanness only makes it more difficult for each of us to get the job done.
- Each of you has a story to tell that's bound to be interesting to someone outside this classroom: to little kids in kindergarten, old folks at the Senior Center, or students up at the high school. I want you to get that story onto paper in your own style and then be ready to share your story with others.

I have heard words very much like these from teachers who embody their stance in ways that go beyond words. Both connotations of stance—physical and interpersonal—show up in our tone, posture, nonverbal cues, and inner feelings that we express along with words like these. Your stance as a teacher or parent reflects the beliefs about children that you consciously try to adhere to and the feelings you communicate through words, gestures, and actions.

Insincerity, prejudice, favoritism, rigidity, condescension, impatience, lack of compassion—these are aspects of stance that young people are all too familiar with in their relationships with certain adults and kids. Their antennae are particularly sensitive to such attitudes and pick them out of the static and buzz of the classroom. Our respect for the dignity of young people and our expectations for their achievement have to come through in word and action, or else students will stop listening and no longer see us as people who can be trusted to help them shape their lives for the better.

It's better for our actions be right and our words to fall short than the other way around, because young people pick up much from our nonverbal cues. Better yet that words and actions convey the same message of respect, inspiration, high expectations, pride, seriousness of purpose, and good humor.

A CLASH OF STANCES OVER RACISM AND *HUCKLEBERRY FINN*

Beth, a family friend, got into a bruising battle over just this sort of issue with her high school English teacher in an honors literature class some years ago. She felt that her teacher, who professed high standards of literary criticism and prided herself as an advocate of excellence, was subtly demanding obedience to her own point of view at the cost of encouraging students to relate their reading to their lives.

The battle was fought over *Adventures of Huckleberry Finn*. Beth, who had participated in a seminar on Mark Twain at another school, was asked by her teacher to lead a class discussion on a day that the teacher had to be absent. The issue of racism in the book came up in that class period, and students began to talk about their own prejudices. Beth was excited to see a new energy in the discussion on the part of her fellow students.

When the teacher returned, Beth was asked to summarize the previous day's discussion. To her dismay, she soon found herself being criticized by her teacher for "straying from the text." The message she received was: "It is not what *you* think about racism that counts; it's what Twain is saying in the text."

To Beth, Twain's sympathetic portrayal of Jim, the runaway slave, invites readers to examine their own prejudices. That her teacher could deny this intent of Twain's and also downplay the importance of having students debate these ethical issues was one shock. But she found herself abandoned by her classmates, even the ones who had been actively engaged the day before. They didn't disagree with her—they just seemed to wither before the teacher's authority. Beth was hurt and temporarily silenced by her experience, although she later wrote an excellent paper about it.

Beth and her teacher were exhibiting profoundly different stances—not only on how to engage students' thoughts and feelings but on the meaning of literature itself: whether *Huckleberry Finn* (or any work of art) should serve as a springboard for exploring personal ideas and feelings or whether paying attention to the literal text is the principal aim of the serious student of literature. From one perspective, their dispute was about the legitimacy of a student using her own reflections on literature to engage fellow students in a discussion of ethical values. Looked at another way, it was a dispute over whether it is okay for a student to lay the text aside while pursuing her own agenda.

For Beth, comparisons and reflections make literature meaningful to people, and her stance, accordingly, was to promote a full and free discussion among her classmates. To her teacher, the course was about American literature and textual analysis, not about personal values or prejudices—the task at hand was to help students become more discerning readers.

The failure to acknowledge and address both the teacher's and the students' stances turned what might have been an illuminating class discussion on opposing views into a fight for control of the class, a fight no student is likely to win. The lesson for teachers is that when we take our stance for granted and don't discuss its implications with our students, we run the risk of encountering a strong-willed student like Beth, who will challenge our approach to the material. The larger risk is that we will not have a student like Beth and will face, instead, her mostly obedient and subdued classmates, too ready to accept our unspoken stance and do at least some of what we tell them to do—as long as they don't have to think very hard about it.

I use this incident not to take a side in the debate among English teachers over the importance of close reading of the text versus the value of linking literature to other concerns. I use it, rather, to illustrate how having a stance can help us avoid some unproductive roadblocks. A stance—however deeply felt—should not be fixed and final, a dogma that students have to silently accept. If her teacher had seen Beth's difference of interpretation as an opportunity to refine her own stance and subject it to debate, some valuable educational results could have come out of it, not least of which would have been engaging more of the class.

THE STANCE A SCHOOL TAKES—OR AVOIDS

Let's look for a moment at the concept of stance writ large, as a declaration of what education should mean to an entire community. All school districts have some sort of educational philosophy or mission statement, usually drafted by the school board, superintendent, or a committee appointed by them. Many such statements, once discussed and voted on, are thenceforth ignored. It's different when teachers and community members try to reach consensus on some core values they are willing to advocate for across an entire school or district.

A worthy mission statement obliges everyone to critically examine current practices to see if they actually promote the goals and values written therein. A school philosophy that talks about respect, dignity, love of learning, and hard work means little if these concepts are unmeasurable or are often undermined in practice. But if the core beliefs include, for example, that "all children are expected to perform high-quality work in literacy and mathematical problem-solving," or that "every student has a right to have his or her culture validated as part of the school curriculum," or that "no student will receive a diploma until he or she has demonstrated, at a satisfactory level, the skills and knowledge that the school community has listed as essential for success," then the prospects for aligning theory with practice are likely to improve.

These things are measurable to varying degrees, and they require significant changes in pedagogy and structure. Thus, a school's or school system's stance, if well founded and endorsed by the school and community, can lead to important shifts in the stance that teachers and their students adopt toward the learning process. A number of years ago, Pioneer Valley, a small rural high school in northwestern Massachusetts, decided to eliminate student tracking and instead to begin looking at all of them as people with the potential to learn together at higher levels. In Branford, Connecticut, the high school staff formulated performance-based graduation requirements in place of credits or time-based instructional units, as the basis of their diploma. In both cases, the articulation of a stance came first, followed by the difficult and demanding process of organizational and structural change.

Teachers must work toward a common set of beliefs wherever they can find allies—in the department, at grade-level staff meetings, with respected colleagues in whatever capacity, and, of course, in daily work with students. Your chances for success in changing the school culture are greater when other people, within and without the school, uphold and reinforce your stance. But even when teachers must work alone, the seeds of positive change are planted wherever they can engage students in dialogue about values, standards, and goals.

STANCE MADE PRACTICAL

What are some practical ways that teachers can explore, define, and refine their stances? How can we make this clear to students and colleagues? Stance is a matter of internal discovery. But it is also a public statement that teachers can project in a manner that suits their personality and style.

WHAT JAY SHAPIRO WANTS YOU TO ASK YOURSELF

On the personal side, to help get a clearer picture of the stance you would like to present (so that you might compare it with the stance that you may have previously revealed), here are some questions suggested by Jay Shapiro, who has taught high school for many years in New Jersey:

- What are the five most important values or beliefs in your life? What are the ideas and ideals your try best to live by?
- What are five core beliefs that you hold about children and adolescents?
- If you were the boss of the whole school, what words would you like to see greeting everyone who entered the building? And what message would you like to prepare for every student who walks into a classroom?
- What is it about the subject(s) you teach that connects with your core values and beliefs? Why have you chosen to devote your professional life to this field?
- What might your students produce or demonstrate that would prove to you that they had really benefited from your role as teacher?

Giving honest answers to these questions is not easy. We are often so conscious of the attitudes we feel we *should* possess about kids—that all kids can learn, that they should have high self-esteem, that we should pay attention to both their cognitive and emotional development—that it can be difficult to sort out the beliefs we actually *have*.

Putting our thoughts on paper allows us to share them with colleagues and students and to see how our values and beliefs contrast with theirs. Teachers often do this only in the privacy of their classrooms: They state their beliefs clearly to students, post them on the wall, and provide students with a list of class rules and expectations at the beginning of the year. But if it ends there, the impact of our stance may be limited to our current students, who probably won't remember these beliefs for long.

If we want our students to accept, adopt, and carry forward these beliefs and values, our stance ought to include a willingness to enter into dialogue with students and colleagues about what it all means—how we create a decent and productive climate that respects peoples' differences while encouraging and supporting their best efforts.

INTUITION AND A CLIMATE OF RESPECT

Talking about values, beliefs, and the classroom policies that derive from them is a very practical kind of discussion to have, with potential benefit for all concerned. But that doesn't make it an easy process to carry out, particularly when students have not previously been included in rule making, goal setting, and values-based conversations in school or at home. Teachers must rely on their intuition to give them a sense of what issues students are ready to talk about and deal with, and how to help them participate in risk-taking conversations. Here, too, it helps to have other colleagues engaging their students in similar dialogue so that kids see the grown-ups around them reinforcing these values. Although the class may or may not succeed in reaching consensus on all issues, teachers can remind everyone what they have agreed upon, even while maintaining their responsibility to impose or uphold other rules of the school or classroom that some students may not agree with.

In such a climate of respect for people—for their differences as well as the values they hold in common—students are more likely to respect themselves, their fellow students, and the adults who work with them. The hope is—and it is not an easy hope to sustain in today's society—that when students see other students violating agreed-upon norms, they will find some way of moderating (or at least not joining in or cheering on) such disruptions. But the willingness of kids to uphold decent behavior depends not only on how well they have been brought up at home but on how skillfully and purposefully teachers have included them in the rule-making process.

The stance we take in our homes, classrooms, school, and community grows from the core values and beliefs we develop, articulate, test out, and commit to putting into practice in spite of the obstacles that modern life and society place in our path. A parent's stance in the home, like a teacher's stance in the classroom, is created from feelings and beliefs about who these children are and how much they can produce of lasting value for themselves and society under the parent's guidance. That is our stance, and everything we do flows from that posture. Everything.

15

SOME THOUGHTS ABOUT CLASSROOM DISCIPLINE

No human being is unmotivated. In fact, every living creature is highly motivated all the time. . . . But every living creature, including students, is not necessarily motivated to do what you, I, or anyone else thinks they ought to do.

—WILLIAM GLASSER, *The Quality School*

Here is an obvious question that a classroom teacher might pose: How can we talk about stance and not mention discipline? Don't research, experience, and common sense tell us that concerns about discipline are foremost in the minds of many teachers when they think about how to improve their effectiveness in the classroom? It's as if they are wanting to say, "What kind of stance do you expect us to develop if we're having to contend with kids who don't seem to want to learn—or let anybody else learn, for that matter?"

HOW OFTEN DOES IT RAIN IN YOUR CLASSROOM?

As I write, we are experiencing a string of April showers that would be called a monsoon in other places in the world. In this old house, a heavy rain often produces some roof leaks that wind up as drips on the kitchen floor. Because the roof is basically sound, and the ceiling leaks only once in a while—and when it does it just drips a little and doesn't flood us out—it seems easier to put out a pot or two to catch the drips.

But I don't fool myself about where the rainwater is coming from—it doesn't start from the kitchen ceiling.

For most of the experienced teachers I know, discipline is an occasional problem that can be dealt with as it occurs. An admonition, a quiet conversation after class, a detention, or a call to parents is usually all it takes. On a few occasions, a dispute among students that began elsewhere bursts forth in a class, and then it's time to call for backup support from a colleague or administrator.

Wherever mutual respect has been established among teachers and students, wherever students understand *why* they are learning what they are learning, wherever a teacher models what it looks like to be a learner—aiming high, making some mistakes, and working with others in the classroom to acknowledge and solve problems as they arise—then the issue of discipline is like my kitchen roof: a few leaks once in a while that can be dealt with as they arise. And anyway, it doesn't rain every day.

But there are some schools, and some classrooms in almost any school where the roof seems to leak all the time, and in those places moving the pots around to catch the drips doesn't do the job. Instead, we have to look at the causes, not just mop up the symptomatic outbursts.

FOUR BEHAVIOR PROBLEMS YOUR KIDS MIGHT CONFRONT YOU WITH

I observe four categories of persistent problems with discipline in a classroom. Their origins are very different even though the symptoms, in terms of the disruption of learning, may look the same. We should try to understand how and why they occur.

One cause is clearly outside the school. A student whose life is chaotic, or who is being abused by people at home or in the neighborhood, will often bring this turmoil into class and express it regardless of what else is going on. We cannot expect teachers to cope alone with seriously disturbed students under circumstances like these. Help from guidance or administrative personnel is necessary, even while the classroom teacher remains part of the team seeking a solution. We should try to hold onto students with some behavior problems in the class, as long as they are no danger to themselves or other students, but the support network has to be there or else learning gets interrupted for everybody. In many schools, however, that support is often missing or hopelessly inadequate. When teachers are forced to work in a disrupted classroom, it becomes especially important (and especially tough) to devise ways of engaging all students, in hopes that they—including the disruptive ones—will find school a pleasant contrast to a disordered society. But I won't pretend for a moment that it's an easy task. And I'm not offering much more here than real sympathy and deep appreciation for teachers who must work each day under the threat of disruption or even attack from students whom our society has failed to nurture.

The real solution, of course, is to develop the kind of leadership that can focus the entire school community toward building character and values. I just heard on the radio about an elementary school in Dayton, Ohio, that transformed itself, both academically and behaviorally, by focusing on character development. Each week a theme is chosen: loyalty, respect, friendship, kindness, etc. The entire school works to integrate this concept into its lessons. At week's end, there is a school-wide assembly, and students present written or artistic responses to the theme. Students interviewed spoke of their school as a place of warmth and safety. And, not by coincidence, their reading scores have shot up from among the lowest to among the highest in the city.

A second cause of poor student behavior lies outside the classroom but at least partially inside the school: student cliques who assert themselves by harassing other kids. The opportunities for such agitation are as frequent as the change of periods or lunch period. This is definitely a school-wide and community problem, one that too many school administrators expect teachers to cope with by themselves. (We discuss this further in chapter 16 on dealing with bullying and meanness.) Ineffective leadership in the school can mean unbearable burdens for teachers, as conflicts between students spill into the classroom and undermine teaching and learning. Any solution will require the shared initiative and follow-through of school staff, parents, students, community leaders, and sometimes police or social workers. In particular, the insights and active cooperation of students are crucial to improving the climate of classroom and school alike. But a helpful place to start is by finding ways to break down the anarchy of the hallways or lunchroom by dividing a large school into smaller "houses" with 150 to 250 students per house.

The last two causes of chronic disruption—an ineffective curriculum and a lack of mutual respect between learners and those who teach them—have origins that cannot be located outside the classroom. Students react to repetitive busywork, to assignments unconnected to their lives, to obsessive focus on test preparation, to subtle prejudices they experience from some adults or fellow students, to insensitivity and unfairness, or to adults with an awkward or off-putting personality by finding ways to ignore, circumvent, or undermine and repudiate such teachers or administrators. And a lot of this has to do with a teacher's stance.

Back in my own New York City high school days, we would imitate the sound of sirens to get back at a teacher who bugged us. One kid would imitate the far-off wail of a police car or fire truck, and another would pick it up, until we had the teacher walking to the windows to try to spot where in the neighborhood the noise was coming from.

Dennis Littky once told me: "When I see frequent behavior problems in a class, I look at the curriculum and pedagogy first, and the cause is usually right there. The kids can't stand it when they're talked down to or given busy work, day after day."

Deborah Meier finds that personality has a lot to do with it:

> There are some people, even some who may be uninspired as teachers, downright boring, in fact, who are somehow able to put kids at ease and almost never have trouble with discipline. And there are others in whom kids sense an uptightness, a tendency to overreact, and they have a lot of difficulty maintaining order even though they may be highly qualified in other respects. New teachers may be confused by the differences between how effective they can be with students one-on-one, and how often they get thrown off the track in classroom situations. Of course when a person is both boring and inappropriate, he or she is really in for trouble. But, realistically, many of the awkward or mixed messages teachers give are due to our inexperience, and being inexperienced can only be cured by experience.[1]

WHAT TO SAY WHEN THINGS GET OUT OF HAND

At the center of both these observations is stance. How does a teacher cope with an awkward or unpleasant class environment? Try to "get rid" of the offending students? Adopt a rigid and defensive posture (the old "Don't smile till Christmas" routine)? Or acknowledge within the class that the climate is an unpleasant and unproductive one and try to work with students to improve that climate?

An experienced educator posed this question to a class of student-teacher candidates: "How would you have responded to a student of mine who, clearly upset over being told to stop whatever he was doing that was disrupting the class, yelled out, 'F—k you!'?" The teacher explained that he was aware that this was a momentary outburst, and the student was not otherwise violent or abusive. And yet . . . the teacher had to do *some*thing.

The student teachers were stymied—this was, they knew, one of their worst nightmare scenarios. The rest of the class would be looking to their teacher to react; yet coming down hard on the offending student would likely only prolong the disruption and quite possibly upend the entire lesson. Still, it would be impossible to ignore this. After letting the student teachers struggle with this dilemma, the experienced teacher said, "So, I looked out at the class (not at the offending student) and said, 'Well, *that* was unexpected!' And then I went with the lesson, as though nothing had happened." He remarked that the offending student, happy to have avoided punishment but chastened by his outburst, quickly regained control of himself.

Sometimes even the most effective teachers feel a need to "crack down" or "rein in" the class. Some students need an adult to do this for them if they lack a parent who sets boundaries. But teachers can choose how they communicate to students about the measures that have to be taken.

WHEN YOU FEEL FRUSTRATED, TRY TO GET *FASCINATED* INSTEAD

My best advice to beginning teachers was always this: When you begin to feel *frustrated* with the behavior of a single student or an entire class, try instead to get *fascinated*. Ask yourself: "Why is this happening?" "What are the students trying to communicate?" "How might I adjust my stance so as to move things off dead center and into positive territory?" Student teachers have told me that getting fascinated works to take the pressure off. A teacher's stance determines not only their standards for student conduct, but their willingness to allow kids to suggest ways that everyone's approach, including the teacher's, might be improved.

Once teachers have done the really hard work of rethinking how they want to work with students and what they really want to teach and why, discipline comes down to a few simple rules that almost all students are able to accept—and that many are willing to help their teachers uphold:

- Every person deserves—and owes—respect.
- Nobody may interfere with another person's right to learn.
- School is a place to learn how to settle disputes by talking them through.

JOSHUA CHARD'S APPROACH TO DISCIPLINE

Joshua Chard offers this reflection as a second-grade teacher:

> As young children start to test boundaries, there are times when they reflexively lie. This isn't malicious. Children might jump to lying to avoid punishment for their behavior and getting in trouble. Herein lies the problem with "punishment" as a way to manage behavior.
>
> Teaching honesty can be especially challenging when kids see adults—on the news, in sports, or even in politics—avoiding the truth or not taking responsibility for their actions. Even young children pick up on these mixed messages, making it all the more important that school is where telling the truth is valued and practiced every day.
>
> I start second grade by discussing the difference between a punishment and a consequence. Punishment—like losing recess—can make kids fearful and defensive. As a side note, taking away recess is counterproductive; students need unstructured time to self-regulate and recharge.
>
> A consequence is much gentler and more restorative. You pushed a classmate when you were lining up in the cafeteria? The first step is telling the truth and owning up to the behavior. Then we can work together to decide how to fix what was broken. Maybe you should apologize to that classmate and invite them to get in line in front of you the next time we line up. No one loses face here; everyone feels better after, and students learn that telling the truth and owning up to their mistakes doesn't result in something negative.
>
> The long-term goal is for students to take ownership of their actions and devise their own solutions. These simple second-grade routines lay the foundation for honest, reflective citizens—kids who grow up knowing that telling the truth is always the best choice.[2]

The schools in my town held parent-teacher conferences and a number of teachers in grades 4 through 6 conducted those meetings in a new way, with some surprising and positive results. To begin with, students wrote personal invitations to their parents to come to the conference. And students attended the meeting to discuss their progress.

The first result was that a lot more parents signed up to come. Both *how* the letter was written (students often rewrote it several times to make sure it was accurate and looked good) and *who* had written it (their own kid) caused some parents who rarely attend a parent-teacher conference to come this time. At the session, the student was the moderator, leading the discussion on what was going well and what needed improvement. Often the teacher remained mostly silent, responding only when asked a direct question by parent or student. As might be expected, not only were students likely to be more critical of their own efforts than their teacher might have been, but the message was received with a lot more openness by the parents, who could take some pride in their child's ability and willingness to be self-critical. It also gave the teacher a chance to point out any of the positive aspects of the child's behavior or learning that had been overlooked. Teachers reported a much-improved atmosphere at the conferences, particularly among parents who'd had problems when they were in school. "Some parents left the room with their heads held high, who previously had felt only shame or frustration or anger," said one teacher. "The difference was that their child was now part of the solution."

This is an example of where a teacher's stance can positively influence student behavior and academic performance. The stance is both physical and attitudinal. The teacher sat on the side, not behind a desk facing parents who might easily have been made to feel like they were little kids again facing a judgmental teacher. That the teacher showed enough confidence to place the student in the leadership role in describing what was good, or not so good, about the student's progress, allowed parents to feel pride in their child's role in the conversation.

THE OTHER SIDE OF DISCIPLINE: HAVING FUN

What would happen if teachers and parents resolved to have more fun with the kids in their care? If we can manage to have more fun in teaching, we might thereby give both ourselves and our students an emotional change of pace. How can we teach any subject to a bunch of teenagers and hope to overcome their shyness, their cultural parochialism, their intellectual timidity and skepticism toward us as adults—unless we and they can have fun doing so?

Psychologist William Glasser, in his book *The Quality School*, is much concerned with situations like this. He points out that the usual response of teachers to negative student attitudes toward schoolwork is to simply require them to do it.

> When students do not work, most teachers are frustrated. . . . [T]hey try to choose a managerial behavior that will persuade the students to start working hard. But in this situation, most teachers do not know what to do. Many of them choose to threaten, a coercive choice that often increases the problem and their frustration. But if this is a choice, they also have a choice to ask themselves, "What might be the best way to solve this problem without coercion?" As soon as they think this, they open their minds to better ways to solve the problem.[3]

Glasser offered another way to view the problem: "Fun is nature's reward for learning." He views fun as one of the most basic human needs, along with survival, love, power, and freedom. It's right up there. It is essential to learning, he believes. It ought to be part of our lesson plan. Glasser is right about this, and about the ineffectiveness in the long run of using coercive methods to motivate students. Neither the work teachers get from the docile, obedient student nor the punishment they mete out to the defiant student is likely to spur lifelong learning—no matter how much it alleviates teacher frustration with student resistance.

In a summer workshop for middle and high school teachers held on a college campus, I had the group of eighty or so divide into disciplines—not the ones they were teaching but the subject they had the hardest time with in high school. Their assignment was to come up with a way to make that subject fun. Those who had "hated" foreign-language class hit the jackpot. They proposed asking students, on day one: "What do you want to say in French to your boyfriend, your girlfriend, your older sibling, or your mother that they won't understand, but that won't get me fired?" The idea of beginning a language class by having students come up with snarky phrases would lead, they felt sure, to students flooding the lunchroom with French. A Spanish teacher told me, months later, that he did ask students that question on the first day of class and later overheard, in the lunchroom, a student of his say in Spanish, "Why are you wearing a fish on your head?"

We've certainly trod the path of coercion for enough years; perhaps we ought to give fun a chance to prove itself as one of the routes to learning. Fun may be another key to renewal as passionate teachers. It can't hurt to look at each day's classes with a determination to have some fun teaching. It reminds us that in the learning business, work and play are not opposites, that most of a child's early learning comes from play, and that playfulness is a quality that adults cherish as well.

All true learning involves hard work. There is much serious stuff in the content and the skills we would have students learn, and there are good arguments for discipline and rigor in the pursuit of knowledge. Education—especially for students from unsafe, unwholesome, unpromising neighborhoods—can be literally a matter of life and death.

Most successful teachers tell me there is no contradiction between serious study and hard work, on the one hand, and having a good time in class, on the other—especially when it comes to helping students to be less inhibited about showing us what they think or what they have discovered or created. Not a few adolescents view public displays of their learning as having unlimited potential for embarrassment and failure. Speaking out is hard enough for most kids. Doing it in French or on the topic of differential equations or symbolism in literature can seem almost impossible.

What stops them is the potential for embarrassment and ineptitude; it stops most of us from speaking about something we're not sure of in front of an unknown or critical audience. Our job is to convince these kids that nothing really bad can happen to them in our classes. The atmosphere in class must become embarrassment-proof. And that requires that everyone loosen up a bit and figure out how to develop tolerance for making mistakes and how to have some fun while we're learning.

I am reminded here of David Ervin's work with seventh graders on music and theater production. There's no way these kids could put themselves onstage—with their own play, music, acting, and set design exposed to public scrutiny—unless they'd had enough fun in creating, rehearsing, and producing the play to cushion their natural anxiety about making fools of themselves in public. I think of Janice Weisberg, goofing with students in math classes as the kids stretched themselves to think out loud in the unfamiliar language of algebra. And I think of the middle school kids in Sturbridge, Massachusetts, who were challenged by both their industrial arts teacher and their history teacher to research and design models for catapults that might have been used in medieval warfare. After the students chose a winning design, they constructed it as a full-size model and lofted a watermelon across the length of the high school football field.

By contrast, I remind myself of the complaints I've often heard from foreign-language teachers that students seem so unmotivated to learn and so unwilling to speak French, Spanish, or German. If we want young people to learn a second language, isn't fun absolutely essential? Unless they are having a good time, why should any self-conscious teenager wish to look and sound foolish forming unusual verbal patterns in front of their classmates? It's just this reticence that leads many language teachers to focus on reading and writing. Yet it is the enjoyment of *speaking* a language that prompts us to continue to learn that language once we are no longer required to do so in school. The most successful language teachers I've met are those who have found a way to have a lot of fun with students while they are learning to make those awkward, goofy sounds.

Joining with students in aiming for high standards in learning and personal responsibility, while also making room for a lot of fun in the process, is as important to a teacher's stance as anything else we might think of. Maybe we should view discipline as an opportunity for us to teach values of respect, mutual respect, principles of a democratic society, good-naturedness, fairness, and decency toward one another. Ideally, a curriculum will capture the attention and the energy of students so that they, too, will have a stake in maintaining an orderly, supportive learning environment and not wait around for someone to make a scene. Let's also remember to take pride and pleasure in the hours and days when what we have organized has gone well—days without crisis or turmoil, days when we, too, can relax and enjoy ourselves.

16

CREATING AND MAINTAINING RESPECT AND CARING IN THE FACE OF BULLYING AND MEANNESS

Each one of our students has an important place and role in our classroom. Their behaviors are forms of communication. Their learning results in wiring and re-wiring in their brains. When the learning is authentic, students will take what they have learned and connect that learning to subjects and places outside of our classrooms. For students, teachers create the connections that last and that matter most.

—CARLY MALONEY,
2024 Utah Teacher of the Year

CREATING A CONTEXT FOR PRODUCTIVE LEARNING

Every highly successful teacher I know has assimilated the axiom: relationship first, task second. For them, the first job is to get to know their students and establish a climate of trust and respect as a prerequisite for productive learning. Each in their own way creates an atmosphere of welcoming, inclusiveness, curiosity, adventure, challenge, and fun. This may take a few days or several weeks depending on what students bring with them into class, based on how respectfully or disparagingly they have been treated previously. Your approach should never be fawning or condescending or excessive—kids know insincerity when they hear it. And it should always be more about them than about you, as is wonderfully exemplified by the teachers whose stories comprise the heart of this book.

ANDREA LEVIN: SOCIAL AND EMOTIONAL LEARNING IS NOW JUST PART OF THE JOB

But, as twenty-four-year veteran teacher Andrea Levin, points out, having a stance that promotes adventure and excitement in the classroom, as important as that is, is not enough. She echoes the reflections I've heard from many teachers about how the nature of teaching has changed and how those changes have impacted the way we approach our students:

> Anyone going into teaching right now needs to understand that fostering social and emotional learning is part of the job. While it may be one's opinion that this should be the job of parents, the reality is that cultural trends connected to technology have created unforeseen circumstances for which many parents are not prepared. If teachers want students to learn, they need to accept that they will be instructing students in areas that used to be outside their purview. There is now research that supports the idea that factors such as ACE (adverse childhood experiences) scores, the degree to which there is a sense of community in the classroom, and healthy connections to adults in the school community all affect student learning.[1]

I've collected a few suggestions, below, for creating a good environment for productive learning. Hopefully, some of these will align with your personality and be appropriate for you to share with your students—depending on their age, culture, and previous experiences. Begin with those you think will produce the best results.

Here is an approach for elementary grades from Joshua Chard of Portland, Maine:

> Second graders come to school with a strong sense of what they believe to be wrong and right. They are just beginning to develop a sense of fairness and a new understanding of what it means to have empathy. In fact, learning about empathy is an important part of social-emotional learning in second grade.
>
> My classroom has a jewel jar filled with students' kind and helpful choices. When the jar is full, we might have an extra recess or a pizza

snack—twenty dollars' worth of Domino's pizza buys much goodwill. Early on, I give out glass jewels, celebrating the acts of kindness I observe from my learners. Students catch on quickly and start pointing out acts of caring they see, which they consider jewel-worthy. When that starts to happen, we go to the next logical step: removing my role in distributing jewels and turning that power over to the children in my classroom. A friend helped you understand the math assignment? How many jewels would you like to give them? Your tablemate helped you clean up the milk you spilled? Grab some jewels for them. Because of this minor procedure, students focus on the good things in our classroom and can't wait to celebrate and to be celebrated.

When students take responsibility for creating a warm and supportive environment, it becomes a natural part of what they do in the classroom and other settings.

By giving students the power to recognize and celebrate kindness, empathy becomes more than a lesson. It becomes a habit. When children take ownership of their community, a culture of care naturally grows.[2]

FINDING THE RIGHT BALANCE

There is, of course, such a thing as being overly focused on social and emotional learning. You don't want students to feel embarrassed or patronized by your preoccupation with their feelings. But if you can find a way in your own words and activities to let them know that their ability to do productive work may depend on their feeling welcomed, respected, and free from fear of ridicule or intimidation, you have definitely made a good start. So this is not just about kids "feeling good," or "being safe"; it's also about setting the stage for doing good work.

The opposite approach, of course, is to make students feel intimidated, ignored, anxious, or unwelcome. We all know horror stories of students being ridiculed, humiliated, or ostracized because someone saw them as "different," with the schoolmaster condoning or even leading the abuse. When a child I know was in third grade, his teacher—who grew up in a family where children were expected to show deference to their elders—was unable to understand that this child and several of his classmates had been raised to question anything that seemed unfair and to argue their points respectfully but with vigor. She reacted with barely concealed anger, and she responded with sarcasm under the presumption that "if you kids think you can argue like grown-ups, you should expect to be treated like grown-ups." But, of course, they were still children and not yet capable of coping with sarcasm from an authority figure. The boy began to twist locks of his hair until they fell out. This symptom disappeared when he and his classmates entered fourth grade.

LEADING WITH CURIOSITY

But let's assume that foisting sarcasm on young children is far from your style and your stance. Depending on the age, maturity, and cultural backgrounds of your students, you might begin with one or two of the approaches below. And remember, these are not recipes; they are suggestions on how you, in your own way, can establish your stance.

- *Lead with curiosity.* Nothing is as inviting as letting students know you are interested in who they are, what they already know, and how they think. It can be as simple as spending time early in the school year talking about things your students know as much or more about than you do: favorite places in the community, local walking trails, best shops to get ice cream. Depending on their age and maturity, let them talk about their pets, their favorite games or shows. Or, if you are new to the school, ask what they especially like (and don't like) about the school, cautioning them not to complain about other adults since you want to be free to form your own impressions about the people you work with. Pay particular attention to them when you ask: "What do you like to learn that nobody ever has to try to make you learn?"
- *Ask students to describe a classroom where they have felt appreciated and respected.* If several mention the same teacher, invite that person into your classroom to talk about how they create a classroom that's a good place to learn. This will make both the teacher and your students feel special. Teachers rarely get invited to such informal settings where they are appreciated by students. If more than one teacher is so nominated, all the better.
- *Have students make a list of the classroom characteristics that help them enjoy learning.* Encourage them to discuss these characteristics and maybe vote on their top five. Make up your own list,

and then compare. This will show your students that you not only value their opinions but are willing to share yours in an atmosphere of mutual respect. Do a classroom environment check every once in a while by seeking confidential feedback from students about the classroom environment.

- *Don't be afraid to take on the question, "Why do we have to learn this stuff?"* It's going to be out there, even if it never gets explicitly raised. So, raise it yourself, and see if your students' sense of what's valuable in the lesson, unit, or course has any relation to what you—and those who've designed the curriculum—think is vital. If you feel especially brave, let your students know that, at the end of the course, they will get to weigh in on how it might have gone better and that you will consider their feedback as you plan for the next unit or course.

DEALING CONSTRUCTIVELY WITH MEANNESS AND BULLYING

Now that bullying and meanness are being taken seriously as more than random incidents of pushing or name calling on the playground, and now that social media is recognized as playing an especially nefarious role in ways children and youth can harm one another and themselves, there are many good books, articles, and videos that discuss these issues in depth. What we will confine ourselves to here are preventive measures that reduce the likelihood of having these behaviors show up in your classroom but also quickly putting a stop to bullying and meanness when it occurs—without your always having to be the one who intervenes. Remember, too, that those who bully are also victims who need help (as, of course, do those they bully). You want to emphasize in your approach that everyone needs to be free from ridicule in order to exercise their right to learn.

- Talk with your students in advance about the kinds of comments that hurt people's feelings and how to find other ways of expressing frustration or anger. Point out, and practice, ways that allow students to express those feelings without hurting others. It's up to you whether you should wait until you see or hear mean or other hurtful comments, or try to preempt them by raising the issue yourself. To avoid snarkiness from older students, it might be wise to have students write down bullying comments they've heard, whether in your class or elsewhere, and place them anonymously in a large envelope or shoebox. You can then screen them and perhaps invite a trusted school counselor or favorite coach to open the envelope and lead a discussion.

- One of my son's middle school teachers required any student guilty of a put-down of a classmate to come up in front of the class and give that student a "put-up," a compliment or positive remark. If the "put-up" seemed insincere, the class could insist that the offending student keep at it until they were convinced of the speaker's sincerity. This introduced a playful yet effective way of enlisting peer pressure to create a more convivial and less intimidating class culture.
- For situations where a student violates agreed-upon class norms regarding bullying and meanness, Karen Ball offers her own technique: "I have found that when a student is not making good choices, talking to them privately is always more productive than addressing it publicly. And when I forget, and say something I shouldn't say publicly, I apologize publicly, too. Most of the time, I will ask the student to step into the hall, and give them a few minutes to calm down, and make sure that I am also calm before I join them in the hall. I usually start the private conversations by asking the student if there is something going on, because they usually don't do x, y, or z. This has a way of melting defensiveness and sending the message that I am there to help, not to invoke punishment. After listening to the student's perspective, I move the conversation to the student's behavior towards others and how it has affected the learning environment for everyone. We talk about ways to get back on the right track and make a plan that hopefully allows the student to own the offense, rather than denying or placing blame on others." Thus, a general approach that many teachers employ to deal with disruptive behaviors could help an offending student take responsibility for restoring a safe learning climate in the classroom.
- For students who persist in violating the norms that you and the class have decided upon, a combination of any of these might work: having a quiet chat with the student after school to try to

find out what's causing the bullying; meeting with the student and parents to explore how to respond to the student's need for attention in ways that don't hurt others and, at the same time, finding ways for the student to take responsibility for a kind of "restorative justice"; having the student identify someone the student trusts (a guidance counselor, assistant principal, coach, or another teacher) and invite that person to join the conversation.

- Ultimately, bullying or meanness toward another student is a violation of that student's right to learn. If you are able to shift the focus from bad behavior, criticism, and punishments to the principle of every student's rights, the intervention becomes less volatile and more a question of fairness, an idea all kids understand.

AN EPIDEMIC OF MEANNESS IN OUR LAND

There is, in our times perhaps more than previously, an epidemic of meanness in our land, reflected in the politics that confront us and the media our students are exposed to—both of which are often brought into our schools and classrooms. As former *New York Times* columnist David Brooks reminds us, "All humans need to grow up in a secure container, within which they can craft their lives. The social order consists of a stable family, a safe and coherent neighborhood, a vibrant congregational and civic life, a reliable body of laws, a set of shared values that neighbors can use to build healthy communities and a conviction that there exists moral truth."[3] Our public-school system, a vital part of that "secure container," has—with all its shortcomings—provided a healthy community for many millions of American children over more than a century, and has in turn contributed to that essential social order. It is now under threat, even as some or more than some of the students who come to us have felt the loss of that security. They bring their insecurities and anxieties with them to school, sometimes resulting in feelings of hostility or victimhood. It may be too much to expect individual teachers to redress these social deficits, but we can try our best, by including, as Andrea Levin argues, "fostering social and emotional learning" within the environment we and our students create to make our classroom a place of security, respect, and fellowship.

PART FOUR

THE STUDENT

17

HELPING STUDENTS TAKE OWNERSHIP OF THEIR LEARNING

I really believe everything relies on authentic engagement. How do we engage and spark students' curiosity and passions while also bringing them into the conversation about their learning? I'm blunt with my students when I tell them—learning history does us no good unless we are actively doing something with it! It's important that young people know that their learning is more than the acquisition of information and the regurgitation of facts. It is more of a call to action to be the best person they can be. In this sense, I focus less on the content/topic and more on the inspiration behind getting students to engage and become active participants in their educational journey. If I exude passion for learning and exploring wonder, my students will be more likely to engage in academic adventures that help them connect with their humanity.

—TAYLOR BUSSINGER, Kansas 2024 Teacher of the Year

REDESIGNING AWAY FROM THE FACTORY MODEL

In the late summer of 2025, on the NPR podcast *On Point*, the subject was "How to Redesign Schools for the AI Age." And while this book does not attempt to tackle this huge question (leaving it to other, more knowledgeable authors), the discussion included two scholars who believe that schools needed to be greatly "redesigned" long before AI. One of them was Linda Darling-Hammond, a distinguished author and professor emeritus at Stanford University; the other was Rebecca

Winthrop, coauthor of *The Disengaged Teen: Helping Kids Learn Better, Feel Better, and Live Better*.

Darling-Hammond talked about how obsolete is the "factory model" of schooling, based on nineteenth-century pedagogy and how, although a number of schools across the nation are moving toward project-based learning and authentic assessment, most are still locked by state and local regulations into outdated ways of treating knowledge and students. She said that, notwithstanding the challenges of AI, "The goal is to develop learning ability and the ability to make good judgements. The human side of learning is going to be very important. There's also the unique human skills, creativity, critical thinking, emotional intelligence, the ability to work and collaborate with others." In other words, AI may revolutionize how we deal with information, but teachers are needed even more to help students learn how to shape their lives creatively and collectively.

LEARNER TYPES: "RESISTERS," "PASSENGERS," "ACHIEVERS," "EXPLORERS"

Winthrop focused on types of learners that she and her coauthor were able to characterize, based on a finding that far too many kids are currently "disengaged" with school. She said that they "went on a deep dive around why kids don't like school. And one of the main things we found is that they're super disengaged. And we see that in chronic absenteeism levels, mental health, we see it in poor academic performance."[1]

Winthrop went on to describe four student "modes of learning":

1. Resister mode: kids in this mode avoid learning and disrupt the class.
2. Passenger mode: kids in this group tend to coast and do the bare minimum without caring about quality.
3. Achiever mode: these kids are "trying to get gold stars on everything, but . . . often are actually fragile, risk-averse learners [who] don't want to try anything new for fear of getting a bad grade."

And, finally, the mode of learning we should nurture in the hopes that all students may spend time in it:

4. Explorer mode: kids who "are really motivated, really engaged, they're following their curiosity, even in a very structured environment."

But what was really shocking was Winthrop's finding that "less than 4 percent of middle and high school kids spend regular time in explorer mode." But, we know that children don't start out as disengaged learners. "Kids are actually all born in explore mode and we slowly beat it out of them. Seventy-five percent of kids in third grade we found in our research loved school, and by the time they were in tenth grade, 25 percent. It had flipped."

When we visited our youngest son's kindergarten teacher on Parents' Day some thirty-seven years ago, she told us she had recently observed Peter busy at his desk, drawing. "I went over to him and said, 'Are you going to be an artist when you grow up, Peter?' and he told me, quietly but seriously, 'Missus Blazon, I already *am* an artist.'"

What Peter was saying amounted to an affirmation that his learning was in his own hands. Amid all that he was being taught, among all the procedures he was expected to conform to, creativity was still his business. Fast-forward seventeen years. As a senior in college, Peter was melding philosophy, psychology, and neuroscience courses into an interdisciplinary concentration called "Cognitive Studies." Peter was a pretty laid-back kid, one who loved the Drama Club and hanging out with his friends. By no means driven to excellence or perfection, he took only one AP course and never bothered taking the AP test. Yet, as with his brother, Zach, he was determined to be the subject of his learning, rather than the object of the teaching agendas of others.

Trent Van Leuven, Idaho's 2024 Teacher of the Year, knows student "ownership" when he sees it in his high school tech ed students. And he doesn't sit back and wait for it to appear.

> The fastest way to reignite passion is to let students take the wheel, even briefly. Give them a microphone, a problem that matters, and a chance to teach others. I've seen tired teachers come alive again when their students plan a field trip, teach a lesson, lead a service project, or present to the school board. When students own the learning, it stops being just your

> job to light the fire. It becomes something shared. That shared ownership—messy and unpredictable as it may be—is where the magic returns.[2]

WHAT STUDENT "OWNERSHIP" MEANS

But what does it really mean for students to "own" their learning? Shouldn't we rightfully expect them to perform the learning tasks we set for them—doing their homework, reading required texts, writing papers and studying for exams—all of which constitute the work of schooling? On that last item—exams—Zach's biology teacher allowed students to put as much information as they could fit onto a five-by-eight-inch card and bring that into the exam room for the final. Cramming took on a whole new meaning, not trying to memorize everything, hoping to guess what would be on the test, but rather "cramming" what they saw as useful stuff onto the card. This incentivized the students to review the course and synthesize what they believed were its most important aspects, which enabled them to have a significant degree of ownership, even in a traditional course with a traditional final exam.

If most students were permitted and encouraged to truly own their learning—as our best coaches inspire their players to take responsibility for getting in shape, practicing, and going out on the field to do their best—we'd see a lot fewer Game of School behaviors that plague teachers: students not caring, cheating on assignments, or passing off AI work as their own; students acting bored, sneaking a look at their phones in class; students rebelling openly or withdrawing subtly in reaction to being bossed around by their teachers (who, in turn, resent being bossed around by administrators or bureaucratic mandates); students acting as captives in an institution run by grown-ups who try to make them do things they'd prefer not doing.

STUDENT OWNERSHIP IN THE EARLY GRADES

Joshua Chard responded to my request for his insights into the challenge of nurturing student ownership:

> When students start the year in my second-grade classroom, they are eager for affirmation and approval. They frequently ask, "Is this right?" or "Did I do a good job?" or "Do you like my work?" At seven, children are naturally driven to seek validation from the adults they trust.

It might surprise people to know that I don't answer these kinds of questions directly. Instead, I respond with prompts like, "Does your work match the directions?" or "How do you feel about it? Why?" or most importantly, "Is there someone else in the room who can let you know how good you've done?"

Consider this: There are twenty or more students in my classroom, each with unique insights, experiences, and inventive solutions—and only one of me. By stepping back and making space for student voice, I empower my learners to become the most insightful and creative educators in the room. This shift requires a leap of faith; both teachers and students are often used to the teacher being in charge. But when students take the lead, engage in productive struggle, and apply their unique knowledge to rigorous tasks, they thrive.

At first, they may crave that instant reassurance. But over time, they learn they can take ownership of their learning. Students' ideas and leadership become the foundation of our classroom culture, and their self-confidence and sense of agency thrive.

Of course, this doesn't happen overnight. It takes intentional scaffolding. But the reward is watching learning unfold naturally—and seeing my students' enthusiasm as they tackle new challenges and grow into leaders for one another. On the last day of school, one of my students beamed, "At the beginning of the year I didn't think I could even do my work, but now I can help my friends do their work." He'll carry that lesson with him forever.

Spend ten minutes in my classroom and you'll see: I am not the "sage on the stage," the keeper of knowledge, or the sole source of affirmation. Those roles belong to the remarkable and insightful seven-year-olds who inspire and teach me every single day.

I once visited a high school in the Midwest, where a dedicated English teacher shared her most vexing dilemma: "Along with teaching English, I'm also the faculty adviser for the student newspaper. When I'm with the kids in the newsroom, I mostly just sit at my desk and wait until someone asks me for help with something. The kids run the show. They do all the writing and the photography, and they work hard to put together each edition of the paper. But I have most of these same kids in my junior and senior English classes, and they sit there like bumps on a log. It's like pulling teeth to get them to discuss their reactions to the novel we're reading, or to share their essays with fellow students."

The answer to her dilemma was sitting right in front of her, but for some reason she was unable to ask her kids to explain the disparity. It is the age-old specter of the schoolmaster standing in front of the class expounding upon something that he has no doubt is of great import, giving orders and disciplining laggards. When we allow ourselves to assume that student resistance to learning goes with the job, we have all but thrown in the towel. We become preoccupied with something called "classroom management," as we imagine ourselves tottering on the precipice of classroom anarchy, hearing the echo of those who warn, "You'd better get control over those students, or they will walk all over you." And, in fact, when we as teachers become the inheritors of young people scarred by years of compliance-based teaching, it can seem true that "control" is the first order of business.

STUDENT OWNERSHIP VS. CLASSROOM MANAGEMENT

After years of teaching education courses to undergraduate and graduate students, my ears still ring with pleas from those about to begin their student teaching—"Please help me with classroom management"—while my colleagues and I tried to fill them with our philosophy. "Teachers teach as they've been taught, not as they've been taught to teach," goes the old saying. If, nearing the apex of their study with us, they still felt preoccupied with their ability to maintain control rather than eager to inspire their students, that was our shortcoming, not theirs.

So, how do we change the balance of power in our classrooms and schools so that our students come to see learning as something they have agency over within a partnership that we have cocreated with them? Let's be clear, we're not talking about students who seek "ownership" of their GPA and who practice "self-advocacy" in pursuit of an undeserved higher grade. We contend that most human beings seek a democratic environment in which they have a high degree of autonomy and choice. The paradox, of course, is that as teachers we attempt to promote democracy within a structure of compulsory education and the residue of hundreds of years of traditional and often autocratic school culture.

DEBORAH MEIER: A QUESTION OF DEMOCRACY

This brings us to the uncomfortable recognition that our schools are very far from being democratic places for teachers and students to work in—and even less so in this politically charged era. My good friend and mentor, Deborah Meier, has made this issue the focus of her thinking for decades and has worked tirelessly to bring democracy into the schools she has led, including Central Park East Secondary School in New York and Mission Hill Elementary School in Boston. Deborah has seen to it that students, teachers, and parents are a vital part of the decision-making process in these schools, even as she has battled against administrators seeking to impose their will on her and her staff. Here is what she has told me in our discussion about her continuing quest to make schools not only more democratic but more capable of infusing democratic citizenship in all students:

> "What's the most important role for our education system today in helping preserve our democracy," you ask? Your question presumes that I want us to "preserve" our democracy, as opposed to strengthening and transforming what we have now into a more *genuine* democracy. The educational system we have now is essentially an oligarchy with important democratic features that allow teachers to manifest a certain degree of freedom.
>
> I am convinced that there is no way we can instill democratic principles in children unless the adults—especially the teachers—also practice democracy. You cannot teach democracy unless you and the members of a school community—teachers, administrators, students, and parents—act in democratic ways. This is our first essential task.
>
> The public school can be an intentional community whose work is guided by habits of mind and heart to address the challenge of making democracy possible. The members of the community—individuals who attend the school, who work in the school, or who have a child in the school—ought to be engaged in cocreating this work. A school that intends to teach democracy must practice democracy in its governance capacity. Time needs to be devoted to the deliberative and reflective process of governing. This includes issues of staffing, curriculum, leadership, budget, safety, and the way we all should conduct ourselves and treat others. That is the best way to encourage democracy in the classroom.

Democracy is not a natural habit. It takes an institutional commitment, along with constant practice, perseverance, and skill—none of which comes naturally. Democracy is a more difficult subject to teach than physics or advanced mathematics.

Schooling is all about influencing students in ways that increase their independence and autonomy. Whether we are conducting a unit or course on arithmetic or writing, all we have going for us is our capacity to enlighten others in ways that change their perceptions of numbers, words, and ideas—and that is how knowledge becomes a source of power. Kids are properly attracted to power, and they seek influence. Our modeling of adulthood needs to show them how this might look. Students need to witness powerful adults unafraid to discuss power!

There is, on one hand, the system role and, on the other, the personal role that each teacher and school plays. It is the system's job to concern itself with the education of all children and to pass on to them knowledge, skills, and values. But we also have an obligation to care about children's personal happiness and confidence in the present. Teaching is a day-by-day commitment, so we are only thinking not only about children's value to society but also their value to themselves, their families, and loved ones.

As a kindergarten teacher in Chicago in the 1960s, what I liked best was helping children enjoy their ideas and develop well-earned convictions. I liked watching the children experience the delight that can come from sharing their convictions with others—ferociously at times, but with pleasure as well. Sorting out conflicting evidence—but not giving in too easily—has always been a fascinating challenge for me. That process turned out to be equally interesting to five-year-olds. I enjoyed the freedom alongside my class of youngsters to rediscover together what the world looked and felt like and how to put our ideas to the test through words, arguments, experiments, photos, artwork, and music.

WHAT TEACHERS CAN DO, EVEN IN "UNDEMOCRATIC" SCHOOLS

I'd like to end this chapter by focusing on what teachers can do, even under a less-than-democratic school structure, to allow their students to experience what it means to have a major role in guiding their learning—despite the requirements that are imposed upon them by standardized testing, mandated curricula, and the regularities of school that are outside their control. If it is difficult to teach democracy in undemocratic school settings, perhaps we can help our students experience aspects of choice, freedom, cooperation, initiative, and self-responsibility that help them be more democratic in their dealings with others. The chapters that follow are devoted to this exploration. Here are a few questions that can help students start owning their learning:

- What's the difference between learning that you have a real stake in (beyond just the grade) and learning that you do to please or obey the people who have the power to reward or punish you?
- What skills and knowledge have you learned outside of school that truly belong to you?
- How can we take the threats out of our classroom, so that each of us can express our opinion without being criticized or made fun of for having unpopular ideas?
- What kinds of games, rhymes, or songs can we create to learn things you don't especially want to learn? This works especially well with younger students, but it can also include aspects of irony and slapstick for older kids.

Likewise, a teacher might say something like this to their class: "Sometimes I'm going to ask you to learn something that I think is important but that you may not think so. I do this because I sincerely believe that it is important, but I will always explain why and try to show you how it will be useful to you. I will try to do this in a way that respects you as a learner."

A final thought: Student ownership of learning is the closest we can come to democracy in the classroom.

18

A PASSION FOR EXCELLENCE

Those of us who are interested in improving education have a habit of paying too much attention to schools and not enough to children.

—HAROLD HOWE II,
Thinking About Our Kids

"THEY JUST DON'T CARE MUCH ABOUT WHAT THEY'RE LEARNING IN SCHOOL"

So far in this book we've been looking mostly at teachers, particularly at those I am calling passionate teachers—who they are, what they do, how they strive to change the Game of School, and what kind of stance they take toward their students. Let's shift our focus to look at things from the perspective of the persons for whom passionate teaching is intended—*students*. The goal of passionate teaching, after all, is engaged, exploratory, productive, high-quality student learning. If it isn't happening much in schools, let's ask why.

The principal of my sons' high school sat down one June day with a group of graduating seniors and asked them to tell her where in their lives they worked hardest and did their best thinking. They listed their jobs, hobbies, and sports. Nobody mentioned their academic classes.

Teachers are often amazed to discover that students who show little effort on classwork or homework can summon tremendous energy and discipline outside of school—whether they're taking apart and rebuilding a car in the family garage, serving as assistant manager at a local fast-food restaurant, organizing a charity drive for a church, or forming a band, finding a place to practice, and getting gigs.

When my son Zach was in tenth grade, he illustrated this as well as any. He would breeze through his homework as an irritating inconvenience way before booting up his computer and entering a world of technical engagement and intellectual challenge that his teachers and I could scarcely fathom. Others among his classmates probably paid as little attention to homework as he, while they devoted mental energy to other things—music, athletics, jobs, relationships—that truly engaged their minds and their spirits.

As a tenth grader, my son was not usually bored with work in school. He respected most of his teachers. Their pedagogy simply did not connect with his interests. Their curriculum rarely drew him out. They didn't find much for him to do that he felt was worth devoting his energy or his intellect to. Some of this was undoubtedly due to a normal adolescent resistance to adult agendas; some to a social environment that makes it hard for kids to appear excited about school. But whatever the causes, school had not yet found a way to inspire the many like him to discover meaning in the lessons. For many of our students, the result of their efforts is far less than what we believe their potential to be. How they perform in school is not indicative of what most of these kids are truly capable of.

What teachers get to see, far too often, is not students' enterprise and enthusiasm, but the Game of School compliance or lack thereof. Kids do such work chiefly out of obedience. The more obedient they are, the more homework and schoolwork they do. Teachers complain when students are disruptive or indolent. But it's almost as bad when students offer us their obedience at the expense of the quality of their thinking and the caliber of the work they produce. When we get compliance instead of thoughtfulness, submissiveness in place of high-quality work, we all lose. We do get something, some work out of them, but it doesn't seem to stay with them, and we find ourselves having to reteach the same skills, to correct the same errors, year after year.

Most teachers I've talked with have much loftier goals for their students than getting them to comply with deadlines and pass tests. Most seek another quality of response. What they really want is excellence or mastery. Although they often don't get it even from their most promising students, teachers keep looking for it, as they should.

WRONG—AND RIGHT—PLACES TO FIND STUDENT EXCELLENCE

The wrong place for us to find excellence is at the high end of a classic bell curve—treating as "excellent" only what the top achievers in the class do: score the highest on a test, hand in the neatest and most error-free papers, get furthest in the textbook, or have perfect rates of attendance or homework completion. Schools have traditionally defined "excellence" by such attributes; we rank students numerically by how high their grade-point average is. And these are good qualities for a student to have, to be sure. But they limit excellence to a select few individuals. I don't deny that some of our most obedient students produce some of the highest-quality work we see. It's just that we lose too many creative and talented students when teachers make it apparent that compliance is what they're after. A lot of kids in most schools take one glance at the way the top scorers act and decide it's not worth it to compete or comply.

A somewhat better but still inadequate way to define excellence is as a product of student exertion: the "A for effort." This approach has gained favor among those who champion heterogeneous grouping of students, the inclusion of students of different skill levels and/or students with disabilities in classes, and those who want all students to have a fair shot at doing well, regardless of limiting circumstances. As a parent, I often hear myself telling my kids: "I don't care what grade you get; I just want you to do the very best job you can." Most kids don't believe that line for a minute, even though it's at least partially true.

Most of us would agree that rewarding students for diligence and improvement—regardless of results—is vital for young learners and continues to be important as they grow. But at some point we've got to help students contend with real-world standards where quality of performance counts every bit as much as a willingness to work hard.

EXCELLENCE EVERY STUDENT CAN ASPIRE TO—AND ACHIEVE

Let me suggest a third definition. Excellence may be found in the results students attain by doing work that

- is intrinsically important, concerns things that matter in the world
- involves both discipline and a stretching of students' minds and actions beyond what they think they can do (i.e., effort)
- shows creativity and individuality that reflect a student's view of the world
- makes a contribution to the learning or well-being of oneself and others and has use beyond the completion of an assignment

Every student, of any "ability level," has the potential to do excellent work under these criteria; yet no student can do so casually, simply because he or she is smart, talented, eager to please, or has well-educated or highly motivated parents. Such a definition of excellence can also help us focus more closely on a short list of crucial questions, challenges, tasks, skills, and student outcomes. The real distinction, then, might be between a student who gets 100 percent on a history textbook chapter quiz and one who compares chapters in an old and a new textbook to point out the biases in each—or between a student who gets all right answers on the math homework and one who can explain the faulty reasoning that led to a wrong answer.

A teacher's focus on excellence should not have to mean requiring a steady, unbroken, high level of performance from students. The best baseball players in the world fail to hit safely seven times in ten. We're after excellence—or, as author Tony Wagner would argue, "mastery"—not near-perfect completion of mediocre tasks, and we should not create unrealistic obstacles for a large number of potentially excellent students by confusing the two. Doing a truly outstanding job on a paper, project, or experiment, and getting full recognition for it, is arguably more important than turning in homework every day—and it may have a greater influence on a student's willingness to stay engaged in learning and foster pride in hard work.

WHAT YOU MUST GIVE UP TO GET EXCELLENCE FROM MORE THAN THE TOP FEW

If it is excellence/mastery we're after, if we want to see the best students can do in the humanities, sciences, arts, and other fields, then we have to give up something. Students should not have to keep doing everything their teachers ask them, day after day, just in order to be seen as "excellent." Excellence is not an everyday thing, and mastery is a step-by-step reaching for an identified operational goal. Both are special, earned, and reflective of a pride and confidence that are the student's own. We may have to sacrifice quantity of compliant performance if we want students to achieve quality of achievement.

Our traditional methods of grading—I will expand on this later—give the opposite message: three missed homework assignments, two failed quizzes, plus a terrific term paper that's four days late add up to a pretty mediocre grade in many courses. Too many talented young people lose interest in learning and lose faith in school because their teachers won't accommodate inconsistent excellence. And far too many students from economic or educationally disadvantaged backgrounds give up on school because teachers cannot abide their inconsistent performances, which may be due to hardships and obligations beyond the school. Teachers who succeed in getting high-quality work from at-risk kids are often those who can inspire them to do a few wonderful things occasionally and who thus hold onto kids who haven't yet developed the kind of work habits they will eventually need as successful adults.

This is not to deny the value in this world of regular, high-level performance, or our role in helping students build solid work habits. We don't want our chemists or air traffic controllers, accountants, surgeons, or postal clerks to turn their standards of performance on and off. Punctuality and consistency do count for something. But when our main job is to help students develop their minds and increase their confidence and engagement in learning as a lifelong affinity, we have to choose our battles. As every parent knows, we can't expect to win with kids on all fronts, not when there are so many forces competing for their attention and allegiance, and when their resistance to adult demands is essential to their becoming adults themselves. When we don't ask for everything, we stand a greater chance of engaging their energy and perseverance and of getting them to want to show us their best.

WHO ARE THE EXCELLENT STUDENTS?

I believe the genesis of excellence is within each learner: in the individuality, creativity, diligence, honesty, and sensitivity that each student may choose to bring to learning tasks of substance and value. Not all of us are alike in our inclination to do excellent work on a given learning project. Excellence, as I am defining it here, is not a birthright, as are respect and dignity; it must be earned.

But to speak of differences in inclination is not to argue that only some of us have an innate or God-given capacity to achieve excellence; nor does it suggest that everyone has a place along a spectrum of ability such that we can predict who is likely to do excellent work, who will do average work, and who will do poorly. That dreadful fallacy has been embraced, by and large, by the general public, and often induces a sense of hopeless resignation in parents whose child has been dubbed a "slow learner." Millions of Americans are walking around whose natural desire for learning was cut short by their school's labels of "general-level student," "slow learner," or "non-college material." The "innate ability" way of appraising, sorting, and grouping students—rarely challenged by educators until the late twentieth century—has contributed to massive rates of failure and mediocrity in our schools, particularly in areas of urban and rural poverty. But its effects extend to almost all students: We all tend to think of ourselves as "dumb" in at least one subject, when the truth is that we may simply have gone about learning a subject (or had it taught to us) in a way that has led to a feeling of failure or incompetence. We are not all talented violinists, mechanical geniuses, or lyrical poets—but we can all make music, fix things, and put our feelings on paper.

I once took a large college class of Intro to Education students out onto the quad and asked them to line up according to how their interest in classical music, art, and dance compared with their interest in sports. They had fun with this. Then, I asked them to line up based on those who preferred to spend time alone versus those who always wanted to be with a group of friends. This, too, they were willing to do, accompanied by much banter. Finally, I asked them, rather casually, to line up in order of smartness, with the smartest at one end and the least smart at the other. After milling around in confusion for a minute or two, they told me they refused. I brought them back inside and congratulated them on their refusal. Then I added, "But think of how your future students will feel about an education system that seems to want to do exactly that to them, year after year, school after school."

As Howard Gardner points out in *Frames of Mind*, we should work with children and young people so that each can strive for—and achieve—excellence in projects and tasks that take their unique pathways to excellence into account and offer them multiple avenues for displaying their skills. Teachers will want to strike a balance between those basic skills—such as reading, writing, numeracy, thinking, problem-solving, working with diverse people—that we expect all students to learn and demonstrate proficiency in but also in other areas of learning that allow students to show us how their unique personalities create meaning.

Even within that short list of basic skills, teachers and students can find lots of ways for students to show their stuff. With good coaching, staff development, peer support, and attentive teachers, students can work diligently and creatively both to build skills in "the basics" and to show off in other areas of personal excellence. For teachers, taking a look at what excellence and mastery mean, and how we can promote these qualities in the full range of students we see, enhances the spirit of enterprise and creativity for ourselves and for our students. How teachers define excellence—and how we apply that definition as we assess students' work—is the key to everyone's success.

19

THE PRACTICE OF EXCELLENCE

The logic of the school mind is that it is better to leave school with a tool kit of superficial jargon derived from economics, sociology, natural science, and so on, than with one genuine enthusiasm.

—JOHN TAYLOR GATTO, *Dumbing Us Down*

OUR THREE BAD HABITS

As with talk about passionate teaching, reflections on producing excellence in student learning can sound utopian to today's classroom teacher. How can we make it real? What practical steps can teachers take to inspire and cultivate the kind and quality of student attitude, effort, and performance that we have just talked about? Allow me to suggest three traditionally bad habits in teaching that are obstacles to the pursuit of excellence in learning:

1. We often don't teach students what's most important.
2. We rarely give them real jobs to do.
3. We are more likely to judge their work instead of guiding and coaching them.

This is the antithesis of passionate teaching. The problem is that we teachers help perpetuate the Game of School when we teach things because we are "supposed to cover them" rather than because we recognize them as intrinsically important; when we ask students to perform tasks that they see as exercises in compliance rather than tasks that accomplish some clear and worthwhile purpose; and when we appear to students as rewarders or punishers of their efforts rather than as allies in their achievement.

As for teaching what's most important, the areas of our disciplines that we feel passionate about and committed to are often—but by no means always—linked to what we feel students must learn to be successful in life. There must be room in lesson plans for these essential skills and for teachers' own passionate areas of interest since both contribute to intellectual development. Poetry, philosophy, and the classics may appear to have little practical use for students (although a case can always be made for their value in "training the mind"), but that need not diminish their importance within the curriculum—so long as there is a teacher who loves to teach them.

In the wake of national and statewide efforts—heralded by some, reviled by others—specifying what "experts" believe are the most important things students should know and be able to do in the core curricular areas, it's our professional duty, as Andrea Levin points out in chapter 6, to become familiar with such criteria. We should confer with colleagues, college admissions folks, local employers, and others about what they think our students ought to be learning—and, most important, we should talk this over with the students themselves. The payoff for this can be great: When students are confident that their teachers know what's essential for them to study and have explained to them why, students tend to work harder and produce more.

STUDENTS CONNECT THEIR LEARNING TO THEIR WORLD

Helping students pursue meaningful, real-world learning begins when teachers help students discover how classroom learning connects to important issues, challenges, and projects outside of school. But teachers can go even further by structuring assignments so that students can see the impact of their work on audiences beyond the classroom in a real-world context. Some of the most astute critics of American education argue that this is where we are most at risk in comparison to other nations' school systems, in which kids spend more time each year applying what they learn to realistic situations. American kids, too, take a lot of pride in doing a job well when they know that the work is meaningful and useful—and that somebody outside the class will be observing or reviewing their work. Such pride is the mother of excellence.

Lastly, the whole cycle of judging and grading represents a colossal drain on everyone's mental and emotional resources. Most teachers despair of ever changing the grade-book routine, either because they believe it is necessary to hold students accountable for the work they are assigned or because they haven't found something to replace it with that will satisfy parents, school officials, and students themselves. How much of what currently goes into grading is truly instructive and helpful to the student? How much is regulatory, administrative, or unnecessarily judgmental? Our challenge is to get off that wheel, to lessen the impact of grading, and to do more coaching and guiding of students while inspiring them to produce works of high quality. The need for giving some sort of letter or number grade may persist for quite some time, but we can do much to make assessment an integral part of learning, rather than the end of learning. When students work for a grade, most of them fix their gaze on mediocre compliance, and most teachers have to accept that mediocrity.

Let's look at each of these three arguments in greater depth.

TEACHING STUDENTS ONLY WHAT'S MOST IMPORTANT

We've already talked about this in chapter 4, but it is worth remembering that the gap is huge and growing larger all the time between what our students need to know to prosper as healthy, thoughtful individuals, citizens, workers, and family members and what we can be confident they do know as they pass from course to course, from one level of school to the next. Certainly, little happens in school on an average day that can give us a good answer to the question: "Of all the things we ask students to do in school each day, how much will stay with them and be really useful to them as adults?"

We sometimes like to say that the answer to this question is unfathomable—that it's all part of the mystery of learning, that everyone is different so even if we had the answers, they wouldn't apply to all students. So why even ask? Yet we can easily state what a course syllabus covers, what material we are presenting in a unit, or what of this information the students are expected to recall on the midterm or final exam. We ought to be able to determine what, among the things we have required students to study, they have actually learned and taken to heart and how well their learning will equip them for the challenges ahead in their lives.

We pay a big price as educators for not trying to answer questions like these. Too many of our students don't take school seriously; the community always seems ready to criticize its schools; teachers underestimate their own importance to young people. How well does our curriculum reflect what we want our students to know, be like, and be able to do? Are we teaching the right stuff and the right habits of learning?

THE "RIGHT STUFF" AND THE "WRONG STUFF"

Thoughtful educators like Linda Darling-Hammond, Tony Wagner, and Deborah Meier have long championed our inquiry into such questions and have argued that teachers must have both the time and the power to make curricular decisions based on their deliberations. The answers will probably not surprise anybody. The "right stuff" for us to teach, most would agree, are the foundation skills in literacy, numeracy, citizenship, and the arts, plus whatever we can draw on from our own thoughts and experiences in helping students become eager seekers of complex ideas and critical issues in our subject areas and across the disciplines. Most teachers would agree that we want students to

1. take some delight in the discovery of knowledge
2. work hard to understand what they have discovered
3. be able to select aspects of the subject to pursue in depth
4. work to achieve a level of mastery of key concepts and skills
5. make the vital connection between learning and their lives
6. develop a sense of civic responsibility and personal well-being

The "right stuff" is not some minimalist collection of facts or theories. It should contain much beyond what is practical or utilitarian. It has room for topics and themes from our disciplines that we feel passionate about, even when they appear to have no immediate application. But for these topics, we also must share with students why we are drawn to these areas and what we hope they may appreciate in them. A high school chemistry teacher, in a workshop, was shocked by this realization: "I've talked to all the science and math teachers in his school, and—duh—we all mostly want the same things, you know, scientific method, care in recording and analyzing data, making and proving hypotheses. And yet we teach our various subjects as though they were foreign languages, each with its own grammar, syntax, and vocabulary!"

The "wrong stuff" is almost all the discrete information that teachers have traditionally insisted on talking to students about and testing them on, because

1. we're afraid they won't care to discover it on their own
2. we accept short-term memorization from them in place of in-depth understanding
3. we're convinced they simply *have* to learn it, whether or not it connects with anything important in their lives
4. it's the way *we* were taught in school

A colleague asked a top high school student why he was cramming for the final exam. "Why don't you take the time during the semester to really learn this material, instead of waiting until two days before the exam to cram it all in?" she asked. The boy looked up and said, "With all this stuff to memorize, if I tried to learn it the right way, I wouldn't do nearly as well on the test. By cramming now, I can manage to remember more of it for the test, even if I forget it soon afterwards."

Teachers know that much of what has been built into the syllabus over the years remains a fantasy, a wish-list. But they feel responsible to their discipline to cover the important information. "At least," so they say, "I will have exposed my students to knowledge they may someday see the importance of."

Tony Wagner once surveyed graduates from a highly rated high school three years after their graduation. He asked two questions: "What do you wish you had been taught in high school that would have helped you in college?" and "What were you taught that has not been useful to you?" Their answers were quite similar: They wished they'd had more training in writing at a college level, that they had developed better study skills, and that they'd had more experience working collaboratively with other students. As for the second question, they reported that most of their time in class had been "wasted" and that the factual knowledge, in the sciences especially, was repeated by their college professors, who assumed they had not been well taught.

Time spent merely "exposing" students to knowledge could be spent in much better ways. It gets back to the issue of stance. If we are "the exposers," what position does that put our students—"the exposed"—in? While we are busy exposing our students to information, we diminish their enterprise and invention; if they're listening to us, they're not likely to be doing their own learning (and who knows where the mind of the average teenager has wandered during a lecture?). We don't have to sacrifice content when we set students the task of solving problems of significance and making meaning out of experience. Let me give an example.

HUNTING IN THE CLASSROOM: A LESSON IN NATURAL SELECTION

Most of us would agree that it is important for students to know something about Darwin's theories of evolution and natural selection. At Thayer Junior-Senior High School, in rural Winchester, New Hampshire, I watched a science teacher, Dan Bisaccio, introduce Darwin to a rambunctious group of mostly non-college-bound students.

It was the last period in the day, and as the kids filed into Dan's classroom, they had anything but science on their minds. He had laid out on one desk a multicolored patchwork piece of fabric and asked for four volunteers to go "hunting." In a jar, he had collected some tiny circles of colored construction paper that he had made with a hole-puncher. These, he explained, were the prey that would hide in the camouflage of the multicolored fabric. We would find out, he said, which coloring of this species best protected them from being caught.

As the hunters got into position around the fabric-covered desk, some other students made a graph on the blackboard, with a column for every color in the jar. They made predictions about which colors would be easiest or hardest to spot on the multicolored background. Dan asked the hunters to close their eyes and then he broadcast a small handful of tiny circles onto the fabric. The four were then told to open their eyes and hunt for thirty seconds, picking as many circles as they could, one at a time, off the fabric. Another student held the stopwatch.

When their time was up, the hunters separated their prey by color and reported the results to those at the board. Four more hunters sat down, and the process was repeated. The data grew, and questions and theories about protective coloration came forth spontaneously from the class. Did a bland color of background make the prey more visible than a bright color? When Dan was asked a question, from time to time, he would deftly turn it back: "What do you think?"

Soon it was obvious that the kids had taken charge of the experiment. Hunting (if not Darwin) was a subject many knew something about: Winchester boys regularly call in sick on the first day of deer season and take off for the woods with their fathers.

Halfway through the period, Dan introduced the background material that many teachers think they have to present before their students can begin to work with ideas. He had photocopied two pages from a text on Darwin's major theories and passed them out to the students, putting them into groups of two or three and charging them to "see if this makes any sense, or if it's a bunch of bull. Tear it apart. Write in the margins. Decide what you think. Talk it over for a while, and then we'll discuss it together."

The students turned to the text with the confidence of people who were already players in this field of inquiry. They had helped recreate the context for Darwin's theories; now they were checking out the official version to see how it fit with what they had experienced here in the class and also in life.

They came back with lots of questions. One student asked, "How come both of my parents are athletic yet I stink at sports?" Dan would turn each question over to the class before offering his own views. The discussion went right up to the bell, and some kids lingered to examine the data on the board.

Here is what I believe we would all consider the *right stuff*: the discovery, the data gathering and analysis, the critical confrontation with a text, the discussion and debate. Best of all, here is the willing engagement of students with difficult content material—no conflict between process and content, no pushing self-esteem at the expense of intellectual challenge. Just good science. What Dan Bisaccio did was to help his students discover Darwin as amateur scientists, as hunter-gatherers of insights, rather than as passive consumers of prepackaged information. He made the choice to cover less material but to pursue the essential concepts in depth. He opted to teach what's important.

Dan is a talented teacher, but so are many others. His methods and the higher levels of student engagement they produce can be our methods and results if we have the time and the will to integrate them into the curriculum. Throughout the day, in every school building in America, teachers are devising lessons every bit as exciting as Dan Bisaccio's.

GIVING STUDENTS REAL JOBS TO DO

What can kids do? Teachers tell me that they are often surprised at the transformation that occurs when students are unexpectedly challenged by a problem or crisis that comes out of the blue and engages students' thoughtfulness and energy. By contrast, when it's business as usual (lectures, homework, exams), kids often behave as though it's their job to avoid taking responsibility for getting the work done. As adults, we somehow contrive, despite ourselves, to make learning seem irrelevant and end up with a number of kids who trivialize their engagement with learning to the point where school becomes an arena of passive conformity, of tuning out or goofing off. But I believe that teachers can do much to help students take themselves, their community, and their planet more seriously. Perhaps the best thing teachers can do is to give students a real job. Here are a few examples:

- A high school chemistry teacher challenged a group of students in her mid-level chemistry class to write a pamphlet on good nutrition, which would be placed in waiting rooms of local doctors' offices. At first the students responded in a typical, ho-hum fashion. But once they realized that their work had to be good enough to earn the respect of doctors whom they knew, their attitude changed markedly, and they were able to produce an excellent pamphlet.
- I visited an elementary school where the librarian was trying to decide what to do with a load of old books from a school that had been recently closed. She decided to ask the oldest kids, fifth graders, to become literary critics—to read and rate the books as "hidden treasure," or "okay for kids who like: ______________," or "get rid of it!"
- A teacher of Spanish in a rural high school wondered how to help her second-year Spanish students get over their shyness about speaking the language. She also wished she had time

to give younger kids a head start in Spanish so that they'd be more interested in a foreign language when they arrived at high school. She decided to have her second-year students go to the elementary school and teach a Spanish lesson once a week to third-grade classes.

- A teacher of eleventh-grade remedial English asked her students to write stories and read them to first graders at the nearby elementary school. The older students, who had come to see themselves as failures, got an enthusiastic reception from the little kids, who asked to keep the stories to read again, and then wrote some of their own stories to present to the older students. "It transformed my class," the teacher told me. "They began to feel like writers, not recipients of remedial services."

We all know examples like these: students building a ramp at the home of a fellow student who's been disabled, helping operate a soup kitchen for the homeless, assisting local environmental groups to catalog wildlife or analyze water samples from a polluted stream, or working with the police to help younger kids avoid violence. But we know these things as special events, enrichment activities, extracurricular projects. We need to see them as the *main event*, as jobs that replace—not just supplement—those tired old lesson plans. There is hardly an instructional unit that cannot be transformed into a job that students can plan, organize, carry out, and complete for the good of the community. Only then will we feel their pride and see how capable students are. An example of this for an English or language arts class would be to suggest that every major writing assignment should have a real audience outside the school. All student writing should have a "real" audience, whether it involves writing letters to the editor; complaints to manufacturers about shoddy products; stories or poems for older folks or younger kids; speeches for candidates seeking public office; handbooks on topics such as violence prevention, self-respect, cultural diversity, or protecting our environment; or researching and writing about significant persons in their family history.

Once students realize that they are writing not only—not even primarily—for their teacher, they can more easily accept the teacher as a writing coach, as someone who can help them reach their preferred audience. And teachers can avoid finding themselves stuck with assignments that nobody cared about writing in the first place. A story is often told about Robert Frost, then an aspiring poet, teaching English at a high school in Derry, New Hampshire. After collecting essays from his students, he casually asked, "Please raise your hand if you want to get your essay back after I have given you a grade on it." When no hand went up, Frost tossed the whole batch in the wastepaper basket. "If you don't care about what you have written, I surely don't want to waste my time reading it."

It doesn't have to be English, of course. If we are serious about coaching, we can help students become better thinkers and better writers on almost any topic. But it is essential that they understand and accept the concept of quality work and that they take part in fleshing out that concept. It will take time for them to accept that ownership, but the rewards can be substantial.

A teacher might begin by handing her class a sample of student work—a history paper, a lab report, an English composition, or a piece of architectural drafting—that she (and hopefully they) consider worthy of an A. She then asks them to transform that piece of student work into one worth only a B, allowing plenty of discussion of just what might diminish its quality by one grade. The students proceed to turn the work into a C, then a D, and finally into an F piece (if she is still using D and F as grades). This exercise should be a lot of fun, having students for once act as "graders." To save some time, the teacher could divide the class into four groups and have one work on the B model, one on the C model, and so forth. The teacher might also want to do the whole thing backward, starting with an unacceptable piece of work and having the students transform it, by stages, into one worthy of an A.

In the end, the teacher will have brought her students right into the discussion of standards, and they will have provided themselves with valid models to support shared criteria for awarding grades. Not only will it make the teacher's grading seem less subjective and arbitrary to her students, but it may foster in students the habits of self-assessment and self-correction since they will have conceptualized the skills of improving their work. I actually tried this experiment way back in the 1960s when I was teaching freshman English while working on my master's degree. It was great fun.

COACHING, INSTEAD OF GRADING, STUDENTS

It is striking how much testing and grading dominate the atmosphere of learning in the daily life of students, and how destructive this can be to the relationship between students and teachers. Life has many trials in store for today's youth, but rarely will they take the form of paper-and-pencil tests. Life has many rewards for effort and achievement (and sanctions for the lack thereof), almost none of which will involve letter grades. Yet tests and grades drive the machinery of learning in schools: "You'd better write it down—it may be on the test," or "I flunked the midterm; now the best I can hope for is a C," or the omnipresent "Whadja get?" Such discourse reduces learning to symbols that have only fleeting significance. The whole process insults the intelligence of teachers and students.

ALFRED KAZIN'S NIGHTMARE

I just picked up Alfred Kazin's 1951 autobiographical sketch, *A Walker in the City*. Here is a passage that relates his impressions of school as a young student:

> It was never learning I associated with that school: only the necessity to succeed, to get ahead of the others in the daily struggle to "make a good impression" on our teachers, who grimly, wearily, and often with ill-concealed distaste watched against our relapsing into the natural savagery they expected of Brownsville boys. The white, cool, thinly ruled record book sat over us from their desks all day long, and had remorselessly entered into it each day—in blue ink if we had passed, in red ink if we had not—our attendance, our conduct, our "effort," our merits and demerits; and to the last possible decimal point in calculation, our standing in an unending series of "tests"—surprise tests, daily tests, weekly tests, formal midterm tests, final tests. They never stopped trying to dig out of us whatever small morsel of fact we had managed to get down the night before. We had to prove that we were really alert, ready for anything, always in the race. That white thinly ruled record book figured in my mind as the judgment seat; the very thinness and remote blue lightness of its lines instantly showed its cold authority over me; so much space had been left on each page, columns and columns in which to note down everything about us, implacably and forever. As it lay there on a teacher's

> desk, I stared at it all day long with such fear and anxious propriety that I had no trouble believing that God, too, did nothing but keep such record books, and that on the final day, He would face me with an account in Hebrew letters whose phonetic dots and dashes looked strangely like decimal points counting up my every sinful thought on earth.[1]

Is this what people mean when they demand that we get "back to the basics"? Time, tests, and grades are still the currency of schooling. Everything students do in school is calculated as a function of time spent and grades received. Yet time and grades are about the worst incentives we could devise for getting students to think hard and produce work of high quality. As motivators of excellence, grades are awful. Almost nothing in real life gets graded. Eggs, maybe. There is hardly a non-school learning program that relies on letter grades or time spent as measures of achievement. Every corporation, agency, and organization that trains its own employees—from McDonald's and Xerox to teaching hospitals to the US Army—has developed a far more accurate and purposeful measure of learner achievement: it's called *performance*, and it is aimed at producing quality.

Progressive educators have long sought active and realistic ways to display and measure what students know, ways more in keeping with the demands for proficiency that life places upon us. But this has made little difference in our schools. We're stuck, most of us, in an educational system built around time, tests, and grades, and the price we pay is that few students bother to show us their best stuff. Most of the time, they don't even know why we are asking them to do the work. Typically, when teachers hand back assignments or exams, students glance at the grade and throw it away. Their work has no further utility. Learning is over. A teacher's attempt to get students to reflect upon their work, to consider how their ideas might be extended or deepened, is met with polite indifference or with that question, again: "Will it change my grade?"

"Ah," we sigh, "if only you understood the value of learning for learning's sake." But such pieties ignore the dictates of the very system we perpetuate. Teachers are likely to overlook the "learning for learning's sake" their students actually do in their lives if it doesn't fit into the syllabus, if there's no column for it in the grade book or online system.

The closest they get is the notion of extra credit assignments, which isn't very close at all.

THE SAVAGE EFFICIENCY OF PLAYING THE GAME

Whether one is an A student or a hang-on-and-pray D student, the rules of school life demand a savage efficiency: Give the teacher the minimum required for the grade you seek. Anything more is foolish. I first learned this lesson myself in fourth grade. My teacher had put a book report chart on the wall with everybody's name on it, and we got a star for every book read. My first book, *Shooting Star*, was a long and fascinating biography of the great warrior Tecumseh. I loved this book and felt proud of having read all its three-hundred-plus pages. But by the time I had handed in my book report, there were four or five stars next to the names of most of my classmates. I got smart. I understood what the game was about. The very next book I chose was a slim volume with lots of pictures, called *Boats on the River*. It was inane and babyish, but it had the one thing that poor Tecumseh lacked: brevity. I could read it, whip out a book report, and earn my star in a single afternoon. I remember the vaguely distressed look on my teacher's face when I handed in that book report, as if she was just now realizing the "race to the bottom" she had initiated.

GETTING SNARED BY YOUR GRADING

Ironically, much of the impetus for the dysfunctional grading system teachers work under stems from their idealism. Teachers want to be what everyone says life is not—they want to be *fair*. Nothing about their personality or actions is as important to students, it seems, as being fair. And they take that challenge very seriously. It is a rare teacher who has not worked out an intricate and detailed system of compiling, weighting, averaging, curving grades to come up with a schema capable of being carried to the fourth decimal point. But it's a trap—for them and for their students. They get snared by a refrain that goes like this:

If the work is important to student learning, I should *assign* it
If I assign it and they do it, I must *read* it
If I read it, I should *critique* or *edit* it
If I critique it, I must *grade* it

If I grade it, I must *enter* that grade in my book
If I enter it, I must *average* it with other assignments
If I average it, it must *count* toward the course grade

Instead of working with students on a short list of things that really matter, on ideas and concepts and projects of substance, teachers and students end up chasing one-page assignments—work the student did or didn't do, completed but lost, submitted but was misplaced, or that supposedly no longer counted, and so on.

At best, this system offers the teacher some protection against the irate parent who storms in accusing the teacher of condemning the kid to a rotten life all because "she didn't know it counted," or "he's a much better student than his grade shows." Whatever the charge, you're protected by the entries in your grading system—the letter grades, number grades, checks, check/pluses or check/minuses, stars for extra credit, zeros for quizzes missed and not made up, or homework not handed in. Parents or students can accuse you of unfairness, but they can never make it stick. But ultimately teachers are trapped behind their grade books in a fortress that keeps too much student excellence outside. We can't just abandon grades since that would only increase everyone's anxiety and result in making grades—or whatever we've substituted—ever more the focus of attention, ever more a diversion from the true purposes of learning.

CHRISTINE SULLIVAN'S THEORY OF WRITING

So how do we cope with student resistance to doing things carefully, to working hard at something until they master it, to taking pride in setting and reaching high standards of performance? How, aside from holding the threat of grade punishment over their heads, can we get them to work hard? Let's look at how Christine Sullivan—an English teacher who, at the time of my interview, had seventeen years of high school teaching experience in Plainville, Connecticut—managed to break out of that fortress.

> My students compile portfolios of their work. To begin their portfolios, they assess their abilities in a very general way and rank them against the Intended Learning Outcomes that the adults in the school have

established. These outcomes talk about "skills, habits, and dispositions" more than about individual pieces of production. When the semester begins, I show them the Intended Learning Outcomes and they fill out a form entitled "Skills Used in Language Arts" that lists the five areas: Reading, Writing, Speaking, Listening, Viewing. Next to each item or sub-heading are the levels they think they have already achieved: "competent, good, very good" or "super." On the back of this sheet, they formulate three goals to work for this semester. Periodically during the course, they meet with their study group and talk about how well they are achieving their goals. As the year goes on, the whole issue of grades becomes less and less significant and, in fact, is replaced by students trying to demonstrate in their portfolios the characteristics that the class is organized around: Reading, Writing, etc.

Four times a semester students make a goal statement that expresses not the grade, specifically, but the skill development or outcome they are working for. Grades limit what students see as being worth striving for, and grading becomes a wall, a roadblock. If, on the other hand, you say to a student: "You need to show range, flexibility, fluency, to show you've developed the habits and dispositions of a literate person"—then nobody knows what the ceiling is. And, if you reinforce appropriate responses and provide appropriate models, you never arrive at the point where a student can say, "Well, I have a 92.4 average, so I don't have to work anymore!"

Students I had three years ago—now seniors—have become revolutionaries in the classroom. They tend to assert their own learning styles. If a teacher says, "Do it this way," they are likely to respond, "I think that is a better way for me to do it, and the product will be better if I do it my way." Other teachers sometimes see that as impertinent—but the kids talk that way because it is how they see work, how they organize their own attitudes toward work.

It's a very slow process; it doesn't happen overnight. At first, of course, students are often confused. They plead, "Just tell me what to do, and I'll do it." And my answer is to ask, "What are you looking to accomplish? What do you want to produce?" If they respond by saying "I'm just trying to get a good grade," I just turn it around and recast it, time and time again. Some of them who are used to getting A's by doing exactly what their teachers ask of them become full of questions—"Well, is this way you want it, Mrs. Sullivan? Is this long enough? Have I answered your question?"—even when I did not give them a question or a specific length. It takes them, often, a long time to discover that they need to make those definitions—but when they do figure it out, they're wonderful to work with.

I see myself teaching them habits of thinking and of working with knowledge, and I use the grading system as a way to teach learning skills, rather than as a way to measure their compliance. But it's a gradual process. It ends up that I fill out a lot of "grade-change" forms. As I prepare to give them grades for the last quarter, we go back and look at that first quarter report card and I ask, "Does that grade still reflect what you now know about those areas of knowledge and skills? Or have you learned some things you didn't yet know then?" Because learning doesn't always happen by October 28th. In fact, just this week (in mid-December), I had a student hand me work that should have been done the second week of October. But she just got it, she understood it, and she went back and did it.

So, grading is a way for me to build a different kind of relationship with my students, and they with me. But more than that, it's a way for them to build a different kind of relationship to the content area and to their own production within it. I don't want to know if a kid has a 76 average. I want to know if a kid is becoming a literate person and has such a feeling for the literary arts that he can continue to grow as a literate person without someone having to be there to prod him. I think independence, flexibility, and this whole idea of being literate is a whole lot more important than a 76, and I believe that if you leave a door open, if you leave a hole in the ceiling, people will grow right through it, rather than saying, "Okay, I've got my B+, so now I'll stop."[2]

20

THE PARENTS' PERSPECTIVE

What Is My Kid Actually Learning?

> *What the best and wisest parent wants for his own child, that must the community want for all of its children. Any other ideal for our schools is narrow and unlovely; acted upon, it destroys our democracy.*
>
> —JOHN DEWEY, *The School and Society*

WE HAVE NO IDEA

In years past, my wife and I met with our sons' teachers in middle school and high school. Most had taken great care to try to know their students personally, a difficult task when working with large numbers. They told us how our boys interacted in class, and they knew precisely what their grades were and how they had earned them. But we talked little about what our sons actually knew and could do as learners in science, English, math, history, and so forth.

I am reminded of a comment I heard from Ted Sizer, who used to teach high school history: "If you tell me you are taking American history and it is mid-November, I have a pretty good idea what topic you are studying, no matter where in the nation your school is, or whether it is public, private or parochial. But if you say you got a B+ in the course, I have no idea what you know about American history."[1]

The attention teachers and parents should pay to the essential goals of learning—the skills, attitudes, and knowledge we want children to acquire and apply—gets crowded out of the teacher-parent conversation by concerns about grades and behavior. Parents seem to want most to know "How's she getting along?" "Is he a nice kid?" "Is she keeping up with the top students?" "How'd he do on that last test?" as though they will discover through the teacher's eyes some crucial aspect of a child's personality that has eluded them or some confirmation that they are doing a good enough job raising their kid. What parents seem to be looking for is reassurance. And, for lack of more substantial information, that's what they often get.

Teachers are likely to respond with "Nick is a very nice boy, a bit of a loner sometimes, but his grades are right up there. I think you have nothing to worry about"; or "Megan has been slipping a bit lately in her homework assignments, but she seemed to do well on the midterm. If she can get back on track, she's headed for an A or B+"; or "Kenny has shown some improvement in his quiz average since we had a little talk two weeks ago, and it's up to an 82. He contributes regularly in class." And parents are often lulled into believing they have received useful information on a child's progress when, in fact, they have been told very little at all about what their child is actually learning.

It's not that these teachers' comments are unimportant—they often do have insights into aspects of a child's personal development and work habits. But shouldn't we all be mostly concerned about whether, or how well, our kids are *learning*?

As parents, we sometimes feel we are invited into school on parent conference day to take a peek into the Forbidden City—a place from which we are all but banished by our children's reluctance to have us pry into their life in school (where they have a chance to define their personality apart from the family), and by teachers' anxiety about being judged by our preconceptions about what should be happening in the classroom. One can almost feel the tension in the air, during open school night, as teachers who have years of experience talking in front of groups get awkward and nervous with parents in their classrooms for a ten-minute summary of the course.

One problem at the secondary-school level is that the traditional syllabus poorly describes what teachers and students actually do in class or what students are expected to learn. Typically, course catalogs are written in the passive voice, with phrases like "Students will be introduced to . . ."; or "In this course, the student is expected to become familiar with . . ."; or "This course will cover the following topics . . ."—none of which say much about what students will actually know how to do as a result of successfully completing the course of studies.

What parents and students should get from teachers at regular intervals is a list of the key concepts, skills, and performances that their school and teachers expect them to accomplish in each course or program area; some reference, perhaps, to how those concepts and skills are linked to other parts of the curriculum; an indication next to each item of how far the student has progressed in attaining the desired results; and a comment on whether the child is behaving well and working hard.

Communication from the teacher on the skills and knowledge that the student is expected to acquire or master will also help students assume responsibility for actually learning what needs to be learned, rather than continuing to believe that their job is merely to come to class prepared and do what they're told. It will also help parents know where their child might need better supervision or extra help in acquiring or practicing a particular skill that they know is important to learn or an attitude that comports with being part of a community.

A PROGRESS REPORT THAT ACTUALLY REPORTS PROGRESS

Here is my design for a one-page progress report that teachers can hand to students (and send to parents) at the beginning of the course, and that should be updated every six weeks or so. I often used this format in the courses I taught at the university level, but I think this format is appropriate for grades 7 through 12, and even earlier.

Course Title: ______________________________

Grade Level: ______________________________

Date: ______________________________

Skills to Be Learned

Three to five skills areas that are essential to the student's being able to do work in this field: the types of reading expected; verbal skills for class discussions; the use of media, tools, or laboratory equipment; the research tasks to be accomplished; the ability to synthesize information from a variety of sources, etc.

Knowledge/Concepts to Be Learned

The basic concepts, theories, and categories of information that are central to the student's being able to work in this field—the areas of knowledge or content that students are expected to comprehend and really know (not just "be exposed to" or memorize for short-term recall).

Attitudes to Be Demonstrated

The interpersonal attitudes, cooperative work norms, class rules, and other key behavioral objectives; plus the "habits of mind" or "dispositions" that a teacher might want to highlight as necessary to work in this field, and aspects of tact or sensitivity that are viewed as important values to be demonstrated.

Linkages to Other Disciplines and Critical Skills Areas

How this course is linked to departmental, school-wide, or system-wide objectives (such as communication, problem-solving, motivation, etc.), so students and parents can see how the course reinforces essential areas of skill and knowledge.

Achievement Level

At the right-hand column of this page, next to each of the items listed under "Skills," "Knowledge," and "Attitudes" to be learned, teachers can check off how well a student is progressing in each area, using the format or rubric they have decided on, such as:

1 = Beginning level of awareness; student competence unknown or inadequate
2 = Partial competence; student able to apply some information and skills
3 = Basic understanding; student able to apply info/skills to known situations
4 = Sophisticated understanding; student able to find new and/or creative applications

Instructor's Comments Regarding Attitude, Effort, Consistency, and Citizenship

Here's how a progress report for a typical foreign-language class might look, using the 1–4 rubric for Achievement Level. Other examples could be drawn from the course outlines in the following chapter.

A SAMPLE PROGRESS REPORT

Foreign-Language Study (French or Spanish)

Skills to Be Learned:	*Achievement Level:*			
1. Able to speak and make yourself understood regarding basic needs and wishes as a visitor to a French/Spanish-speaking community	1	2	3	4
2. Able to understand basic efforts of a native Spanish speaker to communicate with you about everyday topics	1	2	3	4
3. Able to use a language dictionary to look up common words and phrases	1	2	3	4
4. Able to write simple phrases, using learned vocabulary	1	2	3	4

Knowledge/Concepts to Be Learned:	*Achievement Level:*			
1. Understands present, simple past, and future tenses of the verbs to be, to have, to go, to come, to see, to speak, to understand	1	2	3	4
2. Able to count to 100; tell time, date, and year; and describe yourself simply	1	2	3	4
3. Able to describe your family, your hobbies, and twenty-five objects in a house	1	2	3	4
4. Able to read street signs, danger warnings, telephone instructions	1	2	3	4

Attitudes to Be Demonstrated:	*Achievement Level:*			
1. Willing to take part in discussions in Spanish on topics of interest	1	2	3	4
2. Able to take risks in trying to express simple ideas, needs, or feelings even when you don't know all the vocabulary or verbs	1	2	3	4
3. Shows appreciation and enjoyment of differences between our culture and that of speakers of French/Spanish	1	2	3	4
4. Willing to experience new situations and to help others overcome obstacles to learning a foreign language	1	2	3	4

Achievement Level:
In place of the 1–4 Achievement Level rubric, the teacher could use a simple "Yes/No" checklist, or redefine 1–4 so that 1 = Novice, 2 = Adequate, 3 = Proficient, and 4 = Advanced/Excellent.

Instructor's Comments:

____

____

____

____

____

This progress report contains neither a complete syllabus for a course nor all the factors that determine a student's final grade. (We will examine such a framework in a later chapter.) But it does permit teachers to assess their students' actual learning and to share that information with parents. I believe it helps everyone stay focused on the things most important for students in the long run: acquiring and applying critical skills, knowledge, and attitudes.

When we compare this example with the progress reports most schools now send to parents, we realize how poorly our current models and methods communicate the fundamental purposes of school to students and their parents and how much of the essential aspects of curriculum students are actually learning. Few parents ask for information like this, and few teachers offer it. We are not used to thinking about teaching and learning in these ways; it didn't happen for us when we were in school.

Once students, parents, and teachers begin to think about the curriculum in terms of what kinds of knowledge we want students to have, what skills we expect them to develop and apply, and what attitudes toward learning, work, and citizenship we want them to acquire and practice, a new basis for parent-teacher-student conversations is created. No more will conferences be restricted to "What's his average?" or "How's she getting along?" or "How many homework assignments are missing?" We can talk about, "What is my kid actually learning of the things she is supposed to learn?" or "How can we each do our part to help him accomplish these agreed-upon goals?"

Once teachers have done the admittedly difficult work of distilling their course content into these essential areas and finding authentic ways to assess how well students can perform, the effort to communicate regularly with parents about student progress will allow for a much more useful partnership between home and school. Parents will be clearer about how to help their children meet the expectations. Supplemental tutoring in or outside of school can be organized around the student's acquisition and assessment of core content and skills rather than focusing mostly on raising grades.

Such progress reports (which are actually course summaries) are also useful within the school since teachers can share them with each other and reinforce essential skills and attitudes across the grade and throughout the entire school. It is easier for students to develop the right attitudes and acquire the necessary skills if they know that their teachers agree on what's important. What sharing happens now in schools is mostly in areas of student discipline ("No gum chewing or wearing hats anywhere in school!"), preparedness ("Everyone comes to class with pencil, homework, and text!"), or study habits ("You should keep a notebook for each course where teachers can see the steps you take in solving a problem or the drafts you produce when writing a theme"). We haven't yet reached consensus on what it actually means for students to be able to perform the most important academic things, like thinking, experimenting, creating, synthesizing, and documenting. Students go from class to class, teacher to teacher, reacting to each course as though it were a different country with its own laws, language, currency, and norms. No wonder students and their parents are easily confused as to what "school" is all about.

THE ESSENTIAL SKILLS WE NEGLECT TO TEACH

I saw the effects of such a lack of consensus many years ago when I was asked to assist an after-school science program for gifted students in grades 5 through 8. This program focused on the sea, and, after six weeks, students were asked to develop and present a project of their own on some aspect of marine life. The displays were lovely: wave machines, pollution surveys, papier-mâché sharks hanging from the ceilings.

But when it came to presenting their work to the audience, these elite, motivated students resembled a most ordinary bunch. Some spoke right up, entertaining us with the story of their project, its mishaps and its triumphs. Others read more or less articulately from their notes, keeping to the text. But a significant number of these gifted kids could hardly speak at all: They mumbled inaudibly, eyes averted and feet shuffling nervously, and then sat down. "My God!" I thought, "Nobody's taught these kids to talk! Their teachers must all have decided that it was somebody else's responsibility to teach them how to address an audience."

It's best when teachers, students, and parents can join a school- or district-wide discussion about core academic skills and attitudes. Where such a forum does not yet exist, teachers can get together with colleagues within their grade, faculty team, department, or curriculum block (e.g., math/science, humanities/arts, tech ed/business) and devise common areas of emphasis for students. Who besides English teachers, for example, is responsible for getting kids to write and edit their work? In what classes will research skills or public speaking be emphasized?

If teachers can communicate regularly with parents about such expectations, they gain powerful allies in the struggle for excellence. During the final years of our children's high school, my wife and I received one-page outlines at the beginning of the year from some of their teachers, talking about the purpose of the course and what we could expect our sons to know and do as a result of completing it successfully. The outlines gave us a perspective on what would actually be going on in their classes and how our own family discussions, homework guidelines, vacation trips, and holiday gifts might reinforce what they were studying.

Whether we look at learning from the eyes of the student, the teacher, or the parent, the pursuit of excellence will remain an elusive, highly subjective and confusing endeavor until we are able to talk clearly about what *excellence* and *mastery* mean (as well as other appropriate indicators of achievement). Unless we know what our young people are expected to be able to accomplish, apply, and retain in their learning—unless we communicate regularly about what it means to do these things well—"success" in schooling will continue to be defined by whether kids do what they are told to do by their teachers, with rewards or sanctions tied to their compliance with tasks and assignments that may not mean very much to them. We all deserve better.

PART FIVE

THE COURSE

21

TEACHING HISTORY IN AN INTELLECTUALLY HONEST WAY WITHOUT GETTING FIRED

Today's teachers exist in a long line of great educators who inspired us to make tomorrow better. You do the work that nourishes our society and pushes us towards a better community.

—GEORGE HAWKINS,
South Dakota 2024 Teacher of the Year

This is my tenth year teaching. I was drawn to this profession as an important responsibility, and it feels even more so today. I think the difference is that the work just seems to be more critical. In producing strong and independent and responsible young critical readers and writers and thinkers, the stakes feel higher, especially considering the discourse happening on a national level. Are we preparing them for the world that we exist in?

—TRAVIS NASON, high school English teacher

KEEPING BAYARD RUSTIN IN THE MIX

My nephew's wife, Corey Lynn Fried, is a social studies teacher at a middle school in rural Pennsylvania, not too far from where the renowned civil rights leader Bayard Rustin grew up. (Rustin organized the 1963 March on Washington that gave rise to MLK's "I Have a Dream" speech.) In her unit "People Who Changed the World Through Non-Violence," she encourages each of her seventh graders to pick one nonviolent change leader, study that person in depth, and then share what they've learned with their classmates. Here's how Corey Lynn describes what happened one year:

> After Rustin's death, we learned that he was gay, and when I listed him as one of the leaders my students could choose to research, a parent complained to my principal about my including him, because he was gay. The principal called me down to his office and suggested I find someone else. I objected, saying that not only was Rustin a central figure in the civil rights movement but also someone with local connections.
>
> "I understand," my principal said, "but I'm just hoping to avoid any further blowback from the community." "Well," I replied, "I suppose that kind of concern goes with your job description, but I haven't yet received any objections from any of my parents, so I intend to keep Bayard Rustin in the mix."
>
> "You don't really want to die on that hill, do you?" he asked—to which I responded, "As a lifelong advocate for equality and the mother of two biracial children, if that's the hill I have to die on, it's just as good as any other, I suppose."

Eight years later, Corey Lynn still teaches the unit, and Bayard Rustin is still one of the leaders her students can choose to research.

Not every history or social studies teacher is going to be confronted by an administrator asking—or demanding—that you censor curricula you have thoughtfully designed to teach about America's past and present triumphs and tragedies. But each of you undoubtedly has this question on your mind: At a time when the political rhetoric about issues like civil rights, women's rights, immigrants' rights, the rights of people with different gender identities, questions about the status of our democracy, and the veracity of America's historical record is more inflamed than at any time in recent memory, what's a teacher to do?

You want to be true to your values: to inspire your students to seek the truth and to make up—and sometimes to change—their own minds. You want to help them celebrate what is noble and great about our country but also to understand where we have been unfair in our treatment of various groups in our society—from our depredation of native American homelands, to our centuries of enslavement and Jim Crow, to our struggles over women's suffrage, to imprisoning Japanese American citizens during World War II, to our varying attitudes and policies regarding same sex marriage and the treatment of immigrants.

But you'd probably like to avoid battles with school officials, school boards, parents, and others who believe that what is taught in public schools doesn't comport with their family's religious or political beliefs. You don't want to be cowed or intimidated by people hostile to the teaching of our past and current conflicts, but you also don't want to be a lightning rod for public controversy, having students secretly recording you as you teach and making your lessons fodder for community controversies. In protecting your job or your good standing in the school and community, you are likely willing to make adjustments and compromises. But to what extent? And at what cost?

This, from Andrea Levin:

> If someone is an Advanced Placement US History teacher in Texas, that person will probably feel themself torn between teaching what is necessary to acquire college-level academic skills and their state legislators' belief about the role of public schools in reinforcing a positive American identity based on narratives that may be incomplete or historically inaccurate.[1]

TAYLOR BUSSINGER: NAVIGATING UNEASY WATERS AS A SOCIAL STUDIES TEACHER

Taylor Bussinger has faced this dilemma throughout his career as a middle school social studies teache in Kansas, but perhaps never before as acutely. He recently wrote to me:

> Our schools do not operate in a vacuum. Whether it be divisive rhetoric, technological advancement, or socioemotional needs, it's clear that society's triumphs and shortcomings all trickle their way into our schools. As much as some might want to shield our young people from the political, cultural, or social conversations that might be taking place in our world, we simply cannot afford to do so. Our young people will be hearing and/or taking part in the dialogue in some way, whether inside or outside our classrooms. It seems reasonable that the American social studies classroom should be a safe space to wrestle and grapple with discussions and dialogue happening in our current climate. Here we can protect and

> elevate student voices, model perspective taking, teach critical thinking, empathy, and how to effectively disagree so we can hopefully build common ground. If not in school, where will young people learn to engage in critical conversations?
>
> I believe that social studies educators from across the United States should take the current divisions of our country to heart and work to create more unified and empathetic communities. I know there is push-back to this idea. We hear a lot about indoctrination or stakeholders not wanting the teacher to push an agenda. I do not know a single teacher that is pushing an agenda or seeking to indoctrinate ideology. The teachers I know simply want to promote critical thinking, consensus building, and allow students to converse appropriately. The data behind critical conversations and dynamic dialogue seems clear from national studies: Students who engage in frequent current-events discussions far outscore students who do not.
>
> So, posing the question that was posed to me recently—Is it worth shunning dynamic dialogue in order to stay comfortable while jeopardizing our students' future? Or should we model appropriate behavior in these critical conversations and allow students to engage? My belief is that social studies teachers should be trusted as the professionals we are to navigate the complexities of students' voice, perspective, and opinions.
>
> Two weeks ago, during a Socratic Seminar, my student said something so profound that it will stick with me the rest of my life: "What we learn is who we become and who we become is what we put out into the world." The kids in my class desire to know the truth about our history and they want to engage in dialogue about it. My eighth-grade students know the importance of what they learn and are already reflecting about what version of themselves they are going to put out into the world. They want to be informed, they want to have a voice, and they want to engage with others. We must allow space and provide coaching to help our students meet that challenge.[2]

What this book will not do is offer up a one-size-fits-all solution to this dilemma. Everyone's situation is unique. Do you have tenure? Does your district have a policy that guarantees academic freedom? Have your colleagues and academic leaders discussed this issue and come up with principles and guidelines (and shared them with parents and the community)? How does the political climate in your state and community regard teaching so-called "controversial topics"? At best, perhaps, we can offer a few general words of guidance.

The first is to be open with your students about the pursuit of the truth, asking them (in your own words and as part of building and maintaining trust): "How can we learn about our history and our current events and controversies in America and in the world so we all can still feel safe and respected?" "How can we read and write and talk about controversial issues—like freedom and fairness, like privilege and poverty, like our rights and responsibilities as citizens—and be free to disagree or agree, while always respecting our freedom as Americans to form our own opinions?"

APPLYING PRODUCTIVE LEARNING PRINCIPLES TO CONTROVERSIAL TOPICS

The same principles that guide the creation of a safe and productive environment for learning apply to teaching history and social studies and the controversial issues that continue to surround us. We begin with curiosity and open-ended questions. A good topic to begin with might be how children have been treated at various points in our history. What was it like to be a child in the days when most of us were farmers? When some children were born into slavery? When children worked long hours in factories? When the idea of "child labor laws" was introduced—who opposed such laws, and how did they eventually become the law of the land? What is it like for children in other parts of the world right now who do not have the rights and protections that we have? What's the "right amount of freedom" for children of your age? And maybe even, what role should students play in making and revising school rules?

As you address topics in the curriculum—controversial or not—allowing for choice is essential to create and maintain respect among your students and between them and yourself. When students can choose their own way of responding to academic "requirements," it takes much of the educational bullying out of the learning process while at the same time increasing student ownership of learning. When local or state officials mandate that certain things must be, or may not be, taught that can itself be a form of anti-democratic pedagogy. Faced with such constraints, how can you as a teacher find a way to give your students the maximum freedom to approach required or forbidden topics in a spirit of democratic inquiry?

You have no doubt noticed by now that I am asking a lot more questions while providing few answers. I am expressly modeling how such a stance might guide your teaching of contentious topics. Taylor Bussinger has something important to add here:

> All this being stated, I do feel the pressure and resistance from outside voices. I am nervous to engage in these conversations and fear being slandered by a politician or stakeholder. Ultimately, I rely on perspective taking. I promise my students and parents that I will never share my beliefs or ideas with my students. I reserve the right to challenge ideas from conflicting perspectives and try hard to make sure I am remaining impartial.

Relating what they are learning to people out in the community can be another great way of helping your students "own" their learning. Interviewing family members and relatives or neighbors is one way to allow students to discover knowledge, rather than merely ingest it. Consider bringing in people who have lived through key experiences (e.g., veterans, people who have been involved with various social movements, people responsible for making or enforcing our laws). My mom, as a third-grade teacher working on a unit on American Indians in the 1950s, scoured the New York City telephone book until she saw the name "Red Cloud." She called the number and found a woman of Native American heritage who was willing to come to her class to talk with her students. It is that kind of initiative that makes for a passionate teacher. And it is the courage and determination of today's teachers like Corey Lynn and Taylor to stand up for the truth and defend their right to help students find their truths that will bring us through this period of cynicism and denial.

22

DISSECTING THE COURSE—AND RESURRECTING IT

We enunciate two educational commandments:
"Do not teach too many subjects," and again,
"What you teach, teach thoroughly."

—ALFRED NORTH WHITEHEAD,
The Aims of Education

PRAGMATIC STRATEGIES TO TRANSFORM YOUR SYLLABUS

For a teacher who has reached this point in the book, the tension between its provocative ideas and the everyday realities of life in school may be reaching a breaking point. Let me offer some relief in the form of specific steps and pragmatic strategies to put our passions to work in the classroom, where it counts most.

We begin with the most obvious feature on the pedagogical landscape: the course. In taking apart and reconstructing a typical high school or middle school course, we will put into practice many of the theoretical arguments from previous chapters, especially chapter 5's framework for categories of content knowledge, chapter 7's design for a performance-based unit, and the emphasis in chapters 4 and 19 on teaching what's most important, giving students real jobs, and coaching instead of judging. Elementary grade teachers can apply much of this chapter to the instructional units they teach.

The unit of instruction called the course is under attack for its failure to deliver the goods—taking or passing a course offers no proof in itself that a student has gained much of lasting value. What might be the result if high school teachers were to give an exam to former students who got an A or B on that same exam a year earlier? I recently heard a speaker dare his audience of teachers and principals to sit down and take, under identical conditions, the very exams in math, science, and social studies now given to eleventh graders in their school systems to see how much of their own high school and college learning they still retained. The implication of these challenges is that what we teach in a traditional course may have little staying power, and how we measure learning may be a poor predictor of future academic success.

Many teachers are exploring alternatives to the 45-minute, 180-day course as a vehicle of instruction, such as 80–120-minute blocks of instruction or back-to-back classes on interdisciplinary themes. Other experiments include senior thesis seminars, workplace apprenticeships, research projects, skills labs, independent study, portfolio development workshops, and extended projects in community settings.

But until it is replaced or complemented in your secondary school by other curriculum structures, the 45–50-minute course will likely remain the basic unit of learning. It has certain advantages: It allows teachers and students to focus their attention on a specific body of information and skills over a semester or year. It permits teachers who are passionate about their disciplines to design their work around essential themes, concepts, and experiences. And it's what students and their parents expect. The point is, you need not wait until the entire curriculum is reformed in order to initiate new approaches to the courses you now teach.

Let us revisit "the course" and see how the ideas in this book permit you to focus on what you feel most passionate about, while your students work to gain the knowledge, skills, and habits of mind that will be useful to them over the long haul. A word of caution: Proceed only if you have substantial freedom to define the content of the course and to decide what to emphasize and how to engage students in learning it. If the course you want to change is controlled by a district or departmental syllabus that permits no major deviation, even on an experimental basis, pick some other course where you do have that freedom. You'll have enough to contend with without facing opposition at your back from dubious administrators or colleagues. Or go first to your colleagues and principal, get them to acknowledge that you and your fellow teachers ought to be getting better-quality work out of these kids than what you're getting now, and suggest that you'd like to try a new approach—with their cooperation and support.

WORKING BACKWARD: DAN BISACCIO'S FINAL EXAM GAMBIT

The first change is to plan the course (or elementary grade unit) backward. Start by imagining where you want your students to be when the course is over (or a year or more beyond) and work back from that vision toward the first class. This breaks the habit of viewing a course as a linear sequence of topics or chapters that begins at lesson 1 and adds new information each week. Students should know where they are headed and what they can expect to achieve if they are to see this journey as worthy of their intellectual engagement and not merely their begrudging compliance. When my children were in high school, they were advised, "If you really want to learn chemistry, take the regular chem course—you'll be doing real experiments. The AP chem course is all exam prep."

Some teachers accomplish backward planning by handing out the final exam on the first day of the course. I first saw Dan Bisaccio do this in a biology course thirty years ago. He simply announced to his class: "Here is the final exam; these are the questions that will be on it. I want to show it to you now so you will know what's ahead and what you will be striving to learn." I observed a few savvy students slip the exam into their pocket when they thought he wasn't watching. "But that's exactly what I want them to do," Dan said when I told him. I was as surprised as his students were—until I got a look at the exam. It was tough stuff, what one would expect from a college-level course. Telling his students in advance what they would have to know by year's end allowed Dan to set his sights high. Here is a copy of the exam.

> BIOLOGY—More often than not, you will find the definition of "biology" given in a somewhat clinical manner such as "Biology is the study of life and how organisms relate to their physical environs." However, biologists are in the business of seeking answers to questions, and their search encompasses a much more exciting and broader spectrum than this usual definition implies.

This year, you will be the biologist and, in seeking the answers to the questions posed below (and others that will certainly arise), you will have the opportunity to discover and understand a much more comprehensive definition of biology than the one previously stated.

From time to time you will be given the following questions to answer . . . and, in fact, this is your *final exam* as well. Each time you answer them, your grade will be based on your development as a biologist. In other words, as the year unfolds, it is expected that you will become more and more the "sophisticated biologist," and your answers should reflect this.

1. Define "biology" in your own words.
2. What characterizes life? In other words, What is the difference between "living" and "nonliving," between "living" and "never living?"
3. There are five kingdoms of life. What are they? What is common to all? What distinguishes each as a separate kingdom?
4. From a scientific standpoint, how did life begin on this planet? What characteristics of this planet enabled life to evolve? What were some problems early organisms needed to overcome and how did they do it?
5. Within the five kingdoms, biologists recognize millions of species. What is a "species"? Why are there so many different species? In terms of question 4, how did so many forms of life come to be?
6. Perhaps the most essential biochemical reactions are listed below. In terms of entropy (second law of thermodynamics), discuss the importance of these reactions as they pertain to life:
   $6\ CO_2 + 6\ H_2O + \text{SUNLIGHT} \rightarrow C_6H_{12}O_6 + 6\ O_2$
   $C_6H_{12}O_6 + 6\ O_2 \rightarrow 6\ CO_2 + 6\ H_2O + \text{ENERGY}$
7. From an ecological perspective, analyze Aldo Leopold's essay "Thinking Like a Mountain" from his book *A Sand County Almanac*:

   ____

   ____

   ____

   ____

FOUR STEPS TO COURSE REDESIGN

What I love about this exam is that it captures just what my own high school biology course lost sight of: the importance to every student of questions about life—where it comes from, what it's made of, how to put all living things in some kind of order, and what our job is to protect it—and the opportunity to look at life as an amateur biologist rather than as a beleaguered student wondering whether what the teacher has written on the board will be included in the final exam or not. With this approach as a model, I want to suggest four key steps to redesigning your course backward.

Step 1 should come as no surprise to readers of this book: *Define the essential skills, knowledge, and attitudes you want students to acquire and demonstrate.* Often we attempt in the classroom what would be unthinkable in the marketplace—we put people to work without telling them what their job is. What is your students' "job" in this particular course? What is it that they must learn and take with them when they leave for another job next semester or next year? You can't ask them to learn "content coverage" or "exposure." You've got to decide what the really important stuff is.

The *Essential Skills* are the academic abilities necessary to carry out the job—the reading, writing, research, speaking, analyzing, recording, and measuring skills. You can make as long a list as you like, but then select the top five.

Essential Knowledge comprises the core content of the course, the things you want students to remember when they've forgotten most of the details. Concepts come from categories 2 and 3 in my taxonomy of content in chapter 3. List them, once more choosing only the top five concepts, theories, and laws (fewer than five may be even better).

Essential Attitudes, Dispositions, or Habits of Mind will round out the job specifications for this course. These are the values and attitudes that, put into practice, allow the student to participate in the discipline with the attitude that a professional would bring to the field. Caring, punctuality, collaboration, attention to detail, and so forth, belong here.

Step 2: *Establish the themes of the course by asking several essential questions* (Ted Sizer's term). These questions, which have been described in chapter 7 as "hook questions," are the unknown, open-ended, up-for-grabs kind of inquiries by which you announce to your students that there is room in this course for each of us to pursue answers of our own—while examining some of the ways people have tried to answer these questions in the past. In contrast to a traditionally structured course, in which the assumption is that somebody (the teacher, the textbook, the "experts") has already figured out all the important stuff, posing essential questions invites your students to join the community of scholars in looking for new ways of defining what is important and what has meaning. At first glance, this may seem a frivolous exercise in certain disciplines in which many things are known—the laws of physics, the declensions of irregular verbs, the geometric formulae, the outcomes of major historical events. But a passionate teacher is one who celebrates the living debates and dilemmas that inhabit all disciplines. For his "Senior Seminar: Nature, Environment, and Human Beings," Dan Bisaccio asks essential questions that could as easily be asked in a middle school course as in a graduate seminar:

1. What are the major environmental issues that face us today? Why are they a concern?
2. Can I make a difference? Is it worth it? Does it really matter to me? List at least three essential questions for your course. And invite your students to suggest others.

Step 3: *Outline various options for students to demonstrate their achievement of the essential skills, knowledge, and attitudes listed above.* How much of what you've listed can students demonstrate through projects, performances, displays, debates, research reports, or other situations where students apply their new learning, such as by teaching others? Tests and quizzes can become excellent *diagnostic* tools in this process, allowing students to get a sense of how much they've learned and what they still need to know—without penalizing them. Or, as in Dan Bisaccio's biology final, preparing and practicing to answer sophisticated test questions, known in advance, can be a major part of what happens in the course. List some of the ways students will be able to demonstrate to you that they have actually learned the "essentials."

Step 4: *Set out the bases for assessing students' achievement.* Let's assume that all the standard means of measuring student learning are there for your use: short-answer tests, essays on major course themes, research or response papers, student-designed projects, and in-class discussions. Remember that your objective here is to encourage students to reach for higher-quality work than they're accustomed to. So some flexibility may be necessary. The same test or term paper might not motivate all students. While this makes the assessment job more difficult for you, it allows you to individualize assessment to a much greater degree and promotes a higher level of individual responsibility and initiative on the part of students. You might construct a pie chart to show students how your assessment and evaluation of student work will be apportioned. You might leave as much as 20 percent of the grade for students to apply to *their* preferred means of evaluation. This allows a student to really go to town on a self-designed or group-designed project, or to put extra work into a research report, or to help lead classroom discussions, knowing that such extra work will "count." Such an option promotes the students' sense of taking responsibility for their learning.

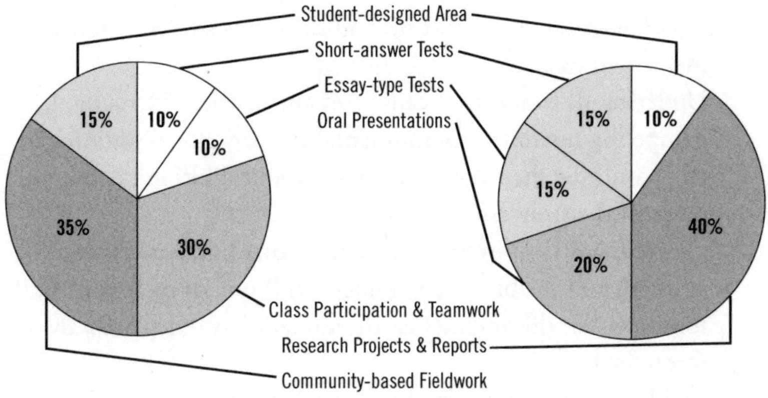

MODELS OF COURSE REDESIGN:
ENVIRONMENTAL STUDIES AND US HISTORY

Here is how the redesigned course outline might look, as far as "the essentials" are concerned. These samples reference the progress reports of the previous chapter.

Course title: Environmental Studies, grades 9–11

As a result of successfully completing the work of this course, the student will have acquired the following skills:

1. Is able to collect, record, and analyze scientific data on environmental topics
2. Is able to read, understand, and distinguish various points of view
3. Is able to relate scientific data to economic, political, and aesthetic consequences
4. Is able to do independent research using materials in the school library and in at least one other information source (e.g., town library, Audubon Society)
5. Is able to share information, ideas, and opinions on the environment with audiences in the school and community

As a result of successfully completing the work, the student will have acquired the following content knowledge:

1. Is able to identify and use correctly the following scientific and environmental terms: [list here all the terms students should identify or memorize]
2. Understands concepts of cause and effect, scientific method, competing interests, environmental impact, global warming, etc. [continue the list but be careful about diluting the importance of the truly essential concepts]
3. Understands the interrelationships among humans, plants, animals, and the biosphere; understands one or more specific topics within this theme that the student has independently researched
4. Is able to apply environmental knowledge to an issue of significance in the community

As a result of successfully completing this course, the student will have demonstrated the following attitudes:

1. Appreciates the vulnerability of life on earth and the role of humans in the stewardship of the planet

2. Acknowledges the complexity of environmental choices and the need to make such choices in their personal life and as a citizen
3. Cooperates with other students and does a fair share of work in groups
4. Contributes to the learning of other people inside and outside of class
5. Takes responsibility for working independently and in groups (comes to class prepared, hands work in on time, and completes any unfinished work within accepted timelines)

Achievement Level and Evaluation Mix

1 = Novice level: Student competence is not yet known or is inadequate

2 = Basic level: Student is able to articulate and apply some information and skills

3 = Proficient level: Student has a basic understanding and is able to apply information/skills/attitudes to known situations

4 = Advanced level: Student shows sophisticated understanding and is able to find new and/or creative applications of information, skills, and attitudes

In this course:

15 percent of the final grade will be based on answers to essay questions that have been given to students in advance of the test

10 percent will be based on a short-answer, sentence-completion, concept definition test that students can retake at intervals during the course

20 percent on a self-designed research study on an environmental topic

20 percent on a group project to improve some aspect of the environment in this community

15 percent on participation in class discussions

20 percent to be applied by the student to any of the above categories (except the short-answer test)

An added option, which I developed as a college teacher, was to add on an extra 20 percent, making a total of 120 percent and giving students the option to do well in most areas, not so well in one or two, and still end up with an A. This option, explained in greater depth in chapter 24, gives students more flexibility in apportioning their efforts (without feeling the pressure to get everything right).

Course title: Twentieth-Century US History, grades 10–12
In successfully completing the work of this course, the student will have acquired the following skills:

1. Read and comprehend historical material from both primary and secondary sources
2. Discuss and debate social issues of life in the twenty-first century and relate them to twentieth-century events and forces
3. Plan, research, and write a 2,000–3,000-word report on a historical theme of twentieth-century United States history
4. Present an oral summary of a research project to the class, and respond critically to the reports of at least two other students
5. Design and present a scenario on life in America if some historical event had turned out differently

In successfully completing the work of this course, the student will have acquired the relevant content knowledge so that they may:

1. Identify the following persons and events from 1900 to 2000 and place them within their approximate time of prominence or occurrence [list them]
2. Identify and describe the significance of the following major themes of the twentieth century and show how they affect us today: the Civil Rights Movement; US role in the century's world conflicts; depressions, recessions, and economic growth; the changing role of women [continue list, but don't overload it with too many topics]
3. Choose one major issue or theme and write an in-depth research report on it

4. Select one major issue or event and develop a scenario on how our lives would be different if that issue or event had turned out differently

In successfully completing the work of this course, the student will have demonstrated the following attitudes:

1. Willing to take an active part in discussions on issues of current and historical importance
2. Willing to take risks in expressing and supporting opinions on historical issues and events
3. Cooperating with other students and doing a fair share of work in groups
4. Contributing to the learning of other people inside and outside of class
5. Willing to take responsibility for working independently and in groups (come to class prepared, hand work in on time, complete any unfinished work within accepted timelines)

Achievement Level and Evaluation Mix:

1 = Novice level: Student competence is not yet known or is inadequate

2 = Basic level: Student is able to articulate and apply some information and skills

3 = Proficient level: Student has a basic understanding and is able to apply information, skills, and attitudes to historical questions

4 = Advanced level: Student shows sophisticated understanding and is able to develop theories and/or creative applications of information, skills, and attitudes

In this course:

15 percent of the final grade will be based on answers to essay questions that have been given to students in advance of the test

15 percent will be based on a short-answer, sentence-completion, and person/event identification test that students can retake at intervals during the course
20 percent on a self-designed research study on a historical topic
15 percent on a group project to design and conduct a lesson in history for lower grades
20 percent on participation in class discussions and debates on historical issues
15 percent to be applied by the student to any of the above categories

Again, adding an extra 15 percent or 20 percent offers the leeway addressed above.

Developing your course outline through step 4 is, in a sense, the easy part: You can do it in your own good time in the privacy of your study. But if you're accustomed to a traditional approach to teaching—in which you organize and present information to students, discuss it with them, assign homework to reinforce the lesson, and then test them on what they have learned—the prospect of putting into classroom practice the outline you have devised can seem daunting. You might find that you have much less control of the movement of the class. There is less predictability to the process. Lots more things can go in a direction different from what you anticipated. And the whole experiment could come crashing to a halt if your students decide not to take their increased responsibilities seriously.

But that's likely only if students working within this new course structure are as resistant, intellectually docile, fixated on grades, or unadventurous as students in a typical class. In this new framework, students will have more choices, more variety, more challenges, more freedom, and more immediate and long-term relevancy than in any course they are likely to have experienced.

23

ROUNDING OUT THE COURSE

Because I have stirred a few grains of sand on the shore, am I in a position to know the depths of the ocean? Life has unfathomable secrets. Human knowledge will be erased from the archives of the world before we possess the last word that the Gnat has to say to us.

—JEAN HENRI FABRE,
cited by science teacher Dan Bisaccio

PUTTING IT TOGETHER IN THE CLASSROOM: DAN BISACCIO AND CHRISTINE SULLIVAN

Let's assume you have redesigned your course around the various aspects listed in previous chapters, and that you have permission to go ahead and teach the course the way you've designed it. We will also assume that you can articulate your stance and that you and your students can create a good working environment in the classroom. Now to the details of making it happen: How will you actually begin the course? Where do you want your students to be by the end of the first few weeks? How will you manage to overcome the initial awkwardness and resistance that may crop up among students who have been used to a very different style of teaching and learning?

I have asked science teacher Dan Bisaccio and English teacher Christine Sullivan to share some techniques that work for them as they teach high school students in courses that are often significantly different in design from what students have been used to. Both have taught for years in traditional as well as experimental ways. Dan and Christine have delineated some key points where helpful hints might be especially valuable, but the suggestions they offer do not add up to a complete set of lesson plans. That's your job, following the course design you have completed in chapter 19. What they provide are some ideas to stimulate your own creative solutions, drawing on your own experience.

GETTING STARTED

CHRIS SULLIVAN: Straight out is the only way. I must trust the kids and let them see that. The big premise that guides me is: This class is all about kids' learning, not my teaching. First, I talk about standards and expectations. I frankly tell them that I have an idea of what is "good work," but I phrase it by describing the floor—the level of competence that I consider minimally acceptable—and then invite my students to soar through any ceiling which might have existed in their minds to block them in their previous expectations of what they can do in English.

At the beginning of any unit, I give them a prepared overview, so that everyone knows where we are headed. It's important for kids to know the type of assessment that the unit will result in and the approximate time period (to help them budget their time, considering that they have lives outside of school).

DAN BISACCIO: I begin by finding a "story" I can create to get the kids excited and involved. I try to be playful with the content in order to create the right context. A good story or question gets the kids messing about with the subject before they get overwhelmed with the content. It creates cognitive dissonance for kids—something they can relate to but that gets under their skin and messes with their preconceptions.

For example, if we begin with a unit on seasonal changes, I might ask them to reflect that in autumn, plants and animals get ready for winter—our harshest season. Most of our birds migrate, deciduous trees drop their leaves, and many animals hibernate. So why do bats, bears, deer, and moose become pregnant in the fall and have to carry their young through this harshest of seasons? In a Biology II class, I may start by asking students to define, biologically, what an "individual" of a species is. After they have come up with some answers, I'll show them a slide of a two-headed snake with two functioning brains and have them defend their definition.

I truly believe a teacher's job includes causing kids to be befuddled, sometimes—especially when they come to class thinking they are the "Knowers of All Knowledge Worth Knowing!" Of course, I need to make sure not to create a level of frustration that is beyond what the students can handle at the time, but I usually avoid that by trying to be playful in science, not just provocative.

BY THE END OF THE FIRST WEEK OR TWO

CHRIS SULLIVAN: In the beginning of the course, you may have to set out the purpose and questions to help students focus on what to look for and what to talk about. Check your unit descriptions—what *is* the focus? Make sure the questions you ask them invite comparison, planning, and practice, instead of one-word or two-word answers. Yes, this kind of introduction takes more time than just telling them what to do—but it prevents your having to tell them the same thing twenty more times.

I rely heavily on goals and objectives. If it's a short-story unit, those are the important features; if the focus is on persuasion, then that's it. No fair sneaking collateral issues like "analogy" or "metaphor" or "persuasion" into the unit without advance notice. I try to blend in the direction so it feels natural: a little lecture, a little "discovery" conversation, a little practice "quick write" and paired commentary. It might take one or two class periods to let them know: "This is what we're going to study, what we're going to learn. Here are some suggestions about how to show you've learned this, some models, some short trials." I try not to have all the introductory sessions in a row, breaking up the "telling and showing" sessions with "practice and conversing."

After a few weeks, I know the class is going okay when I see students beginning to adopt my vocabulary on the language of writing when they are working in pairs or groups—using such phrases as "I see your focus is on . . . ," or "The character in your story is believable," or "Maybe you should try to tie your paragraphs together better," instead of just saying "This is good" or "I don't get what you're trying to say" without being able to pinpoint the problem.

BUILDING STUDENT CONFIDENCE

DAN BISACCIO: Make sure that kids are moving along and not feeling overwhelmed, frustrated, or totally lost. Last year, one of my Biology II students—an exchange student from another country—told me how upset she was by saying, "This is NOT science! In my country, science is dogmatic!" Other students, used to teachers who present curriculum in a more traditional way, may also be a bit confused by my approach. I am likely to respond by

- giving the class short articles to read and discuss in class, which are germane to the investigations they are doing. The students' questions and comments often clue me in to who is having problems and how I might help out.
- asking students to report to the whole class on their findings thus far on the topics they are pursuing. Often kids will suggest options to each other and help clarify—in *real student talk*—what the key issues and approaches are.
- building in short-term assignments such as labs, fieldwork presentations, and journal entries that allow me to both gauge progress and guide a student along. To me, this is what assessment is all about—giving students just enough feedback to adjust their performance as they go (as opposed to nailing down a "grade").

CHRIS SULLIVAN: *Do your best* is the refrain I keep harping on. When students ask how much I want them to do, I turn the question back on them: "How much do you have to do to do your best?" Kids get frustrated, often asking: "Don't you ever give a straight answer?"

I do remind them, as needed, about standards and pride. Most writing in the class is meant to be shared—I tell them that at the beginning. "Any piece of work you don't have pride in, you need to keep working on." I also let kids abandon papers early on in the writing process—I just make sure they tell me why. My comment often is: "Oh, too bad." Nothing more.

A lot of the confidence that kids get is from each other, being able to give and get feedback without feeling "on trial" or vulnerable to humiliation. However, if a kid asks me to read something, I try never to refuse or send him back to his group. I see it as one of those little offerings that kids give you every so often, which is part of their seeking approval.

A DAY IN THE LIFE

CHRIS SULLIVAN: When I think of a typical day, I can't emphasize enough the importance of planning long-range—the longer the better. We all need an idea of where we're headed: the teacher, for bureaucratic reasons and grading; the kids, for a polar star to fix on.

Each day, I break the lesson out from the long-range plan. It took me a while to plan like this (although curriculum is increasingly being organized this way). I find that composition isn't suited to daily lesson plans that fit into the boxes in the lesson plan books you get from central office. Some of this "break out" is just practice writing: daily business in a composition class.

If the course is really about student learning and not about my teaching, daily plans should concentrate on the actions that students can take to improve their performance. It's more a question of "planning in layers"—so that kids are always involved in brainstorming ideas, writing drafts, editing their work, conferencing with me, sharing compositions in small groups, preparing pieces for their portfolio. And even someone as linear as I am won't find this a problem once you put yourself in a coaching frame of mind.

We often spend two or three days per week in a writing lab, equipped with enough computers for everyone in the class. It is here that kids make decisions about what needs to get more development or which pieces should be made ready for presentation in the portfolio.

STUDENTS WORKING TOGETHER

CHRIS SULLIVAN: Sharing work with fellow students is important. It cuts down on interminable teacher-student conferences and allows you to multiply the effect of a few focused comments efficiently. It provides the slower or more timid students with peer role models, and it assures them that ridicule is not lurking around the teacher's desk. I'm flexible about the size of the group, but I enforce rules: one speaker at a time; positive, helpful comments; we're here to give suggestions, not issue orders, etc. We discuss the rules before we begin the first group session.

Because they know I am there to keep peace and enforce the rules of courtesy, students are more willing to work together in what I call "composing alliances." If I have a particularly reticent classroom, I begin with an assignment that must be completed by working with a partner, each of whom gets the credit. As part of their process notes, I make sure they detail what they accomplished working together, separately, etc.

I allow them to choose their own groups. Because I teach in a high school with a stable population of kids, they've worked out the pecking order and alliances long before I come on the scene. If a pair or a group isn't working out well, I allow them to disperse and find others. I am also sensitive to affairs of the heart, or interfering hormones, and I keep an eye out for such distractions.

KEEPING TRACK

DAN BISACCIO: Once I have identified the skills and knowledge I want my students to be working on (based on my own reasons for including these subjects in this unit), I use a list of action verbs to get me thinking of ways that I can both present the material to students and assess their work. Example: "The student should evaluate/distinguish/contrast/connect . . . (the specific skill or area of knowledge)." This doesn't take much time, and it has helped me create my curriculum. The curriculum is never perfect, but it pushes me and my students, I hope, to go deeper into the substance of the material. The action verbs prod us all to think of how students will apply and use the knowledge and skills they've hopefully acquired.

CHRIS SULLIVAN: I try not to show them benchmarks, or examples of superior student work in the beginning—even these can be limiting. Kids may have much better ideas than any models I might offer. If a student really needs to see some samples, I prefer to show them writing with the process notes and editor's comments attached, so the student sees that this piece did not spring up out of the ground in its finished form. Such material may take a while for you to accumulate (make sure to have the student-author's permission), but it can be a powerful motivator.

I write down my impressions of their work in case their writing disappears. But I also ask them to track their efforts in a learning journal or writing log, and I review their journals during class while kids are working in groups. I always leave some kind of note in their journals, and I often have to chant silently to myself so I do not lose my patience and start evaluating them too soon.

The student's learning log and my periodic checking of it (every three weeks or so) helps document that they are doing something. It's important to build in specific interventions—full stops—dedicated to checking what people know, what they believe they can do, and what new learning they are applying. Be brave, and insist that they prove what they claim to have learned with specific written work! Allow yourself to challenge them, make suggestions, prod, have them redo and re-present the next day. But always balance your need for monitoring against the need to build trust with students, and avoid making a holistic evaluation about any specific piece. If something looks and reads like "junk," I'm up front about it, or I'll ask for it to be redone. I do not believe that anything goes—not even at the beginning of the course.

MID-COURSE CORRECTIONS

DAN BISACCIO: I find that as I go along in a unit, it is important to make changes. The initial story or essential question presupposes that the student has some prior knowledge and understanding of the concepts about to be covered. As the unit unfolds, it becomes clearer to me what the kids do know and what misconceptions they may have. Consequently, in planning curriculum, I try to think about when and where I may need to add degrees of difficulty (i.e., challenges to their understanding and/or methodology) or support (i.e., some background reading, short lectures, or a quick hands-on skill-building practice session).

CHRIS SULLIVAN: Turning an intensive, student-centered course around is like turning a battleship in mid-ocean. (It's hard because the kids have a hand on the tiller.) Once, when I felt I had to do it, I ranted and raved, moaned and groaned that they weren't working hard, weren't producing what they'd agreed to do, and that I was going to have to find a different way to run the course. In the end, I didn't have to change—I got the sympathy vote, and better student work along with it.

Now I build change into the structure. I tell them: "After six weeks, we will sit down and evaluate. If it's not working. . . ." (The subtext is that I'll be devastated—but I don't tell them that.) Put this way, change seems part of the process, not a spotlight on their shortcomings. But perhaps most important is finding a time for students to "cull" their writing folders, to make their own notes on their work, to comment on their progress. After they have done this individually or with their editing partner, I have them form groups in which to share their major conclusions regarding their writing.

KNOWING WHERE TO STOP

CHRIS SULLIVAN: I require that anything the students want to develop for their presentation portfolio (the one that gets graded) be well edited, typed, error-free. I also require process notes or earlier drafts of the finished pieces. I don't let them wait until the end of the course to make selections for the portfolio, or else they'd be scrambling to get things typed rather than continuing to compose or make thoughtful editorial judgments.

When does my course end? It's often hard to say since my students and I continue to talk about their writing process until they graduate or find another mentor. My sophomores have a way of showing up at my door as seniors, when they're ready to write their college application essays. My philosophy is that every course gives my students and me an opportunity to participate in a community of learners. The craft part is to help young people forge these learning alliances and take away with them the spirit of the academy, the sense of community. Yes, the student has accumulated a body of material, a portfolio of his or her writing, and we can use that to symbolize a kind of achievement. But, more importantly, they see "composition and revision" as an ongoing adventure.

DAN BISACCIO: This is actually the first question I try to answer before I plan a unit. On my planning sheets, I outline the skills and knowledge that I want to incorporate into it. In working with students, I also focus on communication skills and research skills that I know are important as they prepare to do their senior projects. For example, the unit on symbiosis requires that students learn how to do active research using online tools and presentation software, while the unit on winter adaptation asks students to develop a learning log, interpret data, and take notes on references they are reading.

In the end, I want students not only to know but to be able to act wisely in their daily lives because of what they know. E. O. Wilson, a Harvard University entomologist (and hero of mine), makes a telling analogy regarding the deforestation of tropical regions: "For lack of knowing, burning forests for cattle to graze is like burning a Renaissance painting to cook dinner." It is my passion as a teacher to help prevent another generation of kids from promoting such destruction "for lack of knowing."

24

GRADING FOR MASTERY

"Mr. Slocum, could you tell the jury how Professor Deadman would grade his students?"

"Yes, he would use a curve. We used to call it 'Deadman's Curve.'"

—GARY TRUDEAU, *Doonesbury*

A course must include assessment of student work, and that invariably means giving grades. Redesigning your course gives you a chance to rethink how you want to do that. Any good grading system should:

1. help students accurately reflect how well they have achieved the essential work of the course
2. act as an incentive for students to learn new things and to keep trying even if they don't perform well at first
3. be simple in design and easily understood by students, their parents, academic advisers, and other teachers
4. support the view that assessment is *part* of learning, not the *end* of learning

By contrast, most current grading systems:

1. reflect how well students have obeyed their teacher's directives rather than how much essential knowledge and skills they have acquired, retained, and applied

2. are both incentives and threats and can lower as well as raise students' confidence in themselves as learners—it can be hard for a student to recover after a bad start
3. are complicated, full of intricacies that can lead to endless hassles between students and teachers, and easy for teachers to defend but difficult for others to comprehend
4. encourage students to pursue grades rather than knowledge and understanding

THE CASE FOR—AND AGAINST—CONVENTIONAL GRADING

The case for existing grading systems goes something like this:

- When students do what they are told, they learn important things.
- Without grades as rewards for good work and as punishments for poor efforts, many students would do even less than they do now.
- Grading systems are often complicated in order to be fair.
- Teachers feel they must distinguish between good, mediocre, and poor students.

The case against most existing grading systems is that they hurt kids—talented, well-motivated students as well as students who are less able performers—because the grade and not learning becomes the goal. Students, like all of us, keep their eyes on the prize. If the grade is the prize and the teacher is the giver of grades, then pleasing or guessing what the teacher will accept becomes the focus of students' actions.

I believe most of the grading systems we now use do not help students become mature, self-motivated, and responsible learners. If anything, they encourage student passivity and irresponsibility (like cheating), and they can inhibit the development of better teaching-learning partnerships.

Why not do away with all grades? If grades make students less responsible for learning on their own, why not get rid of them and replace them with a pass/fail or credit/no-credit system or one that provides only a teacher's narrative comments? For most teachers, and for students and parents, letter or number grades are an important part of our educational heritage. They are closely tied in people's minds with values such as standards, merit, and accountability, and they form a basis of comparison among students and schools. Removing grades would in many circumstances be self-defeating. At this contentious stage of educational reform in our nation, the absence of grades is likely to create so much anxiety and confusion that the focus on grading would increase, rather than diminish. Everyone would wonder: "Does this teacher's comment equal a B+ or an A?" "Will my child be at a disadvantage when it comes to college admission?" "Are teachers trying to avoid holding the students—and themselves—accountable?"

So, for the foreseeable future, letters or numbers are likely to remain part of our grading system. But if so, our objective should be to make grades promote student responsibility and real knowledge gain. Following are five concrete suggestions on how to make sense of the grades we give.

LESS IS MORE: THE FEWER THE GRADES, THE BETTER

Let's reduce the number of grades teachers enter into grading systems. We should have fewer grades tied to substantial, longer-term student performances of essential skills and knowledge so that each grade represents a significant piece of learning. This way, students can concentrate on achieving excellence in a limited number of areas instead of focusing on day-by-day compliance.

It's fine if teachers assign, correct, and comment on homework, quizzes, and drafts as diagnostic tools to help students know how far they've come in understanding the key areas of learning for the course. But such diagnostic work should not be counted toward the final grade. These are scrimmages, practices, rehearsals. Our job is to help students learn from their errors, and we can do that best if we're not judging, tallying, and averaging these exercises and drills.

This goes against the wisdom of years of conventional experience that students won't do their homework, won't study for the quiz, if it isn't going to be graded—and the equally compelling student view: "Why should I do it, if it doesn't count?" But experience here is misleading, drawn from the assumption that students are motivated best by the threat of poor grades. This argument underscores a confusion in the minds of students and teachers between means and ends. Homework, quizzes, exercises, and drafts should be means to student performance, not ends in themselves.

We do not go to school to learn how to do homework or take quizzes. Unless the primary purpose of the course is to teach good work and study habits (and there might well be such a course, especially in middle school), teachers should take a more positive stance toward student motivation, as Christine Sullivan has described in her writing classes.

Every athlete and musician knows that practice is critical to performance. Most practice on their own—in addition to group rehearsals and organized practice sessions. Why do we feel we have to browbeat these same kids into practicing their academic skills? Could it be they don't yet see the value of academic performance because we haven't done a good job of connecting such performance to things that students do value—pride, esteem, recognition, career goals? How will students learn to value the lasting benefits of learning if we allow them to get lost in the fog of daily assignments and the grading behaviors that accompany them?

LIMITING GRADES TO A, B, AND C

We can raise standards of student work by making a C the lowest acceptable grade for a course, or for any important assignment within a course. Grades will then be A, B, and C (keyed, perhaps, to the 1–4 Achievement Level rubric on the sample course outlines). We can add a plus or minus if we think such distinctions useful, but there is a trap in trying to be too precise. What's the distinction between a C+ and a B–? If you're sure you know, you may be too focused on minutiae. Good teaching is not about precision grading; it's about high-quality student performance. The message we want to give students is that *quality is expected in all essential areas*. An assignment or project that is not at a level that merits a solid C or higher is one that has not yet been completed.

Limiting grades to A, B, and C must not be permitted to lead to "grade inflation," where what used to be worth a D now becomes a C because we just don't want to fail a student who shows the right attitude or effort. The basic idea of C-or-better grading mirrors the real-world notion of acceptable standards of performance in areas of the curriculum that are vital to a student's future success.

REPLACING D AND F WITH "INCOMPLETE"

I suggest we eliminate grades D and F and replace them with an "Incomplete," which will stay on the books until the student demonstrates sufficient learning to earn a C by doing extra work, redoing inadequate assignments, retaking tests, or attending summer school to complete the work. This may wreak temporary havoc with computer transcripts and will definitely mean more paperwork and follow-up for teachers, but it will be an investment in quality. For one thing, it obliges both student and teacher to remain in the learning relationship. They can't get rid of each other by giving, or accepting, a lousy grade. They have to work it out.

We should expect that at first, a lot of students will test the system, piling up Incompletes to see if teachers will cave in and give them a passing grade for substandard work, or else dish out a slew of D's or F's as punishment. When students finally realize that *they* must take the initiative to solve the problem, the number of Incompletes will be reduced, and students will have learned a valuable lesson about life. To the inevitable question of "How long should an Incomplete sit there, before some grade is applied?" I would answer that after a semester or so, the course would be removed from the student's transcript, and he or she would get no credit for the course.

Two reflections about Incompletes come from our local high school, where the English department has begun to use them. Teachers report some students literally begging them for a D so they can avoid having to complete or redo assignments they find difficult. The teachers are refusing, and the kids are having to produce work they would otherwise avoid. "I'm not going to flunk you," the English teachers are telling these students, "just make you do the work."

A while ago, a student who normally works at a slower pace than her classmates, and who sees herself as a 70–75 percent student (since she can't manage to get enough work finished on time to qualify for a higher grade), came in with her mother to confront her English teacher. The mother was angry: "I've had it up to here with all these Incompletes!" she announced. "It's driving us crazy." Her daughter explained that it had taken her until the end of the second quarter to complete all her work from the first quarter. Then she mentioned that she'd received a 92 percent on her first quarter's work. A light went on, and both realized the connection. By the end of the conference, the teacher, student, and parent agreed to keep trying the new system since the girl was getting much better results in English than she had previously. It was just taking her more time.

TO FLUNK OR NOT TO FLUNK

Some of the teachers I admire most, including a number of those in this book, are firm believers in the need to fail students who don't perform. They tell me: "I never flunk students—the students fail themselves!" I am deeply respectful of the integrity of their standards and am easily convinced by them that students who come into their classrooms (after years of conventional grading) respond to the threat of failing. But I believe just as deeply that this has to change.

An F is a statement by a teacher to a student, suggesting that not only has that student been unable to perform the required work but that he or she is, in this instance, "a failure." If a student "fails" because he or she was disobedient, rude, sloppy, or habitually late, then the problem is one of behavior and attitude, and the question must be asked: "Are these deficiencies best addressed by means of a grade of F, or should the student's problems be brought to the attention of parents and guidance staff and dealt with at that level?" Giving an F ends a conversation that could have been continued for the benefit of the student, although teachers shouldn't have to carry on such a conversation without support.

If, on the other hand, a student fails because of not doing any work, being absent too often, or not learning anything, then the student remains where they were when the course began. Do we begin life as "failures," hoping to be redeemed by our actions? Our course should be an opportunity to learn, not a win/lose gamble for those who enroll. Lack of early success does not equate to failure, or else most great scientists and inventors would have a D average. In fact, most students who fail do so for multiple reasons. They cut classes and show little interest when they do attend; they do little or no work, sometimes interfering with others who want to work. Nothing in this argument against D's and F's is meant to excuse poor behavior and shoddy performance. We do a great disservice to students when we pass them while tacitly understanding that they know little about either the subject or basic courtesy. I just don't believe that educators should be in the failure business. It's not our job. Every F we hand out is a message that students can easily interpret as "I am bad," "I am stupid," or "I am a failure."

The supreme penalty for not learning something essential should be that one has, in fact, still to learn it. The penalty for disrupting a class and preventing other students from learning should be removal from that class until an agreement is reached on how the student can act responsibly.

MAKING TIME THE KEY VARIABLE

In contrast to a grade of D or F, the value of Incomplete is in its neutrality. It is neither a punishment nor a rebuke. An Incomplete is a personalized grade that provides each student with an individual blueprint to complete the work and gain credit for the course during a prescribed period of time. That's preferable to sending a kid off to summer school to take the entire course over again. In schools where teachers give Incompletes instead of D's or F's, students attend summer school only until they have completed the unfinished work of the course.

For the "slow learner" in any class, or for the summer-school student trying to complete the coursework, an Incomplete means that the student can be held to a higher standard of performance while given more flexibility in the time it takes to reach that level. For the class as a whole, time becomes the key variable rather than levels of achievement. The old "grade curve" becomes a "time curve"—it takes different students different amounts of time to reach common (and higher) standards. Some students achieve these skills more quickly than the rest; others take an average amount of time; and a few take longer. This is the foundation of a "performance-based" or "outcome-based" curriculum, about which so much has been written in the past few years. Such a system requires teachers to be much more flexible in how they work with the wide range of students in their classes. In return, teachers need more time, resources, training, and support to make such a system workable for them and their students.

I realize that many teachers may be unable, unilaterally, to implement an "A, B, C, Incomplete" system and may face strong opposition from colleagues if they propose to make this change school-wide. An argument can be made that for low-achieving students who work very hard but can't yet perform at the C level, a D may be an honorable grade.

But a teacher can always discuss with students and parents the rationale for A, B, C, Incomplete and seek their voluntary participation.

At least four objections will be raised to an A, B, C, Incomplete system:

1. Students with learning disabilities might never be able to achieve a C, and that will serve as a rationale to further isolate and label such students.
2. Even non–special education students who've been given several Incompletes might get discouraged and drop out rather than carry that burden around with them as they proceed from one year to the next.
3. The system will extend the time that students have to spend in school, so they might not graduate with their classmates.
4. It will create a paperwork blizzard and a recordkeeping nightmare.

Any of these situations *might* happen, but none of them *need* happen. Students with learning disabilities already have a right to a curriculum modified to ensure an opportunity to succeed. As for students whose report cards now come home loaded with D's and F's, they stand a better chance of success if they and their parents know what has to be learned to achieve a C for the course. All students would be assured a C-or-better average in all the courses they had completed. It will take some students a longer time to finish their coursework. They may have to go to summer school or take an extra semester or two to graduate. Some students may be discouraged to find that their friends are moving on while they are still dealing with Incompletes, but that's already true for students who fail. The stigma of failure will be removed; they will know that neither their teachers nor their school gave up on them by allowing them to flunk out.

Finally, the bureaucracy will need time to adjust, and recordkeeping will need to be overhauled. This will be very annoying. Schools that place a heavy emphasis on comparative class rank will resist factoring Incompletes into the ranking. Teachers who like to wrap up the year by the third week in June will resist having to accommodate students with uncompleted work. Decisions will have to be made about whether a student proceeds to the next course while still working on last semester's Incompletes. It's hard to think of implementing an A, B, C, Incomplete grading system, or other significant changes, in the midst of business as usual. We immediately think of the confusion and the extra work and the lack of public or professional support. All this will be cumbersome and frustrating, like so much else about the job of helping adolescents develop as competent young adults and good citizens. But that's what education is about, and grading systems that are convenient for adults often end up hurting kids.

JUDGING PERFORMANCE FAIRLY

Here are two examples of how conventional grading sabotages excellence:

1. In an English class with four major writing assignments, Samantha hands in one paper that is fairly well written and another that's even better but two weeks late. She never does get the third one in, and she spends too much time on the fourth—producing an outstanding paper that she slips into her teacher's mailbox a week after grades close. Her classmate Charles hands in all four papers on the day they are due—each one a grammatically correct but mediocre, uninspired effort.
2. In math class, Charlotte routinely does every homework assignment and hands it in the next day, studies for each quiz and gets 7 or 8 out of 10 problems right, but she does not really understand nor is able to retain what she learns so she barely passes the final exam. Sam, by contrast, does his homework infrequently and has very inconsistent quiz results but gets in gear toward the end of the term, masters the course content by studying very hard for two weeks, and ends up getting a 96 on the final.

Can we guess which pair—the steady but uninspired Charles and Charlotte, or the erratic but high-performing Samantha and Sam—will end up with higher course grades under a traditional grading system? If all four of them were to receive a C in each course, would that grade accurately reflect the extent of learning these students had achieved? More to the point, has the grading system helped any of these students come to grips with their individual strengths and weaknesses, or focus their energies on performing well the essential course objectives? Yet giving each a C is justified under most existing grading policies and would be seen as fair by teachers who had clearly outlined the rules and expectations of their courses.

I won't defend Samantha's or Sam's erratic performance by pretending they've developed solid work habits, just as we shouldn't chastise Charles and Charlotte for abiding by course rules and expectations. But the truth is that two of these kids know the stuff, and two don't! And a C is probably an inaccurate rating for all four of them. If we want to reward or reinforce punctuality and other good study habits, we can simply add a "+" onto the grade of any student who submits a completed project on time, or we can give a maximum of 110 points (out of 100) to those who perform a difficult task right the first time, rather than reduce the grades of those who take more time.

Most of our grading systems tacitly assume that all students are alike in how they learn and how they show their achievement—contrary to what child development studies and our experience with children tell us. These systems impose a regimen that stifles creativity and masks incompetence. And all in the interest of *fairness*.

Late assignments are discounted out of fairness to those who hand them in on time, and all students must turn in test booklets at the same time—regardless of how different kids work under pressure. Likewise, students who correct mistakes later are marked down in fairness to those who got it right the first time. And a tangle of equivalencies reveals the convoluted logic of the traditional grading: Six homework assignments end up being equal to two quizzes, which carry the same grade weight as one short paper, which is worth half of a research project and counts just as much as class participation. Our grading system, which we've meticulously engineered to "take everything into account," ends up imprisoning us all in its machinations and fails as a motivator of excellence.

GRADING FOR NEW LEARNING, AND FOR MASTERY

What we need are fewer grades and more encouragement for students to keep working on their projects and key learning tasks until they get them done right. And that may mean easing up a bit and taking some of the pressure off, especially with exams. More and more, teachers are allowing students to do open-book and take-home tests, and that is a very good thing. In this way, teachers can ask tougher questions and can better see how students' minds work.

Every one of us remembers taking a test and messing up on a key question that we know we could have answered better had we not been panicked by the clock. I recall a final exam in a classics course during my freshman year at college when I suddenly forgot which was a metaphor and which was a simile, and everything I had studied and learned for that exam turned to mental mush.

The message teachers should give their students, as Christine Sullivan points out, is that we are always ready for students to revise and improve the work they have done in a course. This need not be an impossible burden if we limit ourselves to a handful of graded assignments and thoughtful exams, with everything else treated as practice. Grades for major assignments should be entered in the grading system in a way that allows for revisions when students produce better work. The door should always be open for students seeking to demonstrate excellence.

Isn't this coddling them? Won't some students try to dupe us by allowing a few eager beavers to do all the work so that they can then essentially copy their results and hand in paraphrased versions a week later? Won't teachers be set up, under this system, to be conned by certain kids who will lose whatever impetus they may have to do their work on time? Won't teachers be seen as a bunch of patsies, at the beck and call of every teenager's erratic work schedule and weird study habits?

Yes to all of this—if we change only our grading procedures and continue business as usual in everything else about our teaching. No to any of this—if we integrate our grading practices into a stance that motivates students to reach high standards and take responsibility for their learning.

I have no illusions about the challenge of reforming our traditional grading systems, dysfunctional and counterproductive though they be. I used to ask teachers: "If your house were on fire, and your wedding pictures were at one end of the house and your grade book at the other end, and you only had time to save one of them . . ." There is a burst of laughter and a shaking of heads. "Let the wedding pictures burn," I hear from them. "Without my grade book I'm dead." But that's just why the system has got to change.

GRADING ON A BASE OF 120 VS. 100

Another approach to grading, one that I have used with some success in introductory college courses, uses numerical grades but with a twist: Instead of 100 points being the base, I've used 120. All the criteria for A, B, and C grades remain the same (e.g., 92+ is an A; 85–91 is a B+, etc.), but students know that they don't have to get everything perfect to receive an A. In whatever way I might apportion the various elements of the course (papers, projects, tests), students have 20 points to put toward work they find most meaningful. They can also "flub" some aspect of the course without ruining their chances for a high grade (an A). So, it's possible for students to get up to 120 for their total. They would still get "only" an A. "But is that fair?" some would ask? My answer is, "Anything beyond 92 you do for your own satisfaction and pride." None of my students complained that their A based on 105 or 110 points was somehow devalued by another student's A based on 92 points. To the contrary, they seemed proud of having worked to a higher standard than what was required. It's another way of rewarding inconsistent excellence and downplaying the tendency of high achievers to focus solely on what the teacher wants, while gently reminding them that self-reward for their learning is a big part of what it means to be a learner.

25

WHAT TO DO NEXT MONDAY

"Would you tell me, please, which way I ought to go from here?"

"That depends a good deal on where you want to get to," said the Cat.

—LEWIS CARROLL,
Alice's Adventures in Wonderland

STARTING OUT AS A PASSIONATE TEACHER

Here we are: It's Sunday evening. You and I are winding up this extended conversation. And next week's lesson plans are yet to be written. What to do? Declare some kind of revolution here and now, and turn your lesson plans upside-down? Or shove my book aside and get back to reality? Monday morning won't be postponed. As of 7:42 a.m., you're going to be on!

Something has to change—but in a way that respects your experience and gives you and your students time to adjust. We all need a safe way to begin. Everything can't change, not all at once. You might prefer to begin by selecting one or two things from the following list, keyed to the central themes of the book. If your interest is focused on forging relationships of trust and respect, you might choose to:

- Make a list of the aspects of your work with students that give you the most satisfaction, as well as the things that students and fellow teachers seem to appreciate most about you. Think about what it would take for you to do more of these satisfactory things and to be more like the way you are when you're at your best.

- List the names of students in at least one of your current classes, and next to each, identify an aspect of that person's potential for good work or helpfulness that you would like to see more of, something you already appreciate and respect in that student. Then see if you can find a natural and unembarrassing way to let each student on your list know what you most appreciate about them. Don't try to do it for all students at once, but make up your mind to acknowledge two students or so each day.
- Find some time, or build on a student's spontaneous comment, to begin an informal discussion with students about the kind of learning they like best, ways they would like to see your school improve before their younger brothers or sisters get here, qualities they like most in other teachers, or anything you can think of that lets students know you are keenly interested in what they think about school and how to make things better.
- Pick a fellow teacher whose approach to students you particularly admire and invite yourself into that person's classroom to see what you can learn from the kind of relationship your colleague has established with students. You may also wish to invite that person to sit in on one of your classes, and then compare notes over a beer or a cup of coffee some day after school.
- Ask some students to volunteer to meet with you during a study hall or free period to design a simple, one-page, informal evaluation of how students think the class is doing and what they think might be improved. Try to put the questions in a positive tone. Then let them administer and tabulate the results, and announce that you will repeat this in five or six weeks to see if things have improved as a result of their feedback.

These initiatives require a mutual commitment. If students seem hesitant or start to ridicule the conversation (out of a reluctance to share their feelings or take responsibility), you may have to cut short the conversation by saying something like: "Well, not enough of you seem to be ready to talk about this now, so let's get back to our regular lesson. Maybe we can bring this topic up later, if you are interested."

It may be a while before a critical mass within the class realizes that they do have a stake in a friendly but serious conversation. Few students have had much experience talking with adults in situations where power is more or less equally shared (i.e., where either side can end the conversation, and both sides must take it seriously for it to continue or move forward). It's our role, as adults, to help young people learn to become responsible citizens and decision-makers. It's one of the most important skills we can teach them—in any discipline.

GETTING TO THE HEART OF YOUR SUBJECT

If you're feeling pretty good about how you and your students relate to one another, you may prefer to focus on getting to the heart of your subject as a passionate role model. Here are some possibilities:

- Imagine that because of a sudden budgetary crisis, your school is closing in two weeks and you have to teach an entire semester's worth of material in that time. What material will you focus on? Take that short list and try to build an entire semester-length course around only what's on it. (This is another idea from Ted Sizer.)
- Locate six to ten students who took one of your courses one or two years ago and got a grade of B or better. Ask them what they remember from the course: What ideas or skills or knowledge are they using now or do they feel will be very important to them in the future? If they are willing, let them take the final exam over again (or a shortened version of it), anonymously. Have them trade exam books with one another and score the test. Talk about what has remained with them and, especially, what they would have liked to have learned more about.
- Find something that you absolutely love about your subject or discipline, especially something that is rarely covered in the curriculum or that seems to have no practical value, and substitute it for something that you normally teach but really don't like very much. Try to find a way to share your enthusiasm with students in a way that doesn't overwhelm or intimidate them.
- Invite into class one of your own favorite teachers or someone in your field whose work you especially admire. Tell your students

about it in advance so they can read something by or about that person and think of some questions to ask. When your guest arrives, and after a brief introduction, find a seat in your classroom and join the discussion (so that your students can see you in a learner's role).

- Design a unit from the outline in chapter 7, but begin with item "D. Your Personal Stake" and write a paragraph or two about why you feel especially strongly about this unit. Keep this very much in mind as you teach the unit, and try to set things up so that your students are able to experience, in a personal way, the power of the material and ideas within it. Or you could start with two or three units that you might propose to teach according to the outline, and let your students help you decide which one to develop.

CREATING OPTIONS WITHIN MANDATED CURRICULA

If your curriculum is pretty much set by the department or the central office, or if you don't have the energy to rework your courses, a third point of focus is on students showing what they know and can do through performances linked to real-world challenges. Here are some openers:

- Offer students the option of doing an individual or team project instead of taking the final exam. Explain that this project can be on any topic, approved by you, that involves a key theme of the course and that will be presented to some audience beyond the school (e.g., city council, nonprofit agency, library group, other school). Even if only a handful of students volunteer, that's fine. Invite them to form some kind of group where they can help each other with their projects so you don't have to spend as much time supervising them. Splitting the class like this will mean more work for you, but it's a good way to experiment with a project-centered course without risking getting the whole class involved the first time.
- Present an independent study option for any of the major class assignments of the course so that if students find a related topic

more interesting than what the class will be studying, they can pursue it. Prepare a lesson on independent study to inform the whole class of the challenges and benefits of learning to work on one's own. Then be patient. It may take a while before students start to take you up on your offer.

- Arrange with someone in your department who teaches a different section of the same course to have both sections do a joint research project—or stage a debate that will take up an entire day or half-day (the scheduling problems can be dealt with if you plan far enough in advance). This way, you and your colleague can divide up some of the course material and be able to coach your students to prepare for their presentations. If competition is something that gets you going, you can set up a friendly rivalry between the classes. If not, a collaborative approach can be every bit as effective. By sharing the effort with a colleague, you increase the fun and cut the risks.
- Ask a business group or human service agency in your community to sponsor a research, public relations, or publication project from one of your classes (e.g., an environmental study, a survey of citizens' views on an issue, or a handbook on disease prevention). Arrange for a steering committee of students to meet with you and the sponsoring group to develop a proposal for your class. Have the steering committee lead a class discussion on the merits and risks of taking on this commission and what responsibilities students will have to assume in order to do the job well.

If nothing on these lists seems doable, it may be that the climate in your school has put a damper on faculty experimentation and risk-taking. The sheer weight of regular school business is often enough to depress teachers' energy for anything extra or new, even in the best of situations. Where low staff morale or divisive issues have poisoned the atmosphere, it may be hard for any spark to ignite.

Perhaps the best thing to do at such times is to let it be known that you would like to form a reading group so colleagues can talk about excellence or mastery (or any other topic likely to stir interest). Bring to the first meeting copies of some of the books or articles that you have read and see who shows up. It only takes two people to form a support group (or start a revolution). When teachers are able to discuss with students and with each other how to make learning more enjoyable, such a stance communicates the very essence of pedagogy—an openness to new experience and a willingness to take some risks to create a better environment in which to learn.

JUMPING IN WITH BOTH FEET

Throughout the book, I have attempted to integrate several ideas: that each of us, on our own, can make things happen by working in our classes to create a better teaching and learning climate; that improving teaching and learning will more readily occur when we join forces with colleagues and students, and with administrators, parents, and business and community resources. A third idea is that substantive change requires lots of good ideas and approaches coming together to reinforce one another. Many of us prefer to take our innovations one at a time: "Let me try out this new approach for a few weeks or for a semester before I attempt that one." We're not very confident, most of us, that taking a lot of risks simultaneously is something either we or our students can handle. This is why so many good ideas in the past have failed to catch on. They never had the chance to benefit from a multiplying, or synergistic, effect of other good ideas.

I've been somewhat reluctant to mention a host of issues vital to the pursuit of broad-based excellence in teaching and learning—issues like school governance, system attitudes toward individual and cultural diversity, mandates relating to high-stakes tests, policies and practices dealing with how students are grouped for learning, and the emerging role of technology, to mention just a few. In part, my hesitancy is due to the fact that others have written extensively and well on these issues, and I never sought to write a book about restructuring school systems. My eye has been on what passionate teachers can do to pursue a path of excellence—despite the constraints of their daily routine, which, in these troubled times, includes anti-science, anti-truth, and anti-democratic national movements. And I want to hold that perspective because it is so easy, otherwise, to see change as something that other people have to do for us.

I maintain that the most resourceful and potentially powerful unit of change in almost every one of these transformations is the individual teacher. Movements come and go, but a classroom of eager learners with a passionate teacher to guide them is our best hope for a society of intellectually active minds and finely developed sensibilities.

The irony is that while many of the patterns and practices of daily school life seem to be immutable, many of the dysfunctional aspects would wither under the determined approach of teachers who love to teach and students who want to learn. And we have, potentially, no shortage of either.

I believe nothing short of a revolution in teaching and learning will shake up that system and make it work the way it is supposed to. It won't be new technology. It won't be national standards. It won't be new designs for schools, new arrangements of students within classrooms, or new schedules, timetables, desks, or chairs. It will be what teachers and students are able to do together that will make this revolution.

Only the willingly engaged minds of our students can make great things happen in the schools of today and in the society of tomorrow, and teachers can ignite that fire. The greatest underutilized educational resource in our society is the energy and excitement of our children and youth—students who have the potential to become active, inquiring, and successful learners because of teachers who have found a way to let their passions inspire them.

In the end, our talk must be of both the concrete and metaphysical aspects of teaching. The specific how-to's and the inescapable whys and why-nots must come together in the practices and examples teachers set for their students. For what is powerful about teaching is that we convey to our students not only the wisdom and experience of the past but also the gift of unending discovery and limitless potential. What is unique about being a teacher is that our students can learn as much from the questions we are still vigorously pursuing as from the wisdom we have garnered from years of passionate devotion to subjects and to children.

26

IS PASSIONATE TEACHING FOR NEW TEACHERS, TOO?

I feel like I'm being pulled in every direction—I'm expected to be the psychologist, the nutritionist, the therapist, to be the parent a lot of times, to be the protector, to be the rock. . . . We're expected to cheer and to not punish . . . to cheer and to parent, to cheer and to guide, to celebrate the powerful moments, the successes, but also to console when they're not quite there yet.

—FABIOLA HAMMON, second-grade teacher

Don't be afraid to try something new, even if it might fail. If your students are struggling or you're not enjoying the process, switch things up. Be open with your students by sharing your thinking, your goals, and inviting them into the process. You don't have to be perfect. What matters most is that you're listening, reflecting, and always striving to grow. That's how you make an impact. And in doing so, you model something powerful: that it's okay to make mistakes, as long as we reflect, learn, and keep growing."

—CORY HAFER, 2024 Delaware State Teacher of the Year

THE BEST WAY TO BEGIN YOUR CAREER

For more than two decades, I taught college students, and later, mid-life career changers who were about to enter the teaching profession. I've also supervised student teachers who were trying out their wings in elementary school classrooms, and I've worked alongside middle school teachers in their first year or two of classroom teaching. Those who have read this book often ask, "Is passionate teaching really for new teachers like me, or should I get my feet firmly planted in 'the way things are' before trying any such radical departure from business as usual in schools?"

There are a lot of things I'm uncertain about when it comes to teaching, but not this one. *Passionate teaching is the best way to begin your career as a teacher.* My message to new teachers is this: This whole book applies to you. You don't have to earn your right to be a passionate teacher by spending years proving that you can teach in conventional ways. You may, though, have to be courageous, take some risks, anticipate making lots of mistakes, and commit yourself to the pleasure and pain of intensive learning. You will certainly have to learn a lot about human relationships and something, too, about the politics of schools as complex organizations.

According to the National Commission on Teaching and America's Future, a third of new teachers leave teaching within three years, and half leave within five years. I believe this is largely due to frustration, exhaustion, difficult working conditions, and/or disillusionment. Had these people consciously begun as passionate teachers, their careers might well have persisted. Few people can suffer the abandonment of their ideals without serious consequences. Some become hardened to a culture that disrespects teachers and students, and they often adopt insensitive ways of running a classroom. Alas, society might be better off if they had left the profession early rather than becoming inured to the status quo and, as we often say, becoming "part of the problem." I remember an angry veteran teacher storming into the teachers' room, crossing her arms on her chest, and declaring, "Some of these kids think the whole school is built around them!"

Age has no monopoly on resistance to the idea of passionate teaching and learning. When I talk with principals and head teachers, I am as likely to hear the complaint that "some of our youngest teachers are the ones most afraid of trying new approaches" as "it's our older staff who are stuck in their ways."

Your life as a beginning teacher may well be more challenging and more frustrating than anything you've imagined. As Deborah Meier says,

"The only cure for inexperience is experience," and nobody can rush that process for you. But try not to abandon your idealism as you adjust to the often-painful realities of your first teaching job.

THREE FIRST-YEAR TEACHERS: DIFFERENT GRADES AND CIRCUMSTANCES BUT A COMMON COMMITMENT

Melissa Parent, Mark Knapp, and Kimberly Frazier-Booth were first-year teachers when this book was originally published, although each had some previous experience in working with kids. Melissa Parent taught third grade at the Walker Elementary School, in Concord, New Hampshire, which serves a mostly white, working-class neighborhood; Mark Knapp taught science to sixth and seventh graders at the Josiah Quincy Upper School, in Boston's Chinatown, with a population of mostly Asian American and African American children; Kimberly Frazier-Booth, who was a journalist for ten years, taught English in the City on a Hill public charter school, also in Boston, where her ninth- and eleventh-grade students were largely Caribbean and African American.

All three faced a number of problems in their first year, and yet all three seem to have begun—and remained—passionate about their teaching. I invited them to collaborate with me on this chapter.

"It's really tough if you're not in a school that welcomes and supports new teachers," Melissa Parent commented. "A classmate of mine faces that in the school she's teaching in. She feels all alone; but even worse, all she seems to be getting are these little negative messages—'You should be focusing more on teaching reading' or 'You should pay more attention to math.' I don't think she's going to stay with teaching past this year. And she could be a really good teacher if she were getting a bit of support."

Mark Knapp recalled substitute teaching in public schools in western New York, where "too many of the teachers seemed to be in it only for themselves, not caring about the goals of the school as a whole. Here, at Quincy Upper School, there's much more openness and discussion. If there's a problem, such as scarcity of lab equipment or up-to-date technology, we talk about it, we compromise, and we lend a hand instead of hoarding for ourselves. There [in New York], whenever teachers were asked to cover another teacher's class for a period, they would throw a tantrum in the faculty room. People here [in Boston] want the entire school to work well. It's a 'big picture' approach."

Kimberly Frazier-Booth has found a somewhat different challenge.

> In my school, we have so many young and newer teachers that there are few seasoned teachers to turn to for long-range perspective and experience. I've gotten feedback from my supervisors, who are younger than I am, [saying] that "I'm not quite sure how to assess you—you don't *look* like a first-year teacher." My principal has been principal for two years; my lead teacher is in her first year in that role. So, I need to be vigilant in my *own* reflections because the feedback I get doesn't go deep enough.
>
> I spent the first two-thirds of the year being frustrated about this. Then I sort of kicked myself and said, "Hello—there's an opportunity here to do my own assessment, to look to myself first, and also turn to my students for advice on what works and doesn't work for them." When you ask kids those questions, they are brutally honest. It's more focused than what I might expect from a supervisor. The kids know that what's at stake is their education. And that's when you become a better teacher.[1]

New teachers face lots of challenges and obstacles to their ideals. In this chapter we will examine three really big ones that every new teacher has to cope with:

- fitting into your school's culture—dealing with "the way things work around here"
- having to teach curriculum material you're not familiar with
- gaining control of the class, including dealing with the misbehavior of at least some of your students

Another issue has emerged from interviews with these three teachers—the exhaustion and overwork that new teachers face as they try to learn their new profession. I'm not sure passionate teaching has the answer for that one, but the answer may lie in a new "law of physics about teaching" that I'd like to propose. And all teachers face the same question of how to find a balance between their own views on teaching and the constraints of having to cope with state- or district-sponsored standardized testing.

How you respond to these major challenges will greatly affect the degree of optimism, energy, and joy that you are able to bring to the advent of your teaching career. It may even determine whether you remain a teacher. The stakes are high.

Let's take a look at each of these three challenges in more detail, with the benefit of advice from first-year teachers Melissa Parent, Mark Knapp, and Kimberly Frazier-Booth.

FITTING IN

You arrive at school and pretty soon you are enveloped by that school's particular climate, or atmosphere. A certain feeling in the air tells you, "This is a great place for kids and adults to be." Or it says, "Some of these people like to be here, but some of them clearly don't," or even, "Most of the folk here are pretty cynical and burned out, and the kids show it, too." You sense the degree of staff friendliness and collegiality and the stance that most staff members take toward the students. Do they view them as "a great group of kids who need to be challenged," as "a bunch of rascals who would try the patience of a saint," or as a collection of "good kids" and "bad kids"? You should prepare for the possibility that your initial response to the culture may make fitting in more difficult than you have anticipated.

To a greater or lesser degree, you will feel that this culture—particularly how the people around you seem to feel about the kids and their learning potential—challenges your own assumptions and dreams. You may well feel tempted to hide your feelings, to shove your ideals into the background and quietly find your place within the status quo. *Don't do it!* Now, at the start of your teaching career, is when you must reaffirm your high expectations and values, if only to yourself, to a few close friends, and—most important—to your students. Of course, you must present yourself as a friendly, cooperative, respectful professional, as somebody who acknowledges that they have lots to learn. But it's more than a question of how to survive. It's also a matter of deciding if the culture of the school you're in makes it the right place or the wrong place for you to earn your wings as a teacher.

In these days of teacher shortages, district officials and school principals now see the importance of devoting resources and attention to welcoming new teachers into the profession and helping them survive their first few years.

It was not always thus. My mother, who reentered the teaching profession in the 1950s after the last of my brothers entered first grade, faced the typical initiation of beginning teachers. The district put her in the least desirable school, with the toughest and most unruly kids, in the noisiest or most cramped classroom, with the oldest set of textbooks. She was bullied by a principal famous for driving teachers to tears.

My mom barely survived her first year and then transferred. It was not a nice experience, but she was buoyed by her fierce determination to make a success of teaching and by her down payment, with her first paycheck, on a brand-new dishwasher, a symbol to her of liberation from enforced domesticity. She developed into a wonderful teacher and served for many years.

A beginning teacher once told me that her first job was to replace a teacher who had decided not to return after Christmas, due to illness. That woman got up out of her sickbed to guard her old room from being stripped bare by her colleagues of all her furniture, books, and materials, which she wanted to leave for this new teacher. This was clearly a dysfunctional culture that would no doubt hinder teaching and learning.

The idea that a new teacher has to earn her stripes by having to deal with the toughest kids is still alive. It's a product of teachers who have been disrespected and patronized by administrators for decades. Unempowered teachers tend to treat beginners as the new kids on the block who have to pay their dues in order to join the club. For Kimberly Frazier-Booth, this notion is unacceptable. "I'm thirty-three years old. I've already paid my dues in one profession; I don't want to fall into that same ridiculous mentality. You have to keep reminding yourself of why you've become a teacher. It's all about the kids, and not the politics of the teachers' room."

Mark Knapp remembers, "In the schools I substitute taught in, back in western New York, there were teacher cliques where people would only talk to others within that clique. People held grudges over room assignments that amounted to mutual hatred." If you have to deal with a school culture that is unpleasant, demeaning, or hostile to new teachers, your best defense may be to hold on to your values, try to create a sense of mutual respect in your own classroom, stick close to your friends, and start looking for a better school to transfer to.

Even in a pretty good school, there will be a lot that is unfamiliar. There may be age, style, and cultural differences between you and colleagues old enough to have been your elementary school teachers. You may find yourself calling them "Mrs. McIvey" or "Mr. Flood" even when they call you by your first name. Your way of relating to the kids may reflect differences between how you were treated at home and what older teachers experienced growing up in the 1970s or 1980s. There may be times when you identify more with the kids than with the grown-ups, such as when recess is canceled because of rain or cold but most of the kids still want to go outside. Attitudes toward authority figures may also be different, particularly if your colleagues have had years of kowtowing to administrators (while mouthing off at them behind their backs).

There are the nitty-gritty aspects of fitting in—knowing when it's okay to send disruptive kids to the office, where and with whom to eat your lunch, whether you can go to the bathroom without calling in somebody to babysit your classroom. Details like what to do when you run out of pencils, how many pages you can photocopy for your class, how to respond to an upset parent, or how to leave your classroom blinds at the end of the day may also color how you and your first school relate. The way your colleagues and administrators respond to your inevitable gaffes or foibles will indicate much about how the school's culture treats newcomers.

But the most vital aspect of any school's culture, in my opinion, has to do with stance—how teachers and other staff think about the kids. Melissa Parent, who is happy as a clam with the way adults relate to students in her school, is well aware that things could be much different.

> When I was still in college, I interned in a school that had kids very much like the mix of kids here, many from complicated families or disadvantaged backgrounds. When I arrived there, I wasn't introduced to anyone. Everybody seemed to assume that I was only there for a short while, so I wasn't worth getting to know. And when I did talk to anyone, the first thing they would tell me is that I was brave for coming to work with such kids.

> There was a sense of hopelessness about the place. Teachers were always trying to outdo each other in complaining about individual kids: "You think Joey gave *you* a hard time today? That's *nothing*! Wait till I tell you about Andrew . . ." I felt that the kids were branded—their family life was always brought up; every bad thing they had ever done was repeated; and all their academic difficulties were blamed on the "lousy attitudes" of their parents.
>
> Here, in the school I'm in now, I got welcoming hugs from all the teachers on my first day—even though they thought I was only here to fill in for a sick teacher. Here, teachers give high fives to kids from other classes as they pass them in the halls, and everybody seems to know each of the three hundred kids by name. Instead of blaming the parents, I hear compassion: "Well, you know, his mother's trying really hard" or "His father tries to be there for his kid, even though the couple is getting divorced." Of course, teachers complain if they're having a hard time, but they're always ready to talk about the good things kids do, the funny things that have taken place. They'll say to me, "Wait till you get Dana next year—he's *such* a good kid."

As I write this chapter, the tides of the marketplace have turned. There is now a teacher shortage in many places, and that should keep the balance in your favor as you adjust to your school. It's a lot tougher when you're in a position you must hold on to, however alienating you find the culture of the place. Trust your instincts. Focus most of your attention on your students. You will soon know if this is the right school for you. Don't try to be somebody else. Don't let the culture change how you look at teaching kids. But try to avoid the trap I've seen too many good teachers fall into: They become so devoted to the kids that they allow themselves to be ground down, over time, by a poor school culture.

TEACHING STUFF YOU DON'T KNOW

Inevitably, you will face others' expectations about what to teach or even when and how to teach it. Such expectations have increased dramatically for many teachers due to the demands of standardized testing and the pressures to "teach to the test." Some curricular material will be familiar to you, based on your training and experience. But a lot will be new. Even the familiar stuff will seem strange, at times, since you will have little advance warning of how receptive your students are to it. Not only are you expected to cover subject matter that you are unfamiliar with, but you'll have to devise new strategies to get across the stuff you think you already know.

You will be tempted to hide your ignorance and unfamiliarity and to lean on the text or the teacher's manual or even a colleague's old notes and lesson plans while you try to figure out how to present this material to your students. *Don't do it!* Now, at the start of your teaching career, is the time to define yourself as a learner, as someone with the curiosity and skills to investigate the unknown or unfamiliar. Here is when you begin your career as a model to your students of how people learn.

In a graduate course on curriculum that I taught a few years ago, I learned a lesson: If I want more than a few students to participate actively, I'd better pose interesting questions that students *know* I don't have the answers to. While we were discussing a new magnet elementary school for the university, the issue of cursive writing came up, and I asked them, "As we enter the twenty-first century, do you think that we should still be teaching cursive writing to kids?" The discussion was so much more spirited than anything else we had talked about that I had to ask myself what was the critical factor that prompted almost everyone to jump in.

I'm convinced it was because I had no position on the issue; there was no "right answer" that I was looking for. The normal caution that many students feel about responding to a teacher's inquiry, the fear of getting it wrong, of failing to guess what's on the teacher's mind, was missing. I now try to build such questions into every class session.

Posing such questions is also a good way to deal with unfamiliar material. From my experience of observing new teachers, it's often the least utilized approach. I believe that the most effective way to teach subjects or skills that you are not proficient in is to be both honest and curious about your areas of ignorance. You should be a role model of a teacher who is first and foremost a questioner and a learner. When in doubt, be curious.

It's what most of the passionate teachers in this book do. Yvonne Griffin in sex education, Dan Bisaccio in biology, David Ervin in music and theater—all lead with their curiosity rather than just with their wisdom. Granted, all of them are experienced, master teachers with command of their field. They are convinced that in order to truly engage their students they have to be, first and foremost, learners, even if that has meant throwing away their old lesson plans and starting anew. As passionate teachers, they did not wait until they had full command of their subject before inviting their students into a learning partnership.

You can do it, too. All growth involves taking risks. The risks you take early in your career on behalf of passionate teaching are likely to help you gain more experience and more confidence in less time than if you try to limit your vulnerability by teaching only what you're certain about (or what's in the teacher's edition of the text).

Melissa Parent showed me a newsprint sheet on which she had documented her own attempt to write a paragraph. It had lots of corrections, arrows, new words inserted. It looked like anybody's messy working draft. She explained,

> When I first started teaching writing to them—they're preparing for the state test on paragraph writing—I would try to show them the "right way" by presenting a perfectly composed example. But now, with support from a writing specialist, I'm trying the "writer's notebook" approach, which emphasizes that the only way to get a great piece of work is to start with great ideas that don't come out right at first. But you go back to it, again and again, to build a better piece. And I do that, too, as you can see from this newsprint, I show the kids that my writing starts out as a mess (I even purposely make some mistakes, and the kids love pointing them out).
>
> Kids naturally think that teachers know everything, but when they see me struggling to rewrite, they realize that you don't have to be perfect at the beginning. If we teachers focus too much on getting it right the first time, the kids end up writing these little babyish sentences. They get afraid to take risks, and all the really good ideas are lost.[2]

In exploring new subject areas, Melissa has adapted the old KWL approach—"What do we already KNOW? What do we WANT to know? And what have we LEARNED?" She uses it to build her curriculum:

> For example, in science, with the topic of sound, I tell the kids, "We're going to study sound because we're supposed to, but you get to decide what we actually learn about." This helps me because it allows me to key

> my own lesson prep to aspects of sound the kids have identified as most interesting. For them, it was questions like, "How do we hear?" or "What makes a sound loud or soft? What makes some things sound good and others sound really bad?" I tell them, "You are the designers of this unit. We will learn the things that you are interested in." And I often remind them that I am a first-year teacher and I have a lot to learn. They think it's more fun because then I'm not teaching it to them—we're learning it together.

Mark Knapp gave me another example:

> I decided to do a unit on astronomy with my sixth graders. I know the barest minimum about astronomy, and I told them so. One of my kids retorted, "So now you're gonna teach us something you know nothing about?" and I said, "You bet I am! Any homework that I assign to you, I'm going to do, myself. We're going to have a blast learning this together—so, anyway, what's your sign, baby? What's in your night sky?"[3]

None of this is an excuse for ignorance or unpreparedness on your part. You can't fake your way through teaching. As veteran fifth-grade teacher Alphonse Litz told my class at Northeastern, "There's a world of difference between coming into class with lots of questions about what you want to teach, and being disorganized or unprepared. The one builds curiosity; the other can result in chaos."[4] As a professional, you owe it to yourself to keep learning about the subjects you teach, and with experience you will learn better ways to teach and how to keep old topics fresh and interesting for yourself, modeling how learners act. For now, rather than hide your inexperience or lack of knowledge—and running the risk of turning off your students by dragging them and yourself through the textbook—try using your energy and enthusiasm as a teacher-learner to lead them by example toward critical inquiry and understanding.

Sometimes such an approach pays off in unexpected ways. Ironically, it may not always be your enthusiasm that motivates your students but rather your exhaustion. Even the best-prepared teachers have days when things don't work out as expected. Full-time teacher Kimberly Frazier-Booth faced "the blank wall of the classroom" after knocking herself out by completing a term paper for a graduate course. But in this case, her lack of being fully prepared for class the next day—and her ability to take risks—took an unusual turn:

> I finished my paper last night. I ate dinner and I couldn't even think about preparing a lesson plan on *I Know Why the Caged Bird Sings* for my ninth graders. Five minutes before class starts, I'm staring at the "agenda" list on my blackboard with not nearly enough activities planned to fill an eighty-minute class. So I was just honest with the kids. I told them, "Look, I was just too tired after finishing my paper to make up the test I was supposed to give you, today. And I'm still tired. So I need you to help out. I need some volunteers to present your oral projects on the Black National Anthem, 'Lift Every Voice and Sing,' which you have connected to a scene in the Maya Angelou book."
>
> The tone of the class changed. I didn't have to plead or cajole anybody to present. Every kid—I mean *every kid*—rose to the occasion. It was the first time I saw passion from all of my students, not just one or two. One girl who had been struggling since her transfer to the school, and who had never been willing to stand up and present her work to the class before, did a great job. To have the kids come forward and do their best on the day that I was, arguably, at my worst, was amazing to me. I had to blink back the tears. What it said was that they trust me, that something in my stance is right, because they're not wanting to take advantage of my weakness. Because they see me as a teacher-learner, as someone who is learning with them, they see me as someone they can help out when I need them to.

Was she just lucky this time? Perhaps. But I think Kimberly Frazier-Booth was cashing in on an investment she had been building all year with these kids. I think that there's a key, here, to the third big issue new teachers face.

GAINING CONTROL OF YOUR CLASSROOM

Many new or aspiring teachers tell me that what holds them back in their desire to begin as passionate teachers is this: "How can I be an enthusiastic, idealistic teacher for *all* children, so long as there are a few kids, or more than a few, who seem not to want to learn, or who insist on disrupting the learning of others? How can I be the kind of teacher I want to be and yet maintain enough control so that the kids don't walk all over me?"

Everyone knows of some new teacher who naively entered a classroom anticipating an eager bunch of learners, only to be overcome by some degree of student resistance that went beyond anything the teacher had anticipated or planned for. The response is anger, sadness, tears of frustration, plus a grim determination to "get control of those kids before they get control of me."

You may well feel tempted to hide your true personality behind a mask of sternness and authority—to make sure the students know that you are in charge, right off the bat. There will be teachers who will tell you, straight out: "You'd better come down hard on the kids—at least at the beginning—to show them who's boss. Then, once you have established control, you can relax a little—but not before!"

Don't go down that path without thinking clearly about what that means for you and your kids! What worked for those teachers may not work for you. I'm not even sure it does work for each of them. Look at the students in those "well-controlled" classrooms. Are they excited about learning? Are they taking responsibility for themselves and for their behavior as learners? Or are they held in check in a manner that suggests that as soon as things loosen up—such as with a substitute—all hell will break loose?

There are some teachers whose strictness comes from a deep-seated sense of dignity and respect for their elders, teachers who grew up in a culture that revered authority figures who were unmistakably committed to the well-being of those they led. Such teachers are able to convey compassion and high idealism as part of being strict, and the kids seem to know and respect this. But that is quite different from merely trying to let them know who's boss as a management technique.

There will be other teachers who will try to give you other friendly advice: "Look, honey, my first year of teaching was hell. I cried every night for the first month, and only by April did I realize I would make it as a teacher. Keep your back to the wall, keep your chin up, and plow ahead. You'll survive." *Don't follow their advice, however kindly or well meaning.* Now, at the start of your teaching career, is the time to quietly, firmly—with humor, pride, or however it feels most natural—begin to create the kind of respectful community that will allow you and your students to do their best work. It will take a while for your students to get used to you and you to them. Your skill with various approaches to working with students will improve over time. Don't begin by imprisoning yourself in a fortress mentality.

There may even be college professors who will say to you: "Well, you know your subject and you have the right ideas on multiculturalism, constructivism, gender equity, parent involvement, and full inclusion of kids with disabilities. You'll do just fine in the classroom." *Don't trust that they know what they're talking about.* Having the right ideas is important, but it's not enough. You're the one who has to put them into practice five days a week for 180 days.

The problem with all this friendly advice is that it either assumes that a struggle between your students and yourself is inevitable, or it pretends that ideology alone will carry you through. It won't.

THE PHYSICS OF TEACHING

There must be some law of physics in teaching that goes: If your energy and the kids' energy are moving in the same direction, without major conflicts and continually reinforcing one another, lots of great things can get accomplished. You put a lot into it, you get tired, but it doesn't deplete your energy. When it's going right, teacher and students gain new energy from the pride they feel as they work hard and learn together. They keep surprising themselves and each other. It's exhilarating, renewing. It takes a lot out of you, but it gives you something wonderful in return.

But when your energy and the kids' energy are at cross-purposes—when you try to get them to behave, do their work, speak up in class at a time when they have other things on their minds; when something upsetting has happened; when they don't know why you are making them do stuff; or when there's little sense of community and shared enterprise within the classroom and kids are busy teasing or putting each other down—then the opposing forces will soon deplete and demoralize you, while it convinces some kids that they are "dumb," that you are "mean," or that "school sucks."

The critical moment comes when you first encounter the resistance. Do you push hard against it and try to overcome it by raising your voice or issuing threats? Too many of us do this. Feeling challenged and vulnerable, we reach for those old weapons of threats and sanctions—when what we should do is stop, point out the potential conflict, and move into a collaborative problem-solving mode. It's hard to think straight when we're challenged like that. But that is exactly what's required.

The standard solution is supposed to lie in the area of teaching called behavior management. But this well-worn phrase deserves scrutiny.

Just listen to those two words: *behavior management.* Doesn't this tell you that something's not quite right with the philosophy behind it? Are you a person who takes kindly to somebody *else* figuring out how to manage *your* behavior? Why should your students feel differently?

Nobody wants to be managed by anybody else. It undermines their dignity. It is disrespectful. It says, in effect, "Since I don't believe you see it in your interest to behave well, it's up to me to manipulate you so that you behave well *without* having to do so on your own initiative. You need a bribe, or the threat of a punishment." Whether we're talking about gold stars, pizza parties, extra free time, time-outs, detentions, or phone calls home, if we try to control or manage our students' behavior other than by working with them to make what they are learning about interesting and meaningful, we undermine our power as role models. In *Punished by Rewards*, Alfie Kohn has some very interesting things to say about how rewards tend to diminish students' inclination to do what is in their interest.

You want to be in control *in* your classroom. Not having control isn't an option. But you need something more fundamental than behavior management. You need relationships.

THE CENTRALITY OF RELATIONSHIPS

Here's the mantra. It may sound a bit simplistic, but if you've gotten this far in the book, I'm hoping you won't be offended:

It's the kids. Teaching is about the kids. It's about you and the kids. Teaching is about you helping the kids become powerful learners. For you, a beginning teacher, nothing matters more than your relationship with your students. Nothing else even comes close.

You know your subject matter? Fine! You've organized your lesson plans for the whole first month of school? Good for you! You've set up the room so that it's pleasing, friendly, cheerful? Splendid! You're philosophically committed to seeing each child as an individual, with individual strengths and potential? Terrific! But if you stop there, you may find yourself in big trouble because what it's really all about is you and the kids and the kind of learning community you are able to create for and with them.

One of my former graduate students, Tania, had been an assistant kindergarten teacher for three years. After reading a draft of this chapter, she commented,

> It's important to remember that it *is* "about the kids." I find myself forgetting this, and I have to think back to how I felt right out of college, when I believed children could actually enjoy school and love learning. Although many of the teachers in my school have been very helpful to me, they seem to have forgotten that it is all about kids. They are buried with concerns over preparing for the standardized tests and covering all the state-mandated material, and they don't realize they may be ruining their students' view on education.[5]

This is, by far, the toughest challenge in teaching. There may be a few teachers who start off with a class of eager, confident learners who are at or above their grade-level expectations in reading, writing, and math. For everyone else, some or most of the kids will have self-images as learners that have been damaged by prior experiences in school or at home. This is not to blame teachers or parents; it is to remind us that what we see in preschool and kindergarten and maybe first or second grade—those eager hands raised, those kids ready to do anything and everything their teacher asks—greatly diminishes in the years that follow. I devote most of my second book, *The Passionate Learner*, to the dimensions of and responses to the plight of the child whose natural desire to learn has been blighted by school experiences.

For you, as a beginning teacher, the critical task is to *build a learning community with your students.* You can do that best by gaining your students' trust, assuring them that you really are there for them and that your goal is to help them become more powerful and more capable learners. Neither you nor your students are starting from scratch. Everyone has had lots of experience being a learner—in good and bad situations. A number of students, especially those who have experienced unloving, inconsistent, or untrustworthy adults at home or in school, may not at first see you as someone worthy of trust. They don't know yet that you are on their side.

A number of these students may have been tracked into low-level or remedial classes, or called "disruptive," "immature," "ADHD," or any of the other labels that schools tend to apply to "problem" students, particularly when they don't come from middle-class, well-educated families. Such students may see you at first as just another teacher who will soon get frustrated with them and end up harping on their mistakes, failures, and "poor attitudes." The antidote, for many new teachers, requires a certain openness, a willingness to engage with students on a personal level, as young people who are not solely defined by their in-school behaviors.

Kimberly Frazier-Booth has found that "the valued relationships are often forged outside the classroom. You've got to be there, hanging around the lockers in the hallway, going to a basketball game, leading an extracurricular activity. They have to see you as a person, outside of the classroom environment."

An undergraduate student of mine spent six months working in a middle school, where she was assigned to teach literacy to a bunch of "special needs" boys.

> They hated me, at first. They wanted nothing to do with me or with the reading and writing I was trying to get across. They were angry, mean-spirited, down on themselves and on everything about school—everything, that is, except football (they were the core of their school's football team, the one place where their toughness was appreciated). At my wit's end, I persuaded my roommate to go with me to one of their Saturday football games. We dressed in jeans and sweatshirts, and we waved to them from the stands.
>
> They couldn't *believe* I had come to watch them play! Some of them had never had a parent attend their games, and they all came over to me during halftime. I took notes on what each of them did that helped their team, and when I showed them my notes—on the computer—in class next week, they were really impressed. We spent that whole week doing literacy based on football—a subject they were sure they knew something

> about. We did sentences, paragraphs, vocabulary, everything. They corrected me on the stuff about football that I hadn't understood, but there was no gloating or sarcasm about it; they just wanted to get it right. Our working relationship was completely transformed. They were ready to work with me—that is, until the lead teacher got jealous and told me not to "waste time on topics that aren't in the curriculum." I was furious, and I eventually quit working there—but these "unteachable" kids had shown me how to teach them. I had first to care enough to show up at the place where they felt proud.

Before we leave our discussion of behavior management, there is another approach to behavior that's a lot more useful than advice like "Don't smile till Christmas" or "Have the right philosophy and all will be well." This alternative approach relies on a *procedural*, as opposed to an *attitudinal*, base. A popular approach in working with kids in grades 4–12, for example, is to announce, "The first time I have to speak to you about your behavior, I give you a warning. The second time, your name goes up on the board. If you continue to misbehave, I put a check next to your name . . .," and you proceed to describe the consequences for various levels of disruption (missing recess, detention, emails or phone calls home, conferences with parents).

Another technique, appropriate for younger kids, involves posting cards—one green, one yellow, one red (like traffic lights)—for each child, such that anyone who is out of line is asked to move their card from green to yellow ("warning") and then to red if the misbehavior continues (again, with "consequences"). The idea is to minimize the teacher's having to interrupt the lesson to chastise a student while, at the same time, emphasizing student self-responsibility. I have recently observed this technique in a well-run second-grade class, and it seems to work like magic.

But in discussing these approaches with my class of preservice teachers, we realized that a technique is only as good as the relationship already in place between student and teacher. Techniques may enhance the creation of a trusting and affirming classroom climate but cannot substitute for it. No technique can replace a teacher's role in relating to each student from the heart, and in respectfully conveying their hopes and confidence that everyone is part of the learning community.

FROM "DON'T" TO "DO"

Melissa Parent characterizes herself as "very strict," but it was apparent to me that she carries it with a smile and a genuine openness to power sharing with her third graders.

> I tell them, "There are school rules which all of us have to follow, but we don't have any rules in this class—that is, until we make them up." During the first week of classes, we talked a lot about "rules" and what would happen if we didn't have any.
>
> At first, when we brainstormed our class rules, everything they came up with was "Don't . . . Don't . . . Don't." But then I looked them in the eye and asked: "What do you feel like when you see a sign that says 'Don't'—like when it says 'Don't pee in the swimming pool'?" And they said, "I want to DO it!" So we figured we had to have other kinds of rules, ones that are easy to follow and that you mostly want to do, anyway. We came up with what I call "The Sacred Five": 1. Please keep your hands and feet to yourself. 2. Please be respectful. 3. Listen carefully and follow directions the first time. 4. Always try your best. 5. Please be safe.
>
> On days when things are not going smoothly—lots of disruptions, teasing, everyone seeming to have a tough time—I'll stop everything and say, "Look up at our Sacred 5 and see where we're going wrong." Then we talk about that. It helps that the kids know that these are my rules, too. When I stood up on a chair to reach something, the kids warned, "Ms. Parent, you're not being safe!"

It's unlikely that any teacher walking into a new classroom will be able to avoid some disciplinary tricks of the trade—raising their voice, sending a kid out into the hall or to the principal's office, threatening to call the parents. It may happen once in a while, or every day, as we attempt to establish an effective working atmosphere in our classes. Kids will test us; they will push us to see where or if we set limits. It's how we respond that makes the difference. And, once again, our own experiences as learners are often our greatest source of influence.

The conventional warning to new teachers, "Remember, they don't have to like you; just make sure they respect you," is manifestly *wrong*. Children don't respect people they don't like, although they may, indeed, learn to fear them. There's a difference between a teacher "acting like a kid" to curry favor and one who strives to create a climate where students can like you and respect you. Our own experience as learners often helps us identify with students while still acting as the adults that we are.

For Mark Knapp, the breakthrough happened when the kids noticed and commented on the large scar on his forehead.

> I told them that when I was in junior high school, I dived into a lake, in early spring, and hit my head on a rock. I came out bleeding and almost died while my dad drove me the forty-five minutes to the hospital. It was a real stupid thing—I was showing off. In fact that's what one of the kids said—"You were so stupid!"—but I could tell she said it with affection, imagining me with my head split open. And I could tell them, then, "That happens to all of us, one time or another. Making stupid mistakes doesn't make you a bad person. It's just a poor decision. And hopefully you recover and learn from it. But you have to avoid judging yourself or others too harshly. So, you don't have to say, 'Oh, I didn't do well on that test. I'm too stupid to go to college.' You just learn how to do better next time."

Kimberly Frazier-Booth tells me it was her ability to acknowledge her own teaching mistakes that gained her the trust of her students.

> I've been honest when I've screwed up on something, like when I tried to teach my eleventh graders how to write essays for the school-wide writing competency. I had never been through the process before, and I focused on the wrong thing. I spent hours teaching them how to write a good thesis statement, but not how to pinpoint and answer the question posed. A third of them failed because they didn't respond directly to the written prompt.
>
> I took responsibility. I told them, "I have to share at least some of the blame with you for what happened." The funny thing was, none of them blamed me. But what was more important, none of them looked at themselves as failures. They knew it wasn't just about them. They were learners who hadn't mastered something yet. In my sharing the blame, they were able to look to why they had failed, instead of that they had failed.

We are not operating in a war zone. The kids are not the enemy, not even the disruptive ones. Ignorance, inequality, prejudice, denial of opportunity, and insensitivity to someone's culture or suffering are the true enemies. The kids are who they are. As psychologist Mary Montle Bacon said at a conference, "You *got* what you *got*. The parents aren't keeping the good kids at home and sending you the riff-raff." The challenge for every teacher is to take what you got and, by the example of your own passions, to help the students learn. You may not be able to transform an entire school through your own teaching practices, but you surely can make a difference for the kids in your classroom.

Part of the answer, Mark Knapp believes, lies in the other kind of "discipline," which, for him, is biology.

> Middle school kids are really into all kinds of gross stuff, when it comes to the human body. So we begin at the end, so to speak, with methane from people or animals, and we work backward up the GI tract. It's by far the best way to get them interested in nutrition—rather than to harangue them with what they're supposed to eat, you know, the food pyramid. Putting issues that they are concerned about—sex, drugs, bodily functions—out in the open is one of the best ways to get and hold their attention. I tell them they can bring up any legitimate question about their bodies. And they are always asking me what I was like at their age.

TEN TIPS FOR AN ASPIRING PASSIONATE TEACHER

As someone who helps prepare people for teaching, I believe there are things that may help you hold on to your enthusiasm while gaining the necessary experience that comes only with time. It is crucial that these challenges strengthen rather than overwhelm your ideals and values. Here is my list of critical factors in coping with the challenges every new teacher faces.

1. *Stay alive as an active learner.* Keep reading books and journals that contain both philosophical and practical suggestions for the issues that you face. Nothing, for example, is more useful in helping you deal with the pressures of standardized testing on your approach to teaching than to see how other educators wrestle with this challenge to teacher autonomy and school-based decision-making.

2. *Remember that you are not your kids' first teacher—you're not responsible for how they come to you.* Remind yourself that the kids in your class have had other teachers before you (even if you teach kindergarten) and that the attitudes they bring to class—both positive and negative—have been nurtured elsewhere. Don't blame yourself for any bad habits or poor attitudes they display—or the fact that they don't rush to join you in your enthusiasm.

   But neither should you feel compelled to accept the norms that previous teachers have enforced, such as yelling or using threats or bribes to keep the kids "on task" and "in line." Don't knock yourself out trying to change every dysfunctional aspect of every kid. Let your students know, both as a group and individually, that you are concerned about aspects of their attitudes or behavior and that you will work with them to improve as learners. In time, you'll earn your share of the credit (or blame). Right now is your chance to begin to create with them the kind of work environment you think will help them succeed.
3. *Be aware that all schools are not alike.* Take stock of positive and negative aspects of your school's culture (e.g., morale issues, levels of staff cooperation, administrative practices, policies that may discriminate against students or staff, and attitudes toward parents). Your teaching is greatly affected by the climate and culture of the school you are working in *now*. Your teaching effectiveness will change—for better or worse—should you decide (or be obliged) to teach elsewhere. Do your best where you are, but keep looking for the right school.
4. *Visit other classrooms and invite other teachers to visit yours.* Now that you are a teacher, you should remain a scholar of good teaching. Use a free period, staff development day, or other excuse to visit classrooms in your school and in others where teachers with more experience have worked out effective and engaging approaches to their work with students.

   Even if you end up learning what not to do by watching the effect of other teachers' practices on their students, you will have improved your own teaching. The same is true for inviting other teachers in to see your work. Many schools have mentoring programs for new teachers, and these are often very useful. Good mentors respect the individuality of the people they are working with.

5. *Build a network for yourself as a person and a professional.* Don't try to go it alone. And don't wait for things to get bad before you reach out for support. Before you even set foot in the school, create a network of other new teachers in the district, college classmates who are also new teachers, and/or colleagues at your grade level or in your discipline whose work you admire.

   As a new teacher you will, of course, feel vulnerable. That's unavoidable. But having a network of support—such as a group of fellow teachers who meet for coffee every other Wednesday—can help keep your vulnerability at a tolerable level.
6. *Build strong positive relationships with the parents of your students* (especially in elementary and middle school). Reach out to parents, even if there is not much parental involvement in your school. The earlier you contact parents—do it during the months before school begins and in the first few days of the school year—the more cooperation you will have. Send home a one-page weekly newsletter to tell parents what's happening and how they can help. Let your students help write it.
7. *Think more about procedures and less about rules.* Students of all ages like to think of themselves as grown up. Once they know how to operate independently as members of a classroom community, your job as disciplinarian is much reduced. As Harry and Rosemary Wong point out in *The First Days of School*, the less your students depend on you to get things moving each day or class, the more they will develop positive and productive work habits. I have visited elementary school classes where students calmly and quietly place the tongue depressor with their name on it in the "restroom" slot before leaving the room without disturbing anyone and other classes where students come in, take their writing folders, and set to revising their work while their teacher is still conferring with a colleague in the hall.
8. *Keep "respect" at the forefront of your attitudes and expectations—but aim higher, for "excellence."* As long as you and your students are still finding your way with one another, a focus on mutual

respect is likely to be the best way to build a good working relationship. Respect, in this sense, is more than just treating people fairly and being polite. It should also include respect for the learning potential in every student.

As you get to know your students better, you want to be able to use respect as a foundation for your work with them. But, as important as it is, respect is not the goal—it's a prerequisite for something better—namely, true partnership in learning and excellence in student performance.

9. *Avoid the most common traps in grading student work.* Teachers get in more trouble with their students—unnecessarily—over grading than over almost anything else (except, perhaps, how they handle disruptive student behavior). I have written about this in *The Passionate Learner* as well as elsewhere in this book. The gist of my argument is that if we believe that students are individuals who learn in differing ways, we need to be flexible in how we grade them so that we don't rely too heavily on a one-size-fits-all assessment.

   Of course, some may view this approach as at odds with the ideals of fairness, objectivity, and consistency that teachers are supposed to adhere to. The solution is to train our students to be largely self-correcting and self-assessing in their work so that we become their coaches, not their judges. We want them to feel free to come to us for suggestions on how to improve their work rather than to complain about a grade that reflects a judgment already made. As coaches, we place ourselves on their side in the challenge to perform well as learners. It's another example of our stance.

10. *Know that student excitement about learning is your best protection against whatever the culture of the school throws at you.* Hollywood understands this: Every inspirational movie about kids and teachers—from *Stand and Deliver* to *Mr. Holland's Opus* to *Dead Poets Society*—underscores the power of students' enthusiasm for learning. Of course, it's never as easy as in the movies. But finding a way to generate such excitement is at the heart of passionate teaching.

So here you are. You've handed in your last term paper, completed your student teaching, and received hugs from the kids. You've received your diploma and been showered with congratulations from those who love you. You've passed that dreaded "teacher test" and received your first certification.

And you've landed your first teaching job—perhaps not at the school you'd hoped for, but at a school that you feel has the potential to be a good place to work. You have, at most, a month or two to try to get your life together and prepare for your new assignment. How will you ever be ready?

Remember, it's about you and the kids. Better to start with blank walls (that soon get filled with kids' drawings and written work) and to have a good plan in your head of how you will build a learning community than to put all your time into decorating your classroom without creating a strategy for you and your students to learn happily together.

Think about what procedures you want to start them off with so that they begin to develop and practice good thinking and working habits. Think about the little rituals you want to use each day, week, or month to help your students feel safe, comfortable, and included. Think about the questions you want to pose—and the groups you want them to form to talk about and respond to those questions—so that your students can become active players in the intellectual work and not a fidgety audience for your nonstop talking.

Hold in your imagination the elements of passionate teaching—love of knowledge, fascination with kids, devotion to ideals and issues of the world—and make a commitment to engage your students as partners in learning. They will respond.

ACKNOWLEDGMENTS

There are so many whose wisdom, generosity, and patience have been of critical importance to me in fashioning both the original and this new edition. I owe each of them more than I can possibly acknowledge in these lines.

Let me begin with the teachers whose words grace this new work: my chief collaborators, Andrea Levin and Joshua Chard, as well as faculty and alumni from the Upper Valley Educators Institute (in my mind, the finest place to become a teacher or school leader), including President Page Thompkins and teachers Deirdre Phalon, Travis Nason, and Fabiola Hammon who are quoted herein and others who shared ideas in a focus group.

Corey Lynn Fried movingly relates her experience defending Bayard Rustin for her class, and Taylor Bussinger adds his wisdom to the struggle to teach history honestly in difficult times..

At the suggestion of my wife, Pat Wilczynski, I reached out to many of the 2024 Teachers of the Year, and a number of them responded generously with inspiring thoughts. Along with the wonderful contributions of Taylor Bussinger (Oklahoma) and Joshua Chard (Maine), I have included insights from Zachary Arenz (New York), De'Shawn Washington (Massachusetts), Astral Battiste (US Virgin Islands), Trent Van Leuven (Idaho), and George Hawkins (South Dakota). At least ten others responded to my query with words of inspiration.

I owe a lot to my colleagues and friends Deborah Meier and Tony Wagner. I have learned much from them over the years, and their interviews add greatly to this book. The depth of their critiques on our educational system deserve wider attention from the educational officials and university leaders who guide our schools, as do the books of my late mentor, Seymour Sarason, who reached out to me when he read the first edition. To this group, I add Linda Darling-Hammond and Rebecca Winthrop, whose "On Point" conversation opens chapter 17, which focuses on students owning their learning.

No one has been a greater champion of *The Passionate Teacher* in its earlier editions than Randy Wisehart, coauthor of the recently published *The Habit of Passionate Teaching*. For almost a decade, Randy brought me to Earlham College in Richmond, Indiana, to co-lead his summer workshops for new and experienced teachers and made my book one of two required texts for his classes.

I have been fortunate in my relationship with Beacon Press to have had two outstanding editors to work with: Andy Hrycyna for the first edition and now Rachael Marks. It seems that all the hard textual bargaining happened thirty years ago, and Rachael and I are enjoying smooth sailing, due to her warmth and enthusiasm for this work. Managing editor Susan Lumenello and Rebekah Cotton have been splendid as copyeditors, and Marcy Barnes helped me greatly in the proofreading process.

I reiterate my enduring and deep appreciation for the constellation of inspiring teachers whose living example as passionate teachers formed the heart of the first edition—Dan Bisaccio, Ed Clarke, David Ervin, Alfredo Fuentes, Yvonne Griffin, Susan Lukas, Maria Ortiz, Christine Sullivan, Tim Sullivan—and those who formed the basis of the new chapter for the 2001 paperback: Melissa Parent, Kimberly Frazier-Booth, Tania Stathoulopoulos, and Mark Knapp.

And there is my family: my wife, Pat, whose faithfulness to this project and to keeping the rest of us well-housed and reasonably sane throughout is matched only by her unerring instinct for what sounds right in the text itself. She has been my most constant reader and adviser. Our sons, Zachary and Peter, read all the parts that mentioned them (and some others besides) and permitted me to take no more liberties with the facts than seemed fair. Their school experiences, ongoing during the writing, continue to challenge my complacencies.

To say that I could not have gotten the book done without the support of all of these people is stretching it—I could surely have finished it all by myself around the middle of this century—but it is vastly better because of their knowing and their kindness.

NOTES

PREFACE TO THE 2026 EDITION

1. Zachary Arenz, email message to author, summer 2025.
2. Joshua Chard, email conversations with author, summer 2025.
3. De'Shawn Washington, email message to author, summer 2025.

CHAPTER 2: THE ART OF ENGAGING YOUNG MINDS

1. Tim Sullivan, interview by author.

CHAPTER 3: PASSIONATE TEACHING REVEALED

1. Maria Ortiz, interview by author.

CHAPTER 4: THE CONTEXT OF PASSION

1. Yvonne Griffin, interview by author.

CHAPTER 6: DETERMINING WHAT IS ESSENTIAL TO TEACH

1. Tony Wagner, interview by author.
2. Andrea Levin, email message to author, summer 2025.
3. Andrea Levin, in conversation with author.

CHAPTER 7: DESIGNING A UNIT

1. Susan Lukas, in conversation with author.

CHAPTER 8: THE GREATEST OBSTACLE WE FACE

1. Martin Haberman, "The Pedagogy of Poverty versus Good Teaching," *Kappan,* December 1, 1991.

CHAPTER 9: OPENING UP THE DIALOGUE

1. Tim Sullivan, in conversation with author.

CHAPTER 10: MORE WAYS TO CHANGE THE GAME OF SCHOOL

1. David Ervin, in conversation with author.

CHAPTER 11: NURTURING A RESPECT FOR TRUTH AND A DEFENSE AGAINST FALSEHOOD

1. Joshua Chard, email message to author, summer 2025.
2. Karen Ball, email message to author.

CHAPTER 12: DISCOVERING A STANCE

1. Ed Clarke, in conversation with author.

CHAPTER 14: PUTTING YOUR STANCE INTO PRACTICE

1. Alfredo Fuentes, in conversation with author.

CHAPTER 15: SOME THOUGHTS ABOUT CLASSROOM DISCIPLINE

1. Deborah Meier, in conversation with author, summer 2025.
2. Joshua Chard, email message to author, summer 2025.
3. William Glasser, *The Quality School* (HarperPerennial, 1998).

CHAPTER 16: CREATING AND MAINTAINING RESPECT AND CARING IN THE FACE OF BULLYING AND MEANNESS

1. Andrea Levin, in conversation with author, summer 2025.
2. Joshua Chard, email message to author, summer 2025.
3. David Brooks, "The Crucial Issue of the 21st Century," *New York Times*, July 31, 2025, https://www.nytimes.com/2025/07/31/opinion/democratic-republican-parties.html.

CHAPTER 17: HELPING STUDENTS TAKE OWNERSHIP OF THEIR LEARNING

1. "How to Redesign Schools for the AI Age," On Point with Meghna Chakrabarti, WBUR, September 3, 2025, https://www.wbur.org/onpoint/2025/09/03/redesign-schools-ai-student-chatgpt.
2. Trent Van Leuven, email message to author, summer 2025.

CHAPTER 19: THE PRACTICE OF EXCELLENCE

1. Alfred Kazin, *A Walker in the City* (Harcourt Brace, 1951).
2. Christine Sullivan, in conversation with author.

CHAPTER 20: THE PARENTS' PERSPECTIVE

1. Ted Sizer, in conversation with author.

CHAPTER 21: TEACHING HISTORY IN AN INTELLECTUALLY HONEST WAY WITHOUT GETTING FIRED

1. Andrea Levin, email message to author, summer 2025.
2. Taylor Bussinger, email message to author, summer 2025.

CHAPTER 26: IS PASSIONATE TEACHING FOR NEW TEACHERS, TOO?

1. Kimberly Frazier-Booth, in conversation with the author for the 2001 edition of *The Passionate Teacher* (hereafter cited as *PT*).
2. Melissa Parent, in conversation with author for *PT*.
3. Mark Knapp, in conversation with author for *PT*.
4. Alphonse Litz, in conversation with author for *PT*.
5. Tania Stathoulopoulos, in conversation with author for *PT*.

INDEX